Running on Faith:

Timeless Principles for Winning Life's Marathon

By Rick E. Meyer

I read it with interest, since I consider you to be a good friend. I have found it to be very personal, cleverly written, and insightful for people today through the lenses of your testimony. Our testimony is our most sacred sermon, and you have done well with yours.
-- **Lanier Burns Th.D., Ph.D**.
Research Professor of Theological Studies
Senior Professor of Systematic Theology
Dallas Theological Seminary
Dallas, TX

Copyright © 2017 by Rick E Meyer

Acknowledgements

"Rick, you should write a book."
Kent Frieling and Brian Meyer separately shared this encouragement within a few weeks of one another in the summer of 2006. Even though I inhaled books in reading an average of a book every four days, I failed to give thoughtful consideration to creating a book for the nourishment of

others. I was oblivious to the daunting task which awaited me upon commencement. I quickly became aware that the difficulty of this project equaled the difficulty of training to compete at a high level in running.

Giving proper credit for each person contributing to my writing this book necessarily includes each person with whom I have interacted with throughout my life. Because, each interaction affects our thoughts and resulting development. Disagreements challenge our thoughts and behaviors. This either strengthens or alters our previous beliefs and consequential actions. Additionally, while agreements validate our thoughts, more importantly affirmative people challenge us to think deeper, wider and higher.

Credit belongs to each who taught me to read, write and engage in critical thinking. This includes my parents, family, friends, mentors and teammates along with teachers and professors from kindergarten at Gaylord Grade School through Dallas Theological Seminary (DTS).

Those engaging in specific roles include Barb Lehmann, my speech and literature teacher at Smith Center High School, who has encouraged my writing during this project and my ministry newsletters.

I continually considered the advice of longtime friend and former co-worker, Chuck Kahl. "This is your *first* book, *not* your *only* book. You do not have to include *everything*."

I am forever grateful for my running coaches Jim Muck at Gaylord and Smith Center, Bill Blankenship at Smith Center, Bill "Congo" Congleton at Manhattan, Harry Kitchener at Cloud County Community College and Lyle Claussen who I met in Kearney, NE. They each challenged me mentally and physically more than I ever thought possible while seamlessly demonstrating principles of winning life's marathon.

DTS professors and friends such as Dr. Charles Baylis, Dr. Lanier Burns, Dr. Paul Pettit, Dr. Stanley Toussaint, and Dr. Larry Waters provided significant and timely encouragement. They serve as sounding boards for ideas of biblical application. These godly leader servants remind me that our focus of studying and teaching scripture always hinges on seeking God's intended truth of scripture to mold our beliefs instead of our beliefs molding our interpretation and application of scripture.

Thank you also to the Dallas running community. I am grateful for their listening and encouragement. A special thank you to running buddy Dawn Grunnagle, a professional runner for Nike, for her encouragement over thousands of miles and hundreds of post-run coffees.

I am thankful to know God through His son the Lord Jesus Christ by the power of Holy Spirit. Our only limits are those established by God's plans for us to serve and glorify Him through Christ by the power of the Holy Spirit. The only unrealistic goals for Christians are those contradicting God's desires for us.

> They (Paul, Silas and Timothy) passed through the Phrygian and Galatian region, having been forbidden by the Holy Spirit to speak the word in Asia; and after they came to Mysia, they were trying to go into Bithynia, and the Spirit of Jesus did not permit them; (Acts 16:6–7)

I am eternally grateful that God prevents me from exiting His path for me. Because, Romans 1:20-32 explains that He gives those who no longer acknowledge Him and exchange His truth for a lie "over to a depraved mind" and live in sin.

Lastly, thank you to editor Trish Lewis who challenged me in many ways including long-term habits and style to reach a greater readership in terms of reading style. She offered significant vision in manuscript organization - honing in on specific messages.

Dedication

Delmer Meyer

Judy Meyer Nielsen

Elliott Nielsen (step-dad)

Dee Meyer Isaacson

> who fought a courageous battle with bone cancer

Brian Isaacson (brother in-law)

> who supported Dee beyond description during her fight with cancer and continues to point Wyatt towards the light of Christ

Wyatt Otto Isaacson (nephew)

Table of Contents

Introduction..11

   Your Connections 12

   I'm Calling You 13

Chapter 1: Fear Not 17

   Why Jesus?..19

   The Beginning...22

   Growing Up on the Farm 24

   Parents...25

   Farm 27

   Grandpa Meyer 31

   Sam Showed Me the Door 34

   My Race against a Calf..36

Chapter 2: Desire & Goals Power of the Mind—Combined with Faith.............39

   Back to the Farm 39

   Gopher Holes and Irrigation 39

   Power of a Goal during WWII...45

Chapter 3: 1974 Brings Change..51

   Uncle LaVerne..53

   Growing in Wisdom, Knowledge and Understanding................................55

   Visiting my Cousins..57

   Three Steps to Attainment 59

      1. I Can – Ability...59

      2. I Will – Desire...59

      3. I Am – Realization 60

   Attitude 65

   Passion for Athletics 67

      Where are you led, and how do you get there? 67

   My Beginning in Competitive Athletics..67

      Early Cross Country 67

   Farm (more lessons)...70

   Manhattan 75

   MHS – Cross Country...77

      1983 Camp – knee high tube socks & cotton gym shorts.......................77

Fall 1983 81

Offended 82

Time Trial 85

Workouts 86

Pace 88

Manhattan Invite 90

GOAL #2 – Nationally Ranked Team 96

Chapter 4: Complacency..99

Pre-Race Prayer 104

If Winning Were Easy, Everybody Would Do It...............115

Farmers' Faith..117

Living on a farm requires faith! 117

Reading 118

What Size Of Fuse Do You Possess? 120

Hogs 122

Chapter 5: Expecting to Win: Power of Associations 127

Gaylord Friends 127

Basketball..128

Other's Influence On Me 132

Did You Do Your Best?...135

Chapter 6: Power of Associations....................................139

Now Is The Time To Set Goals 139

Auction...144

Chapter 7: Goal Achieving: Greatness Occurs After Logic 147

Goals 1 149

Terrain..153

Internalizing Goals 155

Farmers..157

Chapter 8: Move to Kearney...159

UNK Cross Country..162

Self Talk...170

Formulas of Faith 172

Form 176

Chapter 9: Marathon Origination of Running on Faith 177

    Omaha 1993 179

    Omaha 1994 183

Chapter 10: Boston 1995 VISION—Go the Extra FIVE Miles 185

    You're Getting There 186

    New York 1996 202

    Post New York 213

        Staying Power 214

    Speaking Faith 216

        Imagination 217

    Imagination – Possibilities 219

        Traveling 220

        Radio 221

        Imagination - Music 222

        Humor 223

        Wavelengths 224

        Imagination - Objects 225

    Think Inside the Bible 226

    Humility 229

    Friends Do Not Let Friends Live Complacently 230

Chapter 11: Activities For Permanent Habits/Lifetime Achievements! 235

    Family Changes 235

    Dad: Death and Funeral 242

    Temptation: Responding 246

    Toastmasters - 2008 247

Chapter 12: Ministry 253

    Dee's battle with Cancer and Death 256

Chapter 13: Writing on Faith 259

Appendix Do you Finish God's sentences? 263

    Altitude & Wisdom 265

    Friendships and Corner Posts 266

Bibliography 267

Introduction

The Kearney Good Samaritan Hospital 5K starts in a matter of moments and others are questioning my sanity again! I quip to Erich and Tom, "This'll be a good mental toughness workout."

Perhaps the 5:30a.m. 6-mile run and the 120 weekly miles of training contributed to my intense fatigue, but I'm still on the starting line and my legs already burn with fatigue. The gun fires at 8:06; Kearney High runners shoot out quickly. Former UNK (University of Nebraska-Kearney) cross-country runners Tom Magnuson, a three-time All-American, and Erich Whitemore, join me as our bodies transform potential energy to kinetic.

Tom's experience and strength delay his assumption of the lead until near the quarter-mile mark. Erich and I move into the second and third position after the first half-mile. We pass the mile in 4:45.

"I can hang out at this pace," I reflect while viewing the split. Erich has other ideas; he quickens the pace. At the halfway mark, my legs begin to wobble and buckle. I struggle to remain upright and moving while Tom holds a commanding lead. My mind, exhausted from the focus and concentration necessary for the demanding mileage and workouts, seeks relief and begs my body to stop. Erich looks back at me, and I call out, "Go ahead."

Erich yells back, "Come on!!"

Once again I plead, "Go ahead." This mental toughness workout exceeds my expectations and desire. My legs wobble like a wheel getting ready to fall off a wagon.

Erich bellows a second time, "Come on!!!"

I state consciously but not verbally, *Lord, I need you! I cannot! Christ can! We are. It is not me, rather Christ who is in me.* I repeat this as if playing a continuous loop. Suddenly, my body fills with the strength necessary to continue this hasty and agonizing pace. The intensifying pain resembles lightning bolts piercing my body's every nerve. Our second mile split is 4:37; an excruciating 4:32 vanishes into history before reaching the three-mile mark. Running on faith, I sprint the final 176 yards and pass Erich to win second place.

A Kearney physician approaches me in the hospital parking lot following the awards ceremony. "Congratulations, Rick. I could never run like you do. I hurt when I run."

His words leave me speechless! Little did I realize, 10½ years later, I would stand in this same parking lot, speechless again, with excruciating pain zapping my body and mind: *Running on Faith.*

Your Connections

I experienced similar scenarios numerous times while running over 129,000 miles in my lifetime. I discovered a comparable truth while writing this book. I cannot run fast or far under my own strength and power; nor can I write a book or achieve anything worthwhile with my own abilities. Absent Christ, I am nothing. What is your strength connected with?

> Are we beginning to commend ourselves again? Or do we need, as some, letters of commendation to you or from you? You are our letter, written in our hearts, known and read by all men; being manifested that you are a letter of Christ, cared for by us, written not with ink but with the Spirit of the living God, not on tablets of stone but on tablets of human hearts. Such confidence we have through Christ toward God. Not that we are adequate in ourselves to consider anything as coming from ourselves, but our adequacy is from God, who also made us adequate as servants of a new covenant, not of the letter but of the Spirit; for the letter kills, but the Spirit gives life. (2 Corinthians 3:1–6)

> Abide in Me, and I in you. As the branch cannot bear fruit of itself unless it abides in the vine, so neither can you unless you abide in Me. I am the vine, you are the branches; he who abides in Me and I in him, he bears much fruit, for apart from Me you can do nothing. (John 15:4–5)

Success mandates singular focus on Christ's presence and the indwelling Holy Spirit's guidance. I find this is always guiding my speaking, writing, running and actions at all times. The Holy Spirit saturates my heart, mind and soul, consequently I strive to continually study the Bible, pray, worship and fellowship with other Christians. This provides powerful protection against promptings, thoughts, words and actions which oppose God's Word.

Only the Holy Spirit's guidance of my writing and your reading provides any meaningful value to this book. God graciously places those with wisdom in my path precisely when needed to enable me to overcome my numerous shortcomings in running, speaking, writing and everything else in life. Friends and family provide much-needed encouragement. They are the ones calling out, "Come on!" as I near collapse from life's exhaustive and enduring pace.

I'm Calling You

Are you willing to *Run on Faith* the rest of your life? *Running on Faith* is trusting in the presence of the Kingdom of God. This is the power of God in Jesus Christ by the power of the Holy Spirit, whether it, like the mustard seed, is too small to see ... or whether you see God's power as magnificent as a full grown mustard tree supporting the birds of the air.

If you are willing to let me help you, I promise that you will fight through challenges and rejoice in celebrations far beyond your wildest imaginations.

Are you *Running on Faith?* Do you exchange encouragement with friends, calling out, "Come on!" like my friends? Biblically, **run** (Gk. *trechō*) indicates to exert yourself, striving hard, and choosing to expend every ounce of energy in serving and obeying God. In ancient Greek writings, running also signified the extreme danger required in the exertion of all your efforts to overcome the challenges leading to victory. Throughout history some Christians have faced grave danger in fully exerting their life for Christ.

Why then do we *Run on Faith*? We *run* in response to God's love for us, and our responding desire to please God (1 John 4:19). We strive to fully exert ourselves in obediently serving Jesus Christ because we yearn for an eternal relationship with God. Running life's race with near perfect tactics and effort without Jesus will still result in our falling galaxies upon galaxies short of receiving salvation from God. The Lord Jesus Christ's death and resurrection for the forgiveness of sins for all who believe in Him serves as the only door to an eternal relationship with God (John 10:9).

Are you willing to *Run on Faith?*

> Now faith is the substance of things hoped for, the evidence not seen. (Hebrews 11:1)

The Greek word for substance is **hypostasis**, translated as "Title-Deed or Legal Paper" defined as "a legal document to effect a transfer of property and to show the legal right to possess it."[1] Additionally, pleasing God requires placing your faith, your complete trust, in Him.

> And without faith it is impossible to please Him, for he who comes to God must believe that He is and that He is a rewarder of those who seek Him" (Hebr. 11:6).

This book examines life events involving various levels of trust in God.

> Trusting God necessitates trusting Jesus Christ for eternal life, remaining prayerful, grateful and joyful regardless of your circumstances. (1Thess 5:16-18)

Faith consists of the three components:[2]
1. Information
2. Mental Assent
3. Trust

---

[1] Logos Bible Software
[2] Stanley D. Toussaint, Ph.D., BE 106B Acts and Pauline Epistles, Class Notes Sept 2012.

Faith in Christ begins with information from hearing, reading and studying the Bible.

> So faith comes from hearing, and hearing by the word of Christ. (Ro. 10:17)

The mental assent involves gaining an understanding of the information. You then choose whether to accept or reject the information as true and applicable to your life. Do you trust the information? In order to trust information, you must trust the source of the information. Do you trust the Bible as the word of God? Do you trust God?

> All Scripture is inspired by God and profitable for teaching, for reproof, for correction, for training in righteousness; (2 Timothy 3:16)

Faith in God the Father, the Lord Jesus Christ and the Holy Spirit is proportionally logical to our trusting relationship with Jesus Christ. This begins with gaining information about God through Bible study, worship, prayer, fellowship with mature Christians and God revealing himself through nature (Psalm 8:3; Romans 1:20). The order varies for each person. Followed by increasing our understanding of this information enabled by the indwelling Holy Spirit. The greater our understanding of Jesus and the holiness, righteousness and power of God, the more logical it is to fully trust God regardless of our understanding of His ways. Logic demands knowing that God's perfect will anchored in His perfect character and established before the foundation of the world far exceeds our highest expectations.

Your mind accepts ideas when you trust the credibility of their original source. Once you accept ideas, you then begin internalizing them into your character which guides your thoughts, words and deeds. Internalizing Christian faith and trusting God results in living your trust in eternal life with God through Jesus Christ. This is nicely illustrated in the second chapter of James, a great chapter to read as a supplement to this section. In other words, your character reflects the thoughts that you gain, comprehend and trust. Your faith determines your character. Chuck Swindoll succinctly writes, "Perfect trust is a character building process."

Running on Faith commands fully exerting yourself beyond the secularly logical, previously known limits perfectly illustrated by the men and women written about in Hebrews 11 who fully trusted in the eternal character and plans of God. We fully exert ourselves because we trust God, the author of life and provider of love, power, mercy and forgiveness. Seek gifts where God wrote your name along with His on the title or deed, despite no physical guarantee of their existence.

Are you willing to push yourself to new, higher physical and emotional limits? Imagine the intimate, penetrating relationship with the Holy Spirit when you assertively explore new frontiers with your absolute trust-filled faith in God as the boundaries of human logic dissipate in your heart and mind's rearview mirror.

God's hand dripping with love, grace and mercy will firmly clasp your hand as a father clasps a child's hand when you accept the challenge of obediently serving Him. You will face challenges while pursuing the necessary wisdom, knowledge and understanding to achieve Christ's will for your life. Will you continue the pursuit when the challenges become unbearable? Remember: wisdom, knowledge and understanding exceed the value of gold, silver and rubies (Prov 3:13-15, 8:8-11,18-19).

I challenged my teammates prior to a 1983 state cross country meet, "If winning were easy, everybody would do it." This is the choice I'm showing you in this book and hope you find it motivating to strive for that heavenly finish line.

If *Running on Faith* were easy, if following Christ were easy, everybody would do it. Consider this a challenge and an invitation. Begin or intensify this challenge of fully committing your heart and soul to Jesus Christ and trusting him with every ounce of energy you possess. Remain on guard, extreme peril lurks in the shadows and aims for your destruction like a highly trained camouflaged sniper in the distant landscape as you traverse along this amazing course (Eph 6:12). Continually study and internalize God's Word throughout your journey, remaining prayerful, grateful and joyful (1Thess 5:16-18).

Chapter 1:

Fear Not

Imagine being on a ship in the middle of the frigid ocean, terrified amidst the darkness. The enemy's torpedoes may strike at any moment and sink your ship, your life and your dreams. My Uncle LaVerne and his shipmates experienced this around the Aleutian Islands during WWII. The Japanese lurked in and under the water, seeking to destroy United States Navy ships. My uncle shared that suddenly a distinct voice of no human origin spoke to him and probably others on that ship saying, "Fear Not, for I AM with you Always." Uncle LaVerne received instant, illogical, yet amazing peace. Those sailors lived in the faith of Almighty God just as Abraham and other godly men and women before them.

Dad recalls Uncle LaVerne's initial visit to the Meyer farm following WWII. He wore his Navy attire and searched for Otto and Ida's only daughter, Berniel, whom he had recently met at a dance. A nine-year-old carefully observed this United States veteran and responded, "She's not here." Uncle LaVerne remained determined and encouraged. He visited the farm regularly; having found success when he and Berniel married in May of 1948.

They enjoyed life on the farm. They raised cattle, hogs, chickens, alfalfa, corn, wheat, grain and sorghum. Raising their daughter (named LaVerna after her father) and several non-biological children became their most important mission. LaVerne and Berniel lacked any contention for showing up on the Forbes 400 list. I knew them for thirty-nine years and noticed their contentment. They took life in stride but not for granted. A day or two after Uncle LaVerne's passing, the family asked me to speak at his funeral. That was when I talked to family and friends gathering information for a fitting eulogy and I inquired about his service in WWII. It was only then that I learned of his guard duty on that ship and the crew being bitterly cold.

I grew up aware of their emphasis on faith and their 'fear not' approach to daily life. Faith presided for this couple whether the markets went up or down or the weather was dry or wet. When a massive hailstorm knocked out every window in their farm home, they feared not, knowing their Heavenly Father befriended them every step of the way. They trusted our Lord, who promised and delivered for Abraham and who delivered Moses and the Israelites out of Pharaoh's hand. This same Lord blinded the 'torpedo firing enemy' of the United States in the Aleutian Islands in the 1940s. He held their lives in His loving hands every moment.

They worked hard—and prayed and worshipped even harder. They knew their efforts did not produce a profitable crop or livestock herd, just as our efforts do not produce anything worthwhile. Rather, our Lord Jesus Christ worked through their efforts and our efforts.

> I planted, Apollos watered, but God was causing the growth. So then neither the one who plants nor the one who waters is anything, but God who causes the growth. (1 Corinthians 3:6-7 (NASB95)

Of course, most readers will never have met LaVerne Anderson; however, you may know a veteran or be a veteran with a similar experience. You may have endured cold, dark, terrifying moments. Every follower of Christ lives as a continual target for Satan and his demons lurking about the Earth. These evil demons fire torpedoes of doubt, envy, greed, lust and all forms of sin, seeking to sink our faith in God Almighty and our Holy Spirit-instilled dreams.

> Now the deeds of the flesh are evident, which are: immorality, impurity, sensuality, idolatry, sorcery, enmities, strife, jealousy, outbursts of anger, disputes, dissensions, factions, envying, drunkenness, carousing, and things like these, of which I forewarn you, just as I have forewarned you, that those who practice such things will not inherit the kingdom of God. (Galatians 5:19-21 (NASB95)

> For our struggle is not against flesh and blood, but against the rulers, against the powers, against the world forces of this darkness, against the spiritual forces of wickedness in the heavenly places. (Ephesians 6:12 (NASB95)

Uncle LaVerne and his shipmates saved themselves only after turning to God and giving all trust to Him. We must do the same. We, too, can live a life of *fear not*. Our Lord presides with us always, providing blessings as great as the number of stars in the universe.

Why Jesus?

Jesus Christ is the only source of authentic hope and inner peace amidst life's challenges and our physical death.

> Jesus said to him, "I am the way, and the truth, and the life; no one comes to the Father but through Me. If you had known Me, you would have known My Father also; from now on you know Him, and have seen Him." (John 14:6-7 (NASB95)
>
> I will ask the Father, and He will give you another Helper, that He may be with you forever; that is the Spirit of truth, whom the world cannot receive, because it does not see Him or know Him, but you know Him because He abides with you and will be in you. (John 14:16–17 (NASB95)
>
> But the fruit of the Spirit is love, joy, peace, patience, kindness, goodness, faithfulness, gentleness, self-control; against such things there is no law. (Galatians 5:22–23 (NASB95)

God the Father, the Lord Jesus Christ and the Holy Spirit are one God; three persons, coequal, coeternal. We cannot know the God of Abraham without knowing Jesus as our savior. Jesus is God's spoken Word, including the Word made flesh. God created the heavens and our Earth with the spoken Word.

In the beginning was the Word, and the Word was with God, and the Word was God. He was in the beginning with God. All things came into being through Him, and apart from Him nothing came into being that has come into being. (John 1:1–3, NASB95)

The Bible says all who observe creation are without excuse for failing to recognize and know God. Creation makes God visible or clear to everyone. Jesus later came to earth as a baby in human flesh to die a humiliating and painful death. Through that death, He collected and cancelled every sin ever committed by all humans in the history of the world. Consequently, He descended into hell for three days to suffer the punishment that each person to ever walk the earth deserves. At the end of three days, He conquered death and hell through His resurrection returning to earthly life. His resurrection provides forgiveness for every sin committed in the history of the world. But there is a catch…

Proverbially speaking, the Father requires a signed receipt for entrance into heaven. When you accept Jesus' invitation and acknowledge your dependence on His death and resurrection for the forgiveness of your sins, Jesus effectively signs your heart and soul as a receipt of forgiveness. Your heart and soul, spiritually speaking, network with the book of life. His *signature* simultaneously records your name in the book of life. Succinctly stated, eternal salvation requires the person to believe they have sinned against God and that Jesus Christ is their only source of forgiving those sins.

> For God so loved the world, that He gave His only begotten Son, that whoever believes in Him shall not perish, but have eternal life. For God did not send the Son into the world to judge the world, but that the world might be saved through Him. He who believes in Him is not judged; he who does not believe has been judged already, because he has not believed in the name of the only begotten Son of God. (John 3:16–18; NASB95)

> Therefore we have been buried with Him through baptism into death, so that as Christ was raised from the dead

through the glory of the Father, so we too might walk in newness of life. (Romans 6:4; NASB95)

Additionally, the aforementioned Holy Spirit resides in you once you know Jesus as your Savior.

Or do you not know that your body is a temple of the Holy Spirit who is in you, whom you have from God, and that you are not your own? For you have been bought with a price: therefore glorify God in your body. (1 Corinthians 6:19–20; NASB95)

The Holy Spirit provides freedom from discouragement, resentment, worry, lust and all sins. Sin represents every desire, attribute, thought, word and action opposing God's character. Additionally, the Holy Spirit communicates with our heart and mind, serving as a coach and mentor for each believer. Our willingness to recognize and obey His guidance enables our inner-peace amidst any and all of life's challenges, regardless of the magnitude. Unfortunately, we sometimes ignore the voice of the Holy Spirit, causing us to fail in achieving God's will for us in this moment and to endure the resulting consequences.

The Holy Spirit also convicts our heart, mind and soul of our sins and our eternal death without Christ, while revealing Christ as our Savior. We must acknowledge our complete dependence on Christ and accept his signature on our hearts. The signature is on our hearts as the heart pumps our lifeblood through our bodies.

For the life of the flesh is in the blood, and I have given it to you on the altar to make atonement for your souls; for it is the blood by reason of the life that makes atonement. (Leviticus 17:11; NASB95)

Consequently, imprints of Christ's character, by the power of the Holy Spirit, disperse through our bodies, reflecting Jesus in our thoughts, words and actions. The accuracy of our reflection of Christ increases with our maturity in and obedience of Him while in our human flesh on Earth.

The Bible identifies blasphemy of the Holy Spirit as the only unforgiveable sin. Anyone who curses the Holy Spirit curses the Holy Spirit's message of believing of Christ as the Savior through His death and resurrection.

The Beginning

I entered this world shortly after 2:00a.m. on Sunday, February 12, 1967 in Smith County, Kansas, the heart of America. Smith County is the center of the continental United States and where Dr. Higley wrote the song, *Home on the Range*. Additionally, one may say that this region is the Bible Heart. Although unverified, it is reported that Smith County, Kansas, led the United States in the percentage of residents regularly attending church.

Figure 1: Delmer, Rick and Judy Meyer. Sunday, March 12, 1967

My parents wrote in my baby book that I had distinct preferences in regards to who held me and who did not. Mom, Dad and my cousins Robert and Bruce sat at the very top. Yes, tiny babies possess the traits of discernment, favorites, acceptance and rejection. Do you have similar stories about yourself, your children, grandchildren or other kids you know?

I was walking on my own at seven months old. According to my mom, I began running about a month later. Why depend upon others when God provides the ability to do it yourself? God ignited perseverance in me at a young age. Moreover, God designed each of us to learn and develop at different rates in each area of life. Some may walk later, yet develop another skill at a younger age than most. Regardless of when we begin walking, everyone falls while learning any task. Throughout life we continually fall short in our futile attempts to match God's strides of holiness and righteousness (Romans 3:23). Moreover, God surrounds us with others to teach, support and encourage us along life's race course.

Figure 2: Rick on the move at 10 months old

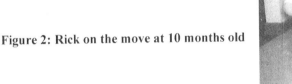

I am immensely grateful for the family, geographical, spiritual, recreational and professional environment encompassing my childhood. Age and wisdom humbly remind me that I did nothing to deserve or earn this childhood. From the beginning I loved spending time exploring outdoors in the trees of the shelterbelt and along the river as well as the buildings, going along with my dad helping around the farm.

Growing Up on the Farm

Your eyes have seen my unformed substance; And in Your book were all written The days that were ordained for me, When as yet there was not one of them. (Psalm 139:16)

God mercifully continued pouring and forming the foundation of my life when He opened my heart, mind and soul by the power of the Holy Spirit to knowing the Lord Jesus Christ as my savior for the forgiveness of sins and eternal life before my first recorded conscious memory. If truth demands memory, how does one explain other non-recallable life events? This formative foundation germinated into a perpetually maturing faith

that has molded my life in every aspect, including my running. We know that God can and has communicated with babies in the womb all the way through the oldest men and women. For example, the Bible tells us that John the Baptist leapt in Elizabeth's womb when Mary visited her cousin while pregnant with Jesus (Luke 1).

Figure 3: My nephew Wyatt Isaacson with a baby lamb. Notice the lamb's apparent peace and contentment in the hands of its shepherd.

When Elizabeth heard Mary's greeting, the baby leaped in her womb; and Elizabeth was filled with the Holy Spirit. (Luke 1:41)

My sheep hear My voice, and I know them, and they follow Me; and I give eternal life to them, and they will never perish; and no one will snatch them out of My hand. (John 10:27–28)

I remain humble, grateful, joyful and prayerful for this gift. If salvation depended on our intellectual ability to comprehend God's complete plan for salvation what *grade* would be necessary to enter eternal life with God?

Parents

Growing up on the farm allowed me to spend a great amount of time with my parents, especially with my dad. I loved being with him – most of the time. The work was often long and tedious, and he expected me to listen and respond appropriately. This enhanced our effectiveness and safety. Over the years, we engaged in thousands of deep, meaningful conversations regarding faith, morality and politics; our conversations revolved around Right and Wrong. Dad and others in the community demanded honesty above all else.

Dad's example taught the gray areas in life arise from either our lacking wisdom or combining the pure white of Christ's truth with Satan's black darkness. Dad's honesty, along with all of my extended family's honesty, influenced my view of the Bible, especially parables. Some claim the parables are fictitious events told by Jesus for an appropriate lesson. If Dad and my relatives, who are sinful humans, strive for truth in their teaching of lessons through stories; why would the Spirit of Truth who possesses infinite wisdom and knowledge of every person's thought and action since creation, avoid speaking anything except pure truth? The Bible says it is impossible for God to lie (Hebrews 6:18); and Satan is the father of lies (Jn. 8:44). Dad taught the necessity of inquisitiveness to prevent premature assumptions. He also demonstrated listening and humility, although my mind and ego were slow to absorb these attributes.

I became a morning person because being with Dad demanded I get up early to shadow him, later he demanded it for work. I despised going to Bible School for a week every summer, wanting to be with Dad; being inside was against my childhood nature and the crafts required in Bible School were boring. Additionally, I despised practicing the Christmas program at church, I am terrible at memorizing Bible verses, acting felt unauthentic; and I wanted to be with Dad.

"Church is very important, you need to go!" Was uttered on numerous occasions. His adamancy of being active in the body of Christ epitomized his core. When Dad and I traveled to the southwest corner of our farm to prepare the sandbar for a Sunday afternoon picnic with friends or family, he whistled or sang *Shall we Gather at the River.* When I complained of the memorization required for Sunday School, Dad assured its significance. When I complained of the required music class, Dad said, "Learning music is very important for church."

Mom possessed the same qualities. Their faith was verbally soft, while screaming in action. The hot Kansas sun in the summer of 1981 elevated the mercury thermometer beyond 100 degrees Fahrenheit. I was cleaning a hog barn with a shovel and pitch fork in mid-afternoon. Suddenly I was interrupted by Mom delivering a huge green plastic cup filled with homemade chocolate malt. The taste and satisfaction of this malt hit squarely on the bulls eye of my thirst and taste buds.

Dad eagerly invited traveling salesmen who stopped around noon into our home for dinner. Mom joyfully added another plate and assured an adequate supply of food. We struggled financially, yet they and others in the area welcomed known and unknown visitors to dine. Mom always had enough extra when friends or family visited during meal time.

Mom sat on the floor with my sister, Dee, and I playing and singing songs such as *Jesus Loves Me.* I viewed this as normal, assuming all children and parents engaged in similar activities of praising our Lord. My grandparents frequently played gospel hymns on their record players. Mom drove Dee and I to non-Sunday church activities and she drove me to baseball practice. When her parents visited once a month she made a cherry pie for Grandpa. Mom continues making my favorites when I visit. To this day, her quiet radiant faith brightens daily.

Farm

What do you first remember? How old were you? Emotion initiates and strengthens conscious memory. What do you believe sparked the emotions to engrain this moment in your memory? My first conscious memory occurs at the age of fifteen months in May 1968, the day we moved a half mile down the road from Martha's where my dad was raised. Martha was a recent widow, who, along with her husband Bill Dannenberg, raised their family in that house. My parents rented the farm and house from Martha after marrying. Since Bill and Martha's sons didn't return to the farm, Bill offered Dad the opportunity to join him in a farming partnership. Bill died before they formed the partnership.

> You shall not move your neighbor's boundary mark, which the ancestors have set, in your inheritance which you will inherit in the land that the LORD your God gives you to possess. (Deuteronomy 19:14; NASB95)

On the day of our move, I stood on the porch on the east of the house. Dad centered the back of the olive green 1951 Ford F-100 pickup between two red brick pillars with white cement tops standing approximately three feet high. The north and south ends contained the same brick features with hand-crafted wood extending to the roof covering the porch. Someone opened both the screen and wood doors connecting into the dining room.

I simply observed as Dad, Mom, Uncle Doug, Aunt Betty and probably others carried household items from the back of the pickup into our new home. Dad and his siblings grew up in this home less than 150 yards from the river. At fifteen months, I lacked the size or strength to assist the adults. Dee and our cousins joined me in the dining room. This was a very emotional day for my young self, filled with the excitement of moving and the company of extended family.

God blessed my sister and me with loving parents and a relationship with Him while we grew up on that Kansas farm along the North Fork of the Solomon River. I loved growing up on this farm. However, I did nothing to earn this privilege of knowing Jesus Christ or living here; rather, God ordained this arrangement just as He does for each of us. My heart, mind and soul cherished life on that farm along the river with an abundance of hunting and fishing opportunities. Each clear night offered an opportunity to gaze into the star-filled heavens, recognizing the glory of God and the work of His hand (Psalm 19:1), providing evidence of God for everyone (Romans 1:20). Knowing God and receiving the fruit of His Spirit which consists of love, joy, peace, patience, kindness, goodness, faithfulness, gentleness, self-control, gratitude, forgiveness and prayer (Galatians 5:22-23) carries us through life's heart shattering, breath seizing moments.

> The heavens are telling of the glory of God; And their expanse is declaring the work of His hands. (Psalm 19:1)

> For since the creation of the world His invisible attributes, His eternal power and divine nature, have been clearly seen, being understood through what has been made, so that they are without excuse. (Romans 1:20)

Unfortunately, our human nature frequently encourages us to question, debate and sometimes argue about God's goodness and methods. Ultimately, this originates from our judging His wisdom, which is us judging God. The more we mature in our relationship with God the greater we recognize God's holy, perfect and righteous character. This also leads to us knowing the absurdity of anyone judging God's actions.

So we moved that half mile down the road to the farm that my grandfather, Otto James Frederick Meyer, purchased in 1918. He and Grandma, Ida Sophie Zabel, married on May 31, 1923 and raised six children on this farm a mile east and two south of Gaylord, Kansas. After fifty years of farming the land and raising livestock along the banks of the North Fork of the Solomon River, Grandpa and Grandma chose to retire and moved a few miles north to Smith Center. They sold the farm to their second youngest child.

My dad, Delmer, visited the bank for a loan. Norm, the banker, reviewed the history of interest rate fluctuations because no caps for variable rate interest existed in the 1960s. He then assured Dad that variable interest rate loans remained historically stable, while also sharing that risks of increase remained possible. Unfortunately, the initial 6% interest rate later soared up to 20% in the 1970s. The additional interest expense created the difference between living comfortably and breaking even or even losing money. The early to mid 1970s were a very hard time for many American farmers.

I became a morning person as a small child because I wanted to be with my dad. This demanded waking up early. Additionally, as a four or five year old, I once slept until 11:40a.m. I do not recall the reason for my extreme fatigue. However, Mom refused to cook breakfast for me since it was almost dinner time. She did let me eat two chocolate chip cookies. I was devastated to miss breakfast for the first time in my life. Do you crave spending time with God enough to get up early each morning? When we miss opportunities for Bible study and prayer, we miss our spiritual breakfast.

I learned from that early lesson; unless I was sick, I never slept in and missed my breakfast again. This once again stresses the fact that a spiritual life demands we take action on our beliefs; not just study. When studying anything, define principles and apply them in your life to reflect those lessons. Initially, the farm turned a profit as indicated by Table 1.

Table 1

Irrigated Corn Yields	
Year	Bushel / Acre
1969	125
1970	130
1971	135
3-Yr Avg	130

Yields proved successful in these years, 1969 being the first full year my parents had complete control of the farm work; and thereby complete responsibility. My dad worked around the clock when necessary, taking fifteen to twenty minute catnaps every three to four hours on the tractor in the field. Yes, he stopped the tractor before snoozing! Sundays consisted of feeding the cattle and hogs, changing the irrigation water when applicable and worshipping God the remainder of the morning. He enjoyed the afternoons and evenings spending time with his family and friends. Afternoon activities varied from visiting with others, viewing crops, hunting, fishing or relaxing on the river following a bonfire cookout in the summers – held on that sandbar we cleared just for these gatherings.

In 1972, our corn yields diminished to about 65 bushels per acre—half of the previous three-year average. There was a disease causing the corn to die, with the plant's death descending from the top down in July. To put the timing in perspective, healthy corn stalks typically mature in September or October as the plant's base turns yellow first, then ascending to the top of the plant. So the early death from the top caused the sickly corn plant to develop very few harvestable kernels which is used to feed cattle. Although unable to assess an accurate diagnosis, plant pathologists studied our challenge. We later learned that our farm became one of the first infected with the disease called Corn Lethal Necrosis (CLN).

The combination of two viruses caused this disease. Before accurately identifying CLN, scientists named it Blue Death because the corn's color turns a blue hue. Dad joked that Blue Death referred to the farmer turning blue because of the financial loss. Plant pathologists later hypothesized that at least one of the viruses necessary for this detrimental disease originated outside of the United States and was transported to north central Kansas by those picking marijuana in our area. Yes, sinful activities have, do and will carry devastating effects on all of society, well beyond those participating in the deeds of the flesh.

> Now the deeds of the flesh are evident, which are: immorality, impurity, sensuality, idolatry, sorcery, enmities, strife, jealousy, outbursts of anger, disputes, dissensions, factions, envying, drunkenness, carousing, and things like these, of which I forewarn you, just as I have forewarned

you, that those who practice such things will not inherit the kingdom of God. (Galatians 5:19-21)

CLN continued spreading across portions of Kansas and Nebraska even into the 1990s. Fortunately, leading seed corn companies developed resistant hybrids. Dr. Ben Doupnik of the University of Nebraska spoke about CLN at a meeting I attended as a crop consultant. A fellow agronomist inquired about the severity of Corn Lethal Necrosis. Dr. Doupnik responded, "The geographical area of CLN is relatively small, but when this disease hits your farm, it is very serious." Would you agree that this is a common truth in life? A situation may not cover a wide area, but significant challenges become very serious when they affect you directly.

Despite these economic setbacks, my parents modeled their internalized faith in Christ. I have frequently quipped, "If I were perfect, I wouldn't need Christ as my Savior for the forgiveness of my sins." One's internalized Christian faith fails to make anyone perfect; humans will never be without fault. Faith transforms our hearts to love God and His people—our neighbors.

Grandpa Meyer

After my grandparents moved off the farm, Grandpa continued helping Dad. As a small child, I eagerly anticipated his daily arrival. He greeted Dee and me at the west kitchen door as we grabbed the pant portion of his overalls before he swung us one at a time between his legs. Our celebration contained extra exuberance if he brought knipp. Grandma made knipp, a German meat combination that delighted our taste buds.

Grandpa arrived every morning driving his 1966 cherry red Ford F-100 four speed, a short box pickup with a Windsor V8 engine. Grandpa putted along on Kansas Avenue, turning south onto Main Street or Highway 281; once outside the city limits he most likely quickly shifted up to fourth gear to assure staying on the top side of the 75 MPH speed limit. He claimed to do this to be sure he removed all the cobwebs from the engine while avoiding being a nuisance on the road by traveling too slow. Grandpa, like many Kansans, lived with joyful urgency.

Grandpa lived a life nearly absent sickness. My father recalls my grandfather's first illness as the stroke he suffered at the age of 71. Dad shares that through Otto's 65th birthday, "I nearly had to run to keep up with his walk." I must have inherited at least a portion of my fast walk and running abilities from Grandpa.

Grandpa's smile appeared as practically a permanent part of him. However, one morning while his two-year-old grandson was helping with chores he (yours truly) locked him in the barn's feed room with no alternate exit...Grandpa's smile vanished. His cheerful voice quickly dissipated. I was unable to unhook that latch attached to the barn door from the staple driven into the side of the barn. Though my grandparents raised six children on this farm, I was the first to lock Grandpa in the barn. His beaming smile returned as my father opened the door, releasing him from bondage and back to the great outdoors.

Grandpa frequently whistled while he worked. We could catch him whistling or singing on the tractor, tapping his toe on the accelerator to the beat of his favorite church hymns. Delmer says the tractor engine's fluctuating response to Grandpa's toe tapping "could be heard a half-mile away."

How true it is when we feel good, we feel good. I frequently invite audiences on cerebral explorations which include the question, "Is it possible to smile and maintain negative emotions?" Smiling and anger oppose one another. Smiling opens our neuron receptors to the chemicals of joy, blocking the anger chemicals. This produces a chain reaction throughout our body. Relaxed muscles are normally healthy muscles.

Our crushed spirit generates negative chain reactions in chemicals in our bodies, resulting in ill effects on our mood and health. Pessimists seldom escape illness.

Though I simplify these explanations, the principles remain true.

What causes cheerfulness in our hearts? The presence of the indwelling Holy Spirit.

So then you are no longer strangers and aliens, but you are fellow citizens with the saints, and are of God's household, having been built on the foundation of the apostles and prophets, Christ Jesus Himself being the corner stone, in whom the whole building, being fitted together, is growing into a holy temple in the Lord, in whom you also are being built together into a dwelling of God in the Spirit. (Ephesians 2:19–22)

I will ask the Father, and He will give you another Helper, that He may be with you forever; that is the Spirit of truth, whom the world cannot receive, because it does not see Him or know Him, but you know Him because He abides with you and will be in you. (John 14:16-17)

However, you are not in the flesh but in the Spirit, if indeed the Spirit of God dwells in you. But if anyone does not have the Spirit of Christ, he does not belong to Him. (Romans 8:9)

But I say, walk by the Spirit, and you will not carry out the desire of the flesh. For the flesh sets its desire against the Spirit, and the Spirit against the flesh; for these are in opposition to one another, so that you may not do the things that you please. But if you are led by the Spirit, you are not under the Law.

But the fruit of the Spirit is love, joy, peace, patience, kindness, goodness, faithfulness, gentleness, self-control; against such things there is no law.

Now those who belong to Christ Jesus have crucified the flesh with its passions and desires. If we live by the Spirit, let us also walk by the Spirit. Let us not become boastful, challenging one another, envying one another (Galatians 5:16-18, 22-26, NASB95).

Additionally, God expects us to continually pray, live with gratitude, and joy.

> Rejoice always; pray without ceasing; in everything give thanks; for this is God's will for you in Christ Jesus. (1 Thessalonians 5:16–18)

Focusing on the desires of Christ while walking with the Holy Spirit creates immense joy. This real cheerfulness prevails though life's challenges, it is a deep feeling that remains even in difficult times. You may have a child or grandchild lock you in a room. That is a small event. Christ sweated blood-like drops as He pondered the crucifixion (Luke 22:44). Christ kept his eyes on the Father's will and love for us. We, too, should focus on the Father's will and our love for others.

Grandpa Meyer suffered paralysis from that stroke in August of 1971. His ill-health continued on for four years. Pictures reveal him still smiling, his cheerful heart remained. His smile lessened during the last few weeks of 1975. As I viewed Otto James Frederick Meyer in the casket, his smile beamed ear to ear. His beaming smile returned as our Heavenly Father opened the door to heaven, releasing him from life's bondage.

Sam Showed Me the Door

Once I began walking, I loved the outdoors and exploring the farm when I wasn't *helping* Dad or Grandpa. Having a dog at my side escalated the joy of my adventures around the farm. My buddy Sam, a brown retriever, fulfilled this role. I began engaging in physical workouts at an early age. During one of these adventures at age three, I became disoriented in the shelterbelt north of our house. Grandpa Meyer planted this shelterbelt consisting of thousands of trees planted in five parallels rows extending a quarter of a mile in length in 1947.

The benefits of reducing the effects of the cold, erosive winds blowing from the north towards our house included reducing soil erosion and snowdrifts. The shelterbelt also protected the house, other buildings, those working outside and the livestock from destructive and chill-piercing winds. This is nearly a quarter of a mile long and roughly twenty-yards wide. Dad shared stories about he and his siblings carrying buckets of water two hundred to four hundred yards up from the river to aid the trees' early growth and development.

It seemed so dark amidst these trees and I couldn't find a way out. Sam led me to the old outhouse used during my dad's childhood. This revealed a path through the trees because a well-worn path existed between the house and the two-seater outhouse. Old Sears and Roebuck catalogs, whose pages once substituted for Charmin, remained in the outhouse.

Dad told a story about his youngest brother Richard seeing a bull snake stick its head through one seat of this outhouse while sitting on the other seat during their childhood. Richard quickly finished and headed for home. By leading me to that old outhouse, Sam saved me from being lost in the shelterbelt. I later told my parents, "Sam showed me the door."

As a youngster, I crawled on Sam's brown back, grab his ears and rode him like a horse around the farmyard. I considered Sam as both dog and motorcycle. Ever the good sport, Sam seemed to encourage the use of my imagination. My slight frame was a light load for Sam. So I am sure he never looked on those romps as a burden.

In 1970, Sam collided with a forage wagon pulled by a pickup on the county road by our farm, though Sam knew the road was off limits for him. We rushed Sam to the veterinarian who examined him, then returned to the front desk where Mom and I waited. "We have to put Sam to sleep." We entered the room where Sam lay on a table. I petted him saying, "Goodbye Sam." I accepted his death as a way of farm life.

The following months I missed having a dog accompany me on my voyages around the farm. In February of 1971, Dad arrived home from town dressed in olive green coveralls, cowboy boots and red winter cap, entering through the west door into our large kitchen. He carried a puppy into the kitchen, kneeling down and saying of the animal, "I just happened to find it..." The timing was more than suspicious. I was elated about my birthday present!

Unfortunately, shortly after receiving the dog, workers constructing the Harvest Store silos accidentally hit and killed my puppy with their pickup in the farmyard. I was concurrently sad about the puppy's death and understanding of the circumstances.

Livestock births and deaths naturally occur as a part of life on a farm. I believe my parents and those whose vehicles hit the dogs, suffered more from the dogs' deaths than I did. Because I heard the word of God at home and while attending church and Sunday school since I was only a few weeks old, I developed a child-like faith very early on.

Faith in Christ enables us to understand that while life is to be revered, death should not be feared. One of my great-grandmothers passed away about the same time as Sam. After her death, I stood in the farmhouse kitchen imagining what would happen if my sister, parents or I died. Would Jesus physically descend thru the roof, the attic and the ten foot ceiling into the kitchen? Would He pick up the deceased in his arms and carry them to heaven? Through deaths of animals and loved ones, I learned about living on the faith of Christ's salvation. I never seemed to have a fear of dying.

My Race against a Calf

I certainly ran early and often during my adventures around the farm. This resulted from my curiosity, sense of adventure, trying to keep up with my dad, and Dad demanding I urgently respond to his commands. Whatever Dad instructed me when performing a task, whether chores, retrieving a tool or getting a vehicle or tractor parked away from our location, he nearly always completed his command with "Run!" Obedient sons and daughters immediately and urgently responded to their parents back in those times. Since it touched an area of joy in my young life, you can imagine how swiftly I complied and ran with intensity.

Decades later, Dr. Stanley Toussaint, one of my favorite professors at Dallas Theological Seminary, illustrated while teaching on Paul, Silas,

Luke and Timothy about them responding to Paul's vision in the middle of the night at Troas in Acts 16:9-10, "True obedience acts immediately."

Figure 4: Dr. Stanley and Mrs. Toussaint. A class picture after Dr. Toussaint's final class of full time teaching at Dallas Theological Seminary. He began teaching in 1960. Rick is in the maroon shirt.

A memorable example of Dad commanding me to run occurred because of a calf. My running gear that day consisted of cowboy boots, Lee stretch denim jeans and a snap-button western shirt. That gear greatly contrasts the type worn by competitive runners today.

This calf's speed and endurance provided a life-long lesson for future races. The cows and calves grazed on the corn and sorghum stalks during the winter. Though we had erected an electric fence to contain them, a calf crawled underneath into the alfalfa field. This calf refused to cooperate and return to the fenced area as we pursued it in the 1966 cherry-red pickup. Finally, Dad stopped and instructed me to climb out to pursue the calf on foot, running to cut it off before it entered the timber along the river. Dad drove on the opposite side of the calf. I ran after that calf for over a half mile, while my legs and arms experienced a sulfurous burn. Even as my lungs burned and lactic acid in the muscles tormented me causing pain in my nerves, I knew I had to keep up the intense pace. I had to succeed! Finally, the calf returned to the fenced area. The chase ended. I bent over huffing and puffing. My legs and lungs continued burning while I rejoined Dad in the pickup to continue our chores. For my young life, that was the most pain I had experienced, but I also felt so grown up and proud of myself for a job well done.

When maximizing our running performances, we must push beyond previously known limits. Just like a seed wanting to germinate, we must figuratively die to ourselves; die to our neurological sensors screaming of the pain. Beyond this sensory death lie the great victories of life. Beyond this intense, tortuous pain resides the great exhilaration of contentment, knowing you challenged yourself more than you ever thought possible. Success in every endeavor requires this extent of personal challenge—only the balance between physical and mental exertion varies.

Chapter 2:

Desire & Goals
Power of the Mind—Combined
with Faith

Back to the Farm
Gopher Holes and Irrigation

Dad raised mostly corn and alfalfa on our farm. These, like all crops, require water to survive and produce a profitable yield. They receive this water from high ground water, rain or irrigation water either singularly or a combination of these sources. Crops such as wheat and grain sorghum need less water than does corn. The typical rainfall during the corn's growing season is insufficient where I grew up as well as into Nebraska. Consequently, farmers irrigate their corn crops with water from a well or from a lake released down canals for gravity irrigation. Fields must first be leveled so that one end of the field is slightly higher than the opposite end with a smooth slope throughout. Gravity irrigation then occurs when farmers intentionally release water from the top end of the field to flow by gravity to the bottom end of the field. We used a head ditch and siphon tubes. Irrigating crops with siphon tubes from a head ditch can zap the joy from life on a farm. This labor and time intensive practice proves physically and mentally demanding on a farmer in the sweltering heat of summer.

Figure 5: August 1974 Judy, Rick and Delmer inspect an ear of corn along the head ditch while irrigating.

Do you remember the movie *Caddy Shack*? Bill Murray played Carl the groundskeeper. Carl decided to rid the golf course of gophers. One particular gopher epitomized a rascal. Carl's numerous attempts to wittingly eliminate this gopher failed.

We, too, had gophers on the farm, especially in the irrigation ditches. Gophers proved challenging pests in and along our farm's irrigation ditches. The released lake water flowed into canals through adjustable gates, placed in the bank of the canals, allowing the appropriate volume of water to flow onto the thirsty crops. However, other cultivation occurs long before the irrigation begins.

During this era in farming, farmers cultivated crops to remove most of the weeds. Weeds are simply plants out of place. The farmers then ditched or hilled the crop, creating small ditches between each row of the crop for the water to flow along the end of fields. Cultivating soil often produces a refreshing aroma that originates from actinomycete bacteria, from the genus *Streptomyce*[3]. This genus also produces antibiotics such as streptomycin, soil microbiologist S.A. Waksman received a Nobel Peace award in medicine in 1942 for this discovery.[4] Soil microbiologist estimate 2,000,000 living biological organisms per square inch of soil.

---

[3] (Clark 1989, 52)
[4] (Clark 1989, 52)

Yes, God places the source of powerful medicines such as streptomycin in soil, frequently referred to as dirt. How many of God's gifts do we miss due to viewing life's thriving soil as simply *dirt*? Additionally, we often find life's greatest gifts through digging through the literal and figurative *dirt* in life.

Because of the limited supply of canal water, each farmer scheduled the receiving of his allotment of irrigation water with the irrigation district's ditch-rider assigned to the region. Consequently, we typically irrigated for a week, and then we shut off for a week. Pesky gophers occasionally capitalized on this opportunity to dig a hole from the inside of the dry ditch to another location; usually along a field road. When water once again ran down the ditch, a portion flowed through the gopher hole in the ditch to where the gopher exited. Farmers then plugged the hole, preventing the waste of water and a muddy mess by the exit hole.

I questioned why we must find the hole in the water-filled ditch rather than filling the hole with dirt where the water exited. This appeared as a much quicker and easier way to solve the problem than finding the hole in the ditch filled with water. However, the permanent solution for each gopher hole begins with first finding the hole in the ditch. We achieved this by either seeing a swirl in the water above the hole or one of us running our hand along the interior of the water-filled ditch. Once found, one of us stood with a foot in the hole while the other irrigator shoveled dirt in the gopher hole and stomped the soil into the hole, plugging it. A child believes that bandaging the gopher hole relieves the problem. Later, I began understanding the necessity of solving the problem at the point of origin and eliminating the cause of the problem from these rascally gophers. Just as in *Caddy Shack*, real life gophers are difficult to eradicate.

Would you agree, resolving issues in running and life engages the same principles as plugging a gopher hole? Find the point of origin and then do everything possible to eliminate the cause. We solve nothing in our masquerade of bandaging the effect rather than the cause. The difficulty and commitment involved in resolving the cause mandates becoming dirty—literally and figuratively. Resolving challenges requires great thought followed by climbing in the flow of life and putting our feet down, just like plugging gopher holes. Great solution-oriented thought requires effort. Henry Ford once stated, "Thinking is the hardest work there is which is why so few people do it."

One sunny July morning, water flowed from the canal into the irrigation ditch, as it should. The two-inch diameter siphon tubes perform their duties of sucking the water from the ditch, through the tubes and into the cornfield. The water properties of adhesion and cohesion properly functioned as the water molecules bound together pulling one another along. My small hands could not help set these big tubes, so I assisted by carrying the tubes from where they ran two days before to where they need to be set that day. In a sense, the irrigation tubes played a massive game of leapfrog. Additionally, carrying an arm full of irrigation tubes across muddy cornrows enhances balance, core strength and strength of legs and feet along with flexibility in the ankles.

Tubes must run at all times to sustain the balanced water level. Irrigating from a head ditch represents simple physics. The volume of water flowing into the ditch must equal the volume of water that the tubes siphon onto the field. If not, the water will overflow and wash out the ditch. Unfortunately, my stepping on top of the ditch, instead of on the side, created two negative results. First, the water eroded the ditch running through the footprint, creating a ditch break. Second, Dad became upset, complete with raised eyebrows, wrinkled forehead and intense amplified voice. He nearly pushed off his cap, his index finger pointing at the water flowing out of control. I became too familiar with this look over the years since Dad never limited this gesture of disappointment to irrigating.

Conversely, setting too many tubes enabled more water to leave the ditch than entered it which caused the water level to drop. If this unbalance continued, the tubes would eventually stop running once the water dropped below the bottom of the tubes in the ditch. Guess what happens when enough tubes stop siphoning water out of the ditch into the field? Right! There is a rapid influx of water, and a ditch break will likely occur. The same thing happens if your kitchen faucet runs water into the sink faster than the drain takes it out— eventually the sink over flows.

The smallest tubes we used had a diameter of one quarter-inch. We did use a few of these on this ditch. Dee and I set these tubes with our small hands. The largest I have seen are the two-inch tubes. Twelve two-inch tubes will keep one acre-foot of water flowing from the canal into the ditch. We usually had two to three acre-feet at one time. Comparatively, the same acre-foot output requires twenty-four 1.25 inch tubes. One acre-foot of water stands one foot deep on one acre, 43,560 square feet.

Irrigating provided valuable lessons regarding our spiritual journey and growth in Christ. We learned the exponential relationship of geometrical area and volume. When we doubled the volume of water, we quadrupled the water's carrying capacity. Similarly, *doubling* our correct understanding and application of scripture, quadrupled our peace, joy and gratitude in our life and the resulting effectiveness of our discipleship. Additionally, optimal spiritual growth, maturity and discipleship occur when we maintain a balance of receiving and serving. The greater our desire to serve and evangelize, the greater input of prayer and properly understanding scripture we need. Conversely, we become frustrated if our input exceeds our output of serving, our applying scripture to our daily lives.

Moreover, the most efficient irrigation systems keep the water below the crop canopy where it is out of sight and less likely to evaporate. Evaporated water does not contribute to the crop's yield. Also, efficient irrigation has minimal water running out the end of the field. The purpose of irrigation water is to soak into the soil and help move nutrients to and through the plants. Nutrients and photosynthesis produce yield.

These same principles apply to evangelism and discipleship. Their purpose exists to draw people to Christ and help those who do know Christ deepen their relationship with Him as well as minister to others by the power of the Holy Spirit. Similar to irrigation, the most effective evangelism and discipleship is often out of sight from the public through elbow-to-elbow conversations and relationships. Unfortunately, secularism and immature Christians measure success on the activities and pontifications they see "above the canopy." Any ministry affected by pride and ego will produce pride and ego. For example, pride and ego drive most donors. Therefore donors prefer the ministries they support irrigate "above the canopy." Instead they should seek real results from people knowing Christ as their savior and perpetually growing in His image regardless of the publicity.

A farmer driving around town everyday blowing his horn and announcing through a bullhorn that he fed his livestock and tended to his crops, doesn't feed very many cattle nor farm many acres.

People and societies bear other striking similarities to gravity irrigation. If we consume more than we expend, our health eventually deteriorates. The more people working in an economy the greater volume of 'water' a society can handle. The economic relationship to increase workers is exponential—just like the relationship of volume to carrying capacity. If capable people stop pursuing Christ's will for their life, then a society's economy will disseminate, just like the irrigation ditch. Because, an economy or society without God's holiness and righteousness is eroding.

Water from the irrigation tubes flow through the fields, infiltrating the soil where the crops' roots absorb it. Water enables crops to stand up straight with turgor pressure, the pressure of water flowing through the plant. An erect plant with leaves fully opened, maximizes absorption of available sunlight. Additionally, water transports nutrients, and ultimately, produces grain which feeds the world. Therefore, grain production is food production. Food and water constitute life. Regardless of the amount of water and nutrients, sunlight is required for grain production.

Similarly, a society only truly receives substantive emotional and spiritual nourishment when its members absorb and live in the Light of Christ. Absorption occurs through a humble heart engaging in Bible study, prayer, worship and fellowship with fellow Christians. Authentic encouragement enhances people as water benefits plants. Encouragement helps people stand up straight. An upright posture, heart, mind and soul in people enables them to perpetually maximize their absorption of the light of Christ (John 1:1-13). Moreover, sincere encouragement enhances the nutrient transporting of a Christ centered heart which enables producing enduring spiritual fruit (John 15:16).

Encouragement is an instrument of divine change. ~ Charles M. Gibbs

Power of a Goal during WWII

The light initiating germination[5] of my pondering the power of the mind combined with the Holy Spirit flashed on my six-year-old imagination while irrigating on the farm with my dad. Dad and my neighbor Richard Horning straddled the property line demarcating their cornfields a mile east and a mile south of Gaylord, Kansas, in July 1973. They discussed crops, weather and irrigation. Wearing green Sears Toughskin jeans, a tank top with blue horizontal stripes, a baseball cap pulled down over my eyes and cowboy boots, I threw clods and chased frogs. Suddenly their conversation captured my attention—ultimately changing my life. Richard began sharing his experiences as a United States Marine serving in World War Two. He described a battle with the Japanese that left him as the only survivor among his group of U.S. troops—I do not recall the number of men in the group. Japanese soldiers walked amongst the U.S. Marine causalities verifying their death by penetrating their heart with bayonets. One Japanese soldier approached Richard, kicking him in the ribs and poking him with a bayonet. Richard played dead! He avoided moving, breathing or screaming—he played dead. Just as the Japanese man prepared to pierce Richard's heart, the enemy commander called for his soldier to move forward.[6]

This story, along with several others Richard told that day, permeated my mind, permanently prompting my curiosity. What forces enabled Richard to remain motionless, breathless and speechless under those circumstances? What caused the Japanese commander to halt his soldier immediately before the bayonet pierced Richard's heart? What prevented the Japanese soldier from quickly completing the motion of piercing before proceeding with his company? Do these forces and causes affect the lives—functionality, performance and health—of typical, non-combat, individuals?

---

[5] **Invalid source specified.**
[6] Verified the event's facts with Richard's son, David Horning, September 2008, Gaylord, Kansas

1. Do your goals agree with the Bible along with promptings and convictions of the Holy Spirit in your heart?
2. Are your goals written in your mind?
3. Do your prayers agree with your goals?
4. Receiving guidance from God begins with studying and internalizing His written word in the Bible.

Do not eat the bread of a selfish man, Or desire his delicacies; For as he thinks within himself, so he is. He says to you, "Eat and drink!" But his heart is not with you. You will vomit up the morsel you have eaten, And waste your compliments. (Proverbs 23:6–8)

Many Christians and non-Christians alike quote Proverbs 23:7, "As a man thinks in his heart, so is he" to illustrate the power of our thoughts. This passage illustrates that our character, embedded in our heart, generates our thoughts and motives. As illustrated, those whose hearts are saturated with selfishness may appear generous through promoting a false façade of generosity. In other words, Proverbs 23:6-8 illustrates that a wolf in sheep's clothing is still a wolf. Just as the nature of animals is determined by their DNA, so the character embedded in our heart determines our thoughts and motives.

Scientifically, our brain and heart health often mirror one another. For example, our bone marrow produces immunity in our body. Similarly, our thoughts originate from and mirror the character residing in our heart. The character of our heart forms our thoughts and motives. These thoughts and motives lead us in setting, pursuing and achieving our goals. Character in the heart that generates good and pure motives is received only from receiving and perpetually submitting to the indwelling Holy Spirit. We receive the Holy Spirit as a result of becoming a Christian.

> That He would grant you, according to the riches of His glory, to be strengthened with power through His Spirit in the inner man (Ephesians 3:16)
> For I joyfully concur with the law of God in the inner man (Romans 7:22)

> Therefore we do not lose heart, but though our outer man is decaying, yet our inner man is being renewed day by day (2 Corinthians 4:16)

The inner man (Gk. ὁ ἔσω ἄνθρωπος) literally refers to the inner person and the hidden person:[7] our heart, mind and soul - these determine our character. The Greek ὁ ἔσω ἄνθρωπος appears 68 times in 17 verses.

Our foundational character is determined by who occupies our *inner man*. Is your inner man occupied and led by selfish desires **or** demons; both of which oppose the Holy Spirit? We live with internal peace, joy, mercy love, hope and power only when the Holy Spirit saturates and guides the heart, mind and soul of our inner man.

These illustrations of our character received from the Holy Spirit reminds us, "For nothing will be impossible *with* God" (Luke 1:37). This Bible passage teaches us that it is God who decides if, when, where, how, why and with whom the *impossible* occurs. Our sinful pride and ego lead us to desiring a self-centered life instead of a Christ-centered life. Pride and ego lead us to believing we determine the if, when, where, how, why and with whom.

Richard's story permanently etches into my thought process because it illustrates the power of the mind when saturated **with** faith in the creator of all who is Jesus Christ (Ephesians 3:14-19; James 4:5). Humble hearts and minds submitted to Jesus Christ and the Holy Spirit know that God's sovereignty and provision in the world and in our individual lives far exceeds the greatest plans conjured up by the accumulation of all mankind.

Contrary to the prosperity gospel, *name it—claim it* preachers, country club Sunday School classes and too many unqualified Bible study leaders; those whose inner man is led by the Holy Spirit seek God's will instead of telling God our plans.

---

[7] Louw, J. P., & Nida, E. A. (1996). *Greek-English lexicon of the New Testament: based on semantic domains* (electronic ed. of the 2nd edition., Vol. 1, p. 319). New York: United Bible Societies.

For example, the Bible gives absolutely no indication of the Virgin Mary sitting in a circle with her friends studying the Old Testament then standing up with her toes tapping, arms waving as if engaging in jumping jacks and boldly proclaiming, "I claim in the name of *Jesus* that the Holy Spirit will impregnate me with the Messiah!! And, wise astrologists, astronomers and scientists will bring us gold, frankincense and myrrh. Can I get an 'Amen'?"

Those with little or no faith in Christ participate in jumping jack like motions while arrogantly telling the Lord what He should give them.

> Humble yourselves in the presence of the Lord, and He will exalt you. (James 4:10)

> The mind of man plans his way, But the LORD directs his steps. (Proverbs 16:9)

However, because we belong to God, we desire only that which He knows is eternally best for us. He gives us the desires of our hearts when we delight ourselves in Him, not ourselves or the possessions of the world.

> Delight yourself in the Lord; And He will give you the desires of your heart. Commit your way to the Lord, Trust also in Him, and He will do it. He will bring forth your righteousness as the light And your judgment as the noonday. (Psalm 37:4-6)

> No one can serve two masters; for either he will hate the one and love the other, or he will be devoted to one and despise the other. You cannot serve God and wealth. (Matthew 6:24)

When we seek the Lord, He will mold our passions, including the specifics of what we should request in prayer. Delighting ourselves in the Lord enables us to squint at His incomprehensible magnificence. Leaving the heart, mind and soul of our inner man singing, "Holy, Holy, Holy..." (Rev 4:8-11).

We may boldly proceed towards the dreams He places within us, knowing He will provide according to His will as opposed to our ability. Nations and militaries do not win wars. God wins wars working through individuals like Richard and Uncle LaVerne in the military of nations. Similarly, we win daily spiritual battles through seeking God.

Richard shared another story of fighting the Japanese. He described the Japanese charging in the middle of the night, screaming at the top of their lungs to scare and deceive their enemy. They hoped to startle the unsuspecting sleeping enemy and create the illusion of a larger attack force. "We didn't know if there were ten or thousands of them attacking."

Would you agree many of our problems in life are like the WWII Japanese soldiers? They catch us off guard, startle us and give us the illusion of being much larger in our imagination than in reality. Sometimes the reality of the situation turns out to be only 1% of our imagined challenge, just like the charging Japanese army.

Would you agree that many attackers in life apply these techniques? People attacking the Bible, a policy or the United States Constitution "scream" as they attack in an effort to shock and disorient their prey. They attempt to deceive in giving the appearance of many more disagreeing.

Veterans provide powerful lessons about human performance and living solely on faith. With WWII vets dying frequently, how many stories similar to Richard's remain untold? We need to hear, internalize, apply and share the lessons from these stories. We need to understand what God is capable of performing through us, even when only death and destruction remain apparent.

Figuratively speaking, Richard stood at the Red Sea believing the enemy would overtake him. His only hope rested in the power of God. Just as God opened the Red Sea for Moses and the Israelites, God opened the Red Sea of WWII for Richard by allowing him to lie there as if dead while the Japanese soldier kicked and poked. God spared Richard's life through a reality showing only death. Numerous other soldiers have certainly faced similar experiences. Like Richard, will you trust Christ while staring at death and destruction? Will you trust Christ when all other hope is vanished?

Chapter 3:

1974 Brings Change

While unrelated to my running at the time, the events of the farm, including diseases, interest rates and the markets later revealed significant learning. Additionally, the Bible offered illustrations of God approving evil generated winds intended for destruction to challenge and guide the sails of our lives in God's intended direction opposing the prevailing current of our desires.

The year of 1974 included components affecting the long-term impact of my life, running and ministry. This included the cattle market crash, a major setback for all cattlemen. On another hot, muggy July afternoon, sweat gushed from our pores as we pulled weeds and stickers in our freshly seeded yard on the east side of the house. I quenched my thirst by taking a swig of delectable mineral filled well-water. During the summer, my parents typically treated us to one 12-ounce can of Shasta pop per day. My favorites consisted of Cream Soda or Coke poured from a quart screw-cap bottle into a six or eight ounce glass that originally held grape jelly.

Eventually the radiant, sweltering afternoon sky darkened as storm clouds rolled through as if on a conveyor belt. Flashes of lightning danced across the dark blue afternoon sky both horizontally and vertically. The rumbling thunder sounded as if God cranked up the bass on His heavenly music. We continued to work while keeping an eye on the sky as the mild storm passed over. I am still fascinated by watching storm clouds develop and move. I fail to remember when I first witnessed one of many developing funnel clouds. Fortunately, the storm passed over our farm that day, yet the air remained sizzling, sultry and eerily calm.

Suddenly, the storm reversed its course. This signified an *east storm*, which results from the atmosphere containing sufficient energy to reverse the winds. Similarly, Bible scholars believe that the vicious wind that killed Job's ten children was a strong wind from the east[8] (Job 1:18-19),

---

[8] Alden, R. L. (1993). *Job* (Vol. 11, p. 60). Nashville: Broadman &

such as an east storm. On this afternoon, the sky turned dark green and a severe hailstorm approached with high winds. Dense hail is to corn as kryptonite is to Superman. After the devastating storm, we could easily see all the way through full-grown cornfields, especially those with east-west rows. Following the storm, the previously hot, muggy weather transformed into a comfortable sun basking late afternoon, with birds cheerfully serenading the countryside.

We, like the weather, will experience major life challenges when opposing nature, the laws of the universe established and governed by God. Converse to nature's storms, we may continue to bask in the light of Christ during life's challenges through studying the Bible, persistent diligent prayer and associating with others who know Christ. If you do fall prey to fear, repent yet stay encouraged, because you share company with the disciples in the boat with Jesus on the Sea of Galilee. Jesus rebuked the wind, calmed the sea and returned peace to the disciples. The biblical word used for rebuke (Gk. ἐπετίμησεν), suggesting that Jesus recognized the power of evil in the storm.[9] Lest we become complacent and justifying in our sinful fear, let us also recall that Jesus admonished the disciples for their lack of faith (Mark 4:39-40). However, Jesus did not "fire" His disciples, nor will He "fire" you when you turn to him and seek forgiveness for your sins.

Truly knowing Christ as the son of God, the crucified and resurrected Savior, necessitates trusting Him. We trust Jesus because we intimately know him as the God of everything ever created past, present or future (John 1:1-4). Satan and his angels chose pride and ego-filled rebellion because they failed to recognize or acknowledge the full identity, power and majesty of God. Their rebellion demonstrates their false belief that they, as created beings, may meet or exceed God in any facet. The Holy Spirit enables our possessing the perpetually increasing knowledge of God's supremacy.

Trusting God through Jesus Christ by the power of the Holy Spirit enables us to know in our inner man that all of creation from the sun, to galaxies

Holman Publishers.
[9] Grassmick, J. D. (1985). Mark. In J. F. Walvoord & R. B. Zuck (Eds.), *The Bible Knowledge Commentary: An Exposition of the Scriptures* (Vol. 2, p. 122). Wheaton, IL: Victor Books.

beyond galaxies, to atoms, quarks and leptons jumps, halts, dances, forms or dissipates at His commands in the blink of an eye.

Uncle LaVerne

Opportunities to observe, learn and grow on the farm consistently presented themselves like a windrow from a dense stand of irrigated alfalfa feeding into a baler or silage chopper maneuvering through a field behind a tractor. One such opportunity arrived through a sickening experience. The flu bug struck me one early spring day in 1975 while I sat in my second grade classroom. The school secretary called my mother to pick me up and take me home. My mom arrived in Uncle LaVerne's dark green Ford F-100 long-box pickup. Mom explained Dad, Uncle LaVerne and Uncle Wayne were using Dad's pickup to hold the vaccines and syringes to vaccinate our cattle next to the loading chute before transporting them to the pasture. I climbed in on the passenger side, placing my feet on and around a tool box sitting on the floor. Mom and I left Gaylord Grade School and drove towards our farm. My stomach felt queasy a couple of times, then quickly settled down. Then, without warning, as we turned west on our driveway, I vomited into the tool box and on the floor of Uncle LaVerne's pickup.

The disappointment of creating this stinky, awful mess in Uncle LaVerne's pickup overwhelmed me. "How could I do such a thing?" "Why did I allow myself to become sick with the flu?" I profusely apologized later in the day. Uncle LaVerne immediately forgave me, and washed away my awful, stinky vomit with water from the garden hose connected to the hydrant next to the old windmill tower between our house and the barn. He assured me in his normal laid back demeanor, "That's okay, it all washed out." Initially, I was nearly too ashamed to acknowledge and apologize for my mess. Perhaps some argue no apology was necessary since I did not intend this. Modern day television programs such as NCIS proclaim that apologizing reveals weakness. My mother believed differently. I am grateful to Mom for requiring me to apologize to Uncle LaVerne, and I remain extremely grateful to Uncle LaVerne for his forgiveness. I felt much better afterwards. He never mentioned this incident the rest of his life.

Similarly, our belief in Jesus Christ as Savior washes away our sins with Christ's blood shed on the cross at Calvary. We repent in our hearts by turning away from our self-reliance to the Lord Jesus Christ. The light of Christ reveals our awful, stinky mess of sin and sinful nature. But why do we allow ourselves to sin? Like my vomiting, we frequently sin despite our desperate attempts to avoid sin.

As disgusting as it is to vomit in someone's vehicle, our sin is exponentially more despicable in our relationship with God. As wonderful and forgiving as Uncle LaVerne was to me and others, Jesus instantly washes away our horrific sins when we turn to God through Christ's death on the cross and subsequent resurrection.

> Then I will sprinkle clean water on you, and you will be clean; I will cleanse you from all your filthiness and from all your idols. (Ezekiel 36:25)

Do we sometimes feel too ashamed to turn to God and away from our sin? Some may argue that repenting and confessing are unnecessary since we sinned unintentionally. We will feel much better after repenting to God the Father and confessing that we are sinful as well as any specific sins revealed to us by the Holy Spirit. The first step of repenting is turning to God which causes us to see God's glory as well as recognize our sins and sinful nature, followed by a horrific feeling, followed by seeing and knowing Jesus who forgives our sin because of His death and resurrection. Additionally, seeing God's glory causes us to submit every aspect of our life to Him - including our family, profession, running, finances, recreation and all relationships with Him.

> As far as the east is from the west, So far has He removed our transgressions from us. (Psalm 103:12)

> When He said, "A new covenant," He has made the first obsolete. But whatever is becoming obsolete and growing old is ready to disappear. (Hebrews 8:13)

Growing in Wisdom, Knowledge and Understanding

To be the *best* we must *think, prepare* and *respond* as the *best*. We learn to *think, prepare* and *respond* as the *best* through reading, recordings and associations by and with the best.

Windmill

I continue striving for the fifth of five goals that I set in June 1975 while pondering by the old windmill tower that remained intact except the head and the pump. I used the attached garden hose and nozzle to spray water on the surrounding ground and flowers, as well as setting up my imaginary irrigation system, while simultaneously imagining pitching a baseball that curved both to the right and to the left all in the same throw. I began setting long-term goals.

1. Be on a state championship team
2. Be on a nationally ranked team
3. Place high in the Boston Marathon
4. Place high in the New York City Marathon
5. *Continuing to pursue this goal*

I had previously set goals in this peaceful locale. The first occurred at the age of sixteen months after I had been walking for nearly a year, when I evidently became determined to climb the ladder up the windmill. I loved heights. I have no conscious memory of this event. Dad said I was 'helping' him when suddenly he saw I had climbed at least 20 feet up the ladder. He instinctively yelled at me to get down! The emphatic tonality of his voice distinctly resembled a drill sergeant. Dad admitted that he immediately recognized his mistake in tone selection because I nearly responded to his commanding voice by leaping to the ground to give immediate compliance. Upon switching his tonality, I climbed down as quickly as possible.

Figure 6: Looking west from the house at the 1966 F-100 pick-up, the windmill tower and the barn. Dee and me, first day of school, August 1974.

The Bible says we are to have childlike faith, one of the characteristics of children is obedience to our parents. I immediately responded to Dad's correcting voice, we should likewise respond to God's correcting voice spoken through scripture, peers, church leaders and our conscious.

Visiting my Cousins

We drove to my grandparents, Kenneth and Emily Kahrs in Nebraska about once a month during my childhood. Dee and I loved seeing them, our aunts and uncles and cousins.

Figure 7: Dee and I held our baby cousins, Deborah Kahrs and Teresa Dorn. Judy and Delmer sit to the left and Grandpa Kenneth Kahrs oversees Dee and me. Winter 1970

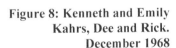

Figure 8: Kenneth and Emily Kahrs, Dee and Rick. December 1968

On a warm afternoon in May of 1975, we visited my grandparent's farm southeast of Bloomington, NE. My cousins and I had been outside climbing around and on top of the barn, corncrib and hog house. The top of the L shaped hog house, formerly the chicken coop, was a terrific spot to pick mulberries from an adjacent tree. We determined too many mulberries were falling on the ground. What was the solution to this predicament? Ours was placing a sheet on the ground underneath the tree, shaking the tree, and then dumping the harvested mulberries into feed buckets.

In need of a sheet to increase the efficiency of collecting the mulberries, we entered the house, realizing that pulling a sheet off of one of the beds in Grandma's house was not a feasible option. She needed those sheets. Fortunately, we found just what we needed in one of the dresser drawers, a brand new, still in the wrapper, snow white sheet.

We anxiously returned to our project, enjoying an abundant harvest of mulberries. However, upon seeing our achievement, Grandma lacked appreciation of our ingenuity. If there is a Grandmother Hall of Fame, Emily Kahrs is certainly among the inductees. This Hall of Fame grandmother had certain expectations for her grandkids, having respect for others and their property was one of them. Grandma and our mothers fully enlightened us about our poor judgment. We fulfilled our goal of collecting several five-gallon buckets of mulberries, though we destroyed someone's property in attaining our goal. We became well informed this method of goal achievement was unacceptable in all situations. We endured the storm of wrath.

This May afternoon served as another monumental day in goal setting for me. My mother called me to the kitchen table during one of our indoor visits for lemonade. We occasionally visited grandma's bowl of lemon drops she kept for her grandkids. Mom was looking at a recent edition of the Hastings Tribune; the Sports section featured an article on the son of one of my grandmother's cousins. Doug Phelps was the first Nebraska prep athlete to clear seven feet in the high jump, achieved during the 1975 season.

This achievement slowly permeated my mind.

Three Steps to Attainment

Three broad steps exist on the path to goal attainment.

1. I Can – Ability

Mr. Cotton stood on his desk during health class during our sophomore year at Smith Center High School. "I told my 1966 basketball team in Wyoming 'you CAN win the State Championship!!!', they won the championship in 1966. In 1967, I told them again, 'you CAN win the State Championship!!!'" Mr. Cotton's message radiated with passion. The first step in setting goals is acknowledgement of your ability to achieve the goal. "Yes, I have the ability!"

This step is the hope stage of a goal. Being informed of our potential, the possibilities surrounding us gives us hope. Unfortunately, too many goals, including New Year's resolutions, remain in this stage.

When I initially set my 4 goals in June 1975, I acknowledged I could achieve these goals. I believed anything was possible with Jesus Christ, if congruent with His will. Seeing neighbors and relatives realize notable achievements strengthened this belief.

2. I Will – Desire

This is the stage of desire, the acknowledgement of both potential and desire. Yes, I know I am capable, I know there are increased possibilities. The I Will stage says, "I am willing." You now are willing, possessing the desire to do the necessary work for goal achievement. Once again, many goals and resolutions are stranded in this stage of goal setting. For those of us who could easily be certified procrastinators, if we ever did the paper work, the I Will stage is often placed in a continual loop. We have a desire to clean our desk and we will. We have desire and ability to increase our physical fitness, and we will. This is also the good intentions stage. I Will'ers intend to do what needs done in achieving their goals but just not at this moment.

A good question to identify I Will'ers is asking how many books they started or own compared to the number they have finished. Before labeling yourself or someone else in the I Will stage as a procrastinator; realize God's plans and timing have precedence over our own, even when we are unable to see the reason for the delay. God's wisdom, exceeds our wisdom. Christ is smarter than the accumulative knowledge of every person to ever live. Abraham Lincoln, with whom I share a birthday (different year!), once said, "If given six hours to chop down a tree, I would spend four hours sharpening the axe." Sometimes the axe is sharpened during the I Will stage.

3. I Am – Realization

I publicly introduced the *I Am* step of goal achievement when speaking to a safety organization at Omaha's Qwest Center in 2005.

Ability and desire are now combined with a crystal clear image of the results. This is the Realization or Achievement stage. The I Am's have internalized the results into the fabric of their souls, of their powerful minds. This stage affects all five senses: vision, taste, touch, smell and sound.

You see the bonus check in your hands with the ordained amount written in the appropriate field, you taste and smell the surrounding air or the cologne/perfume of the person presenting the check. You feel the check in your hands, you feel the shivers of excitement scurrying up and down your spine, and you feel praise, joy and gratitude toward to Lord. You feel the tears of excitement excreting from your eyes. You hear the gratitude and excitement in your voice and anyone else directly involved.

You continue visualizing all of the resulting actions with goal achievement.

I Am opens your mind to possibilities, creativity seeds are germinating, emerging and flourishing. Some seeds, such as velvet leaf, can lie dormant in the soil for fifty years. It only requires one flash of light, one thousandth of a second of light shining on this seed for the phototropic properties to generate the germinating response. This is true of seeds of both weeds and crops. Creativity is one of source of light. However, we must always submit our plans and goals to the great I AM, God the Father (Genesis 3:14).

We strengthen our I Am when we allow our mind, through properties of plasticity, to adapt to the person we have become through spiritual, mental, emotional and physical growth and/or improvement. The brain adapts by forming mental maps of our body as we change. However, some people fail to mentally accept this change, even when the change is significantly positive for them. For example, the author of *Psychocybernetics*, a plastic surgeon, tells of how some people continue having a poor self-image long after requested changes to their nose or any other feature were corrected to their specifications.

Christians suffer from this same challenge. We accept Christ as our Savior for the forgiveness of our sins, yet we continue with a *spiritual schema* (image) of condemned sinners. Conversely, others live with unconfessed sin, rejecting Christ, yet have a spiritual schema that fails to recognize their sins and need for a Savior and forgiveness. Spiritual maturity includes adapting our spiritual schema to match our spiritual image. Once we become saved and forgiven, we need to ask the indwelling Holy Spirit to mold our spiritual mind to recognize our state of forgiveness and our new positioning as children of God with an eternal relationship with Him. The healthy response yields a grateful, joyful and prayerful heart (1 Thess 5:16-18), along with the fruit of the Spirit (Galatians 5:22-23).

Examples

Farmers analyze the soil, length of days, heat units during the growing season and availability of water (rain and irrigation) on their farms, this is compared to the requirements of various crops. This information is evaluated: *I can* grow these crops on my land.

The farmer analyzes their available and attainable resources. This includes labor availability, size and type of equipment, finances, market for product, profit potential.

Goals

1. Assure the goal correlates with God's character
2. Specific
3. Deadline
4. Beyond Reasonable Reach – adjust for different personalities
5. Internalize – claim as your own
6. Without Limits – Brandon Jessop example
7. Requires Prayer – necessity for one to get on their knees

An example of Goal Setting and Achieving from an old blog post of mine follows.

In April 1997, I visited a high school runner at his home who was a multi-state champion in cross country and track and recognized as a competitor on the national level. Brandon set a goal to run 1600 meters (approximately 9 yards short of a mile) in 4:15. Brandon was running 4:16 to 4:18. March and early April weather in the Midwest is often cold and windy; not conducive to fast running on an outdoor track. All around Brandon's large bedroom were notes with his goal – "1600 meter run in 4:15." The previous week he won at a prestigious multi-state track meet in which the race carried the name of the most successful high school miler in history, Jim Ryun. Jim Ryun is the only high school miler to run the Olympic 1500 meters, set the American Record and run within two seconds of the World Record before entering college.

I suggested to Brandon he needed to change the verbiage of his goals to exclude limits - *never set limits on goals*. Verbal limits form mental limits. Rather than declaring 4:15 as his goal, state "4:15 or faster" or "at least 4:15;" enabling his mind to see past the 4:15 limit. Brandon changed the wording of his goals immediately.

Goals with limits have the same effect as instructing someone to pull their car up to a concrete barrier. The drivers will slow down as they approach and stop before contact instead of breaking through to greater destinations and achievements.

Two days later Brandon again ran the 1600 meter race with his goal now properly worded. The following morning, radio sport's reports across the state were declaring a new state record in the 1600 meter run by Brandon in a time of 4:13.3. The state's largest newspaper quoted Brandon that a friend instructed him to "Never set limits on his goals." He surpassed his previous goal by two seconds; 3 seconds faster than his previous best. Brandon and his teammates applied the same principles in setting a goal for their 3200 meter relay. They ran 7:45, surpassing the previous state record by 4 seconds, the fastest in the nation by high school boys for the year until two or three weeks later being bettered by two teams with later state meets and more time to train.

Each of us must take limits off our goals. Instead of stating my goal is to make X amount of sales or Y amount of annual income, rather declare you will make at least X amount of sales or in excess of Y amount in annual income. Eliminating limits on your goals eliminates mental limits on your achievements.

Goals are your road map to your desired achievements.

Anyone can set goals, **achieving** them is another matter. What do you want out of life? How good do you want to be?

We are frequently instructed to set realistic goals. How do you define "realistic?" Is realistic based on *your* abilities and *your* vision? The inner voice inspiring our goals determines realistic. Goals inspired by Jesus Christ reach beyond your abilities and understandings; yet well within Christ's abilities and understanding. What does the Bible say regarding Christ's limits of ability and understanding? The Bible states all things are possible through Christ who strengthens us; with God nothing is impossible.

We limit our vision, goals and achievements when operating within human reason. Inspiration is limited to the source of the inspirer. God inspired goals and visions create vision and action in all whose hearts are open to the Lord. An organization seeking to "Run on Faith," waits upon God's Word in all communication, goals and policies. God's instruction to Israel through Isaiah, "Those that wait on the Lord, shall renew their strength, they shall run and not be weary" remains good advice to us, today. Are you waiting on the Lord when setting personal and corporate goals? Are you waiting on the Lord when communicating with anyone? Are you waiting when determining the policies for your family, business and other organizations?

Have you pondered "Impossible?" Frequently we say, "That is impossible!" Someone often replies, "All things are possible through Christ who strengthens us," or "With God, nothing is impossible." What is Impossible? Impossible simply means the lack of wisdom, knowledge, understanding or strength. God is Wisdom, Knowledge, Understanding *and* Strength. Consequently He never lacks, allowing all things to be possible. He enables us to achieve the impossible by either temporarily opening the gates of impossible for us or gifting us the appropriate Wisdom, Knowledge and Understanding for achievement.

- **G**reatness
- **O**ccurs
- **A**fter
- **L**eaping beyond on Logic

John the Baptist leaped while developing in the womb, while filled with the Holy Spirit. Your Holy Spirit inspired GOAL will also leap while developing into reality. After birth, John the Baptist leapt into the world spreading the word of Christ's arrival. Holy Spirit inspired goals leap into the hearts and minds of your family, organization and customers spreading word of Christ's Blessing through your product or service.

Just as secularism denies and obstructs Christ, secularism will deny and obstruct Christ's GOALs in your life and business. Seeing and accepting the GOALs and Vision requires first seeing and accepting Christ as these GOALs exists in the realm of Christ. An egotistical attitude mocks all that lies beyond understanding. An egotistical attitude claims to know everything, consequently accepting anything beyond its understanding is impossible. Understanding this attitude is essential in maintaining focus, avoiding any distraction from denial and obstruction. Conversely, Christ filled hearts will support you while acknowledging their lack of immediate understanding. This is easily understood in knowing we either accept or deny Christ. Accepting and full understanding seldom coexist. Who among us claims the ability to score a 100% on an exam from Jesus Christ? Answering "yes" is the epitome of arrogance!

I defied the advice of getting a reality check, keeping my GOALS down to earth. I achieved the first four GOALS 8, 9, 20 and 21 years after setting "unrealistic" GOALS in June 1975. I was frequently on my knees pleading for our Lord's assistance. I continue working daily towards the newest 5th GOAL; most likely some still believe it to be unrealistic. I remain on my knees seeking the Lord with all my heart, soul and mind. Upon reflection, I believe God was providing a vision for my life back in '75.

Attitude

One man pretends to be rich, yet has nothing; another pretends to be poor, yet has great wealth. (Proverbs 13:7)

Success is an attitude! During the three year period when I continuously ran 80 to 135 miles per week, in addition to working full time, I valued each minute. If an hour existed between getting off work and my next appointment, I ran 5+ miles, showered and drove to the appointment, meeting or social event. The run would take nearly 30 minutes, leaving 15 minutes to cool down, shower, dress and jump in my charcoal gray T-Bird. Every destination in Kearney, Nebraska, was within a 10 to 15 minute drive. Today, I view every minute as an opportunity to practice or improve a speech, write, work on a speaking proposal, resolve a challenge of clients or run. Transforming every minute into a goal achieving activity enabled me to become a reasonably fit runner, an award-winning speaker and an effective professional.

Other times in life, I have viewed 30 or 60 minutes as not enough time to do anything worthwhile. As you probably suspect, my productivity often mirrors the value I place on a single minute. What value do you place on single minutes in your daily routine? Your minute-to-minute efficiency will increase as you increase the value you place on each minute of your time which is a minute of *your life*. In other words, the more you value your life, the more you will value your time.

Your worldview affects how you calculate the value of time and life. A worldview without God or a limited view of God actively working in your life, places finite values with a heavy emphasis on monetary calculations. When we recognize that God created everything (John 1:1-4) we respect and allocate all time, money, mercy, love, forgiveness and material resources as tools assigned to us for serving God (Mt 25:14-30).

> In the beginning was the Word, and the Word was with God, and the Word was God. He was in the beginning with God. All things came into being through Him, and apart from Him nothing came into being that has come into being. In Him was life, and the life was the Light of men. (John 1:1-4)

The better we understand the correlation between time and life, the greater value we place on the time of other's as well. How one values their time reveals how they value their life. Those who value their life value their time. They will make every effort to keep you from waiting on them. One who habitually makes others wait for them is shouting from the mountain tops that their life is more valuable than those they leave waiting. Obviously, everyone encounters unexpected obstructions causing delays, but the pattern of always being late speaks volumes.

Remember, God quickly forgives us and restores our relationship with Him through the Lord Jesus Christ. Consequently, when we live and grow in God's image we can quickly forgive and restore broken relationships with those who have hurt us and ask for forgiveness. Our ability and willingness to forgive past wrongs and restore relationships with others reveals our relationship with Jesus Christ and our gratitude for His death and resurrection for our eternal restoration and salvation with God.

When I believe that I have all the time in the world, time slips away; leaving me with little to achieve worthwhile goals. Conversely, when I believe that each minute, each second, is precious then my relationships, effectiveness and achievements exponentially increase. Success hinges on our attitude towards each of our gifts of resources from Christ! Do you regularly thank and praise Jesus Christ for each moment, breath and interaction?

Passion for Athletics

Where are you led, and how do you get there?

Several factors fueled my passion for athletics. Gaylord, like many other similar towns, had a long history of athletics; including a semi-professional baseball team in the 1930's. Dad was a pitcher on Gaylord's fast-pitch softball team before and after I was born. He spoke of playing a tough team from Salina in the 1964 State Tournament, telling about one of their pitchers who threw a curve ball that appeared to be coming right at the batter before breaking in for a strike. Gaylord lost the game, enabling Dad to be around the farm when my sister was born in September.

My Beginning in Competitive Athletics

As a baseball-loving boy, I anxiously awaited my 8th birthday in February 1975 to become eligible for pee-wee baseball. However, in 1975 some news arrived with the horrifying magnitude of a Stephen King novel; the age requirement for Pee Wee baseball increased to nine years old! I was stunned and disappointed. Surely the courts would rule this change as cruel and unusual punishment! Unfortunately, when I did begin playing competitive baseball the following year, I quickly realized that I was *lousy*. I lacked quickness, speed, agility or coordination to field a ground ball along with lacking the ability to quickly and accurately throw it to the appropriate baseman. However, the coaches determined that my slow legs and weak arm would do the least amount of harm to the team by me playing in the infield instead of the outfield. Despite my lack of talent, I enjoyed playing. Yes, we may safely assume that the Kansas City Royals never placed my name on any lists of young talent.

Early Cross Country

My first cross country season began at 7:00a.m. in August 1981; we arrived and met on the street at Coach Bill Blankenship's home in Smith Center. Mom generously drove the fifteen miles at 6:30a.m. each morning during practice before school commenced. She called up the enclosed stair well at 6:00 to wake me up. "Rick, Rick, get up, Rick." I struggled to wake each morning. Neither of us imagined the profound impact that cross country would have on my life. Mom occasionally suggested that I received my cross country talents from her because as a child she ran in the pasture to help bring in the milk cows.

I hoped that Kent Frieling would also run cross country, he contemplated it before deciding it was outside of Christ's will for his life. Seniors Dane Devlin, James Azeltine; sophomore Andy Wire; freshmen JC Chance and Rick Meyer constituted the necessary 5 guys for a complete cross country team.

We traveled south on Highway 281 to the Osborne Country Club for our first meet. We arrived an hour early to allow time to warm-up and inspect the 2 mile course, including the finish area. I was excited for the first race, yet nervous about the unknown, including racing against juniors and seniors. The greatest pre-race trepidation resulted from anticipated pain that I would endure during the race. I vividly recall the nerve-piercing pain experienced in the half mile and mile in junior high track. Would I be able to push myself through the pain? Would I continue when the body and mind begged to quit while maintaining a competitive cadence over the rolling hills and prairie? Would I "Run on Faith," trusting in God for the physical strength and mental fortitude to endure to finish line?

The starting gun exploded, the early pace was quick and much faster than I desired. The fiery lactic acid rapidly accumulated in my quadriceps while I ran up the long, north bound hill along the highway. Shortly after the top, I could no longer match strides with Dane. James had already gapped us. Andy and I ran near one another. I remember very little of us running around the remainder of golf course as I mentally focus to endure the burning sensation from the lactic acid. Finally I saw the finish line, I began my slow motion sprint. As I crossed the line, someone said, "One more lap!" I thought, "You have got to be kidding me!" I sprinted too soon. We had to run up a big hill again with another half mile to go.

Eventually the finish line did arrive; I ran about 12:30 on the tough course, finishing well back in the pack. I was amazed during the awards ceremony when they announced that the top two or three finishers ran in the vicinity of 10:30 for two miles. How could anyone run that fast? Our team also placed in the middle of the pack.

The Smith Center Invitational occurred 2 weeks later. Coach Bill Blankenship encouraged us to set a team goal to win the team title. Other Smith Center teams fell short by various margins over the years. I believe 5 other teams competed that Thursday afternoon in mid-September. We began the race by the club house in the crispy fall air, running to the north boundary of the golf course, then turning left towards U.S. Highway 281. We turned again to run south along the highway back towards the club house. I begin feeling pain as we scurried up the first hill near the first half mile. At the top of the hill, we angled northeast towards the far corner, turning south along the creek and passing the mile mark by a par 3 hole. We then turned west to follow the boundary between the course and the creek. The short, yet steep hill provided a painful dose of lactic acid in the legs. I ran as hard as possible without sprinting. We turned towards the south border of the course before making a U-turn to the north. One half mile to go.

Can I hold this pace to the finish? Can I hold off this Pburg runner next to me (Roger Jennings)?

Coach Bill Blankenship drilled into us the necessity of remaining tough and running fast in this portion of the race when the body and mind beg to quit. I continue driving to the north fence, once there we turned back to the south for the final sprint. I somehow held off Roger Jennings. He later won NAIA National Indoor Mile championship, along with running the mile in 4:00 and beat me every time during our sophomore year.

Eventually the meet officials tallied the team scores. We were ecstatic to learn that we won the team title! I could easily adapt to winning team titles. Unfortunately, it would be our first and only title of the season. The following year only 4 boys ran cross country falling one runner short to form a team which consists of 5 to 7 runners.

Farm (more lessons)

Irrigation & KSU

In the late 1970s irrigation water from Kirwin Lake began diminishing. Consequently, the irrigation district restricted the amount of water available for irrigating crops. Whatever could go wrong for my parent's economic survival on the farm did go wrong. Perhaps the temptation grew for my dad to say, "Life is unfair." Yet, I never heard an inkling of those words or any similar messages from either parent. Mom and Dad continued to place their trust in Christ.

Their trusting faith included Dad's involvement in the local irrigation board as well as 4-States Irrigation Council. 4-States consisted of Kansas, Nebraska, Wyoming and Colorado. Dad later served as president and was awarded the prestigious Head Gate Award. During his first adventure to Denver for their annual meeting, he visited with LaGrand Page from Wheatland, WY. Pheasant hunting entered the conversation within the first 10 minutes of the conversation. Dad immediately invited LaGrand to our farm as guests for opening weekend of Pheasant hunting in November. LaGrand and 3 to 4 others drove out and stayed and hunted with us during opening weekend the next 7 seasons. Dee and I gladly gave up our beds and bedrooms and slept on the floor during their visit.

Committing to excellence with maximum physical and mental exertion because of fully trusting God is common for most involved in agriculture. Additionally, in the mid to late 1970's, new plant pathologists joined Kansas State University (KSU) in Manhattan. At least two of these new scientists ranked among the best in the world. Jim Shepard was the first to produce a plant with genetics of 50 % potato and 50% tomato. Jim was also the first to generate an albino soybean plant in the laboratory. Jim also explained cloning in language understandable to me at 13 while pheasant hunting.

The other researcher, Jerry Uyemoto, possessed world-class expertise in numerous plant diseases including Corn Lethal Necrosis. Jerry, along with other KSU researchers, frequently visited our farm near Gaylord. Jerry loved to hunt, especially turtle doves. Dad invited him to hunt along with some of his colleagues. Soon, Jerry brought Jim, Larry Claflin, the Department Head of KSU's Plant Pathology Department, and other researchers to hunt doves and pheasants. Naturally, Dad's invitation included their families. Since God emphasizes family in the Bible, it's only natural that those in God's image also place high value on family in agreement with God. When Jerry, who is of Japanese descent, suddenly stopped shooting at doves, the gun blasts echoing throughout the countryside were quickly replaced with Jerry's roaring, joyous laughter. All hunters within earshot of this laughter shared in the thrill of Jerry's success.

We welcomed Jerry's presence at many meals both when he traveled to our farm for work and when he stayed overnight while hunting. Even though Jerry did not believe in God, we continued our mealtime prayers. Jerry politely avoided participating. Dad and Mom respected his desire to not participate, yet they maintained the necessity of thanking Jesus Christ for our food. Most in Smith County, Kansas, share a simple ministry: love the Lord Jesus Christ with all your heart, soul, strength and mind. They also love everyone encountered along life's journey as much as they love themselves. Despite lacking perfection and a silver tongue, they treated people with respect and welcomed outsiders into their homes as they sought to live the two greatest commandments (Mt 22:37-39).

In 1982 Jim and Jerry discontinued working at the university full time. An investor in Switzerland started a few international research laboratories; one of which ADVANCED GENETIC SCIENCES (AGS), the Swiss investor sought to gather in the world's top plant scientists. He chose Manhattan, Kansas, as one of the sites due to Jim and Jerry's presence.

Economics on the farm continually declined. Finally John, our banker, discontinued loaning additional operating money. In January of 1983, Jim and Jerry offered Dad a position with AGS. Dad's work ethic and critical thinking skills fit in with the world-renowned scientists. Eventually the day of our farm sale arrived, Saturday April 23, 1983! Over 34 years have passed since this emotional day. The grief of losing a family farm is remarkably similar to losing a parent. I was devastated!

My mother remained in the house during the auction with family and friends. She did not like the mandated change, yet she accepted the situation in stride, trying to make the most of the circumstances. She and

Dad practiced what they continually taught their children: just do your best!

Dad stayed near the auctioneer, answering questions concerning equipment as it was sold. At least once he provided an answer that may have hindered the selling price; truth always prevails. I could see the partially camouflaged discouragement on his face. He spent his entire 45 years either on this farm or living in a bordering neighbor's home, whose land he also farmed.

Dad grew up on the banks of the North Fork of the Solomon River: farming, hunting and fishing. His dad taught him to hunt and fish on this farm where he later taught his son to farm, hunt and fish on this same land. Hunting with Dad was heaven on earth as a child. While deer hunting the first two Saturdays of December, he took me to the house to go with Mom and Dee to practice for the church's Christmas program at American Lutheran in Smith Center. I was exceedingly disappointed, I wanted to be with him; especially when hunting! Dad explained the importance of church participation, including the worship of our Savior Jesus Christ.

Dad's lessons delved deeply into life. I typically watched one, maybe two television programs a few evenings a week. I struggled to sit still. The lesson of one particular movie remains fresh on my mind my entire life. The parents in the movie were either divorced or the child was born out of wedlock. The dad and 8 year old son were unable to spend time together. The dad and son visited through the school yard fence near the end of this TV movie. This scene captured my attention because I loved working, hunting, fishing and visiting with my dad. After the movie ended, Dad asked me to stay in the living room before going upstairs to play in my room. I do not recall Dad's specific words, yet his message was clear in referring to the separation of the father and son. If you fall to the temptations of lustful desires, you may have kids that you may have little or no relationship with. I instantly determined sex would only occur when and if I were married. I could not bear considering having children without a daily relationship like I simultaneously enjoyed with both of my parents. Wisdom recognizes that we cannot control everything yet mandates putting ourselves in the best possible position to win.

This lesson's value came from the relationships with my parents. Yes, they spanked me! I needed spankings and other discipline. Rumors abound that I was a little ornery. Once, Mom attempted to give me a well-deserved spanking, I ran out of house yelling, "Child abuse, child abuse!!!" When she caught me, it was! Appropriate spankings and other discipline absent any physical harm are appropriate. Parents' created in the Lord's image discipline those they love.

> For whom the LORD loves He reproves, Even as a father corrects the son in whom he delights. (Proverbs 3:12, Romans 12:6)

Amazing relational memories of Christmas, Thanksgiving, Easter and birthday dinners with aunts, uncles, cousins and grandparents magnanimously swirled through our farm home. These memories include Mom reading Bible stories to Dee and me, along with singing songs such as *Jesus Loves Me*. Because of the time, faith and love daily investment, I always knew deep in my heart of Mom and Dad's sincere love; even when being disciplined. Growing up in Smith County Kansas, one assumed everyone knew of Jesus and his love.

I once laid on the living room floor listening to President Reagan deliver a speech to the nation, remaining there afterwards while CBS gave us their synopsis of what the president said. After listening to the news anchor, I turned to Dad saying, "That is not what President Reagan said tonight!" Dad nodded, "You got it." As a 15 year old, I instantly realized the falsities proclaimed by the major news media.

Leaving his lifelong friends and community after the auction, he perceived himself as a failure to meet the expectations of his father who died in 1976, along with disappointing his mother, four brothers and his sister. Dad continued to farm Martha's land for another year or two. Ron Zabel rented our farm, eventually buying the farmstead. In the late 1980s, with all ties to the farm permanently cut, Dad's last southward turn off of Highway 9 a mile east of Gaylord occurred. He never drove by the farm the remainder of his life. Yes, a farmer and his land are closely tied. Land, as previously illustrated, is a living organism into which a farmer and his family *Run on Faith* pouring in their every ounce of physical, mental and emotional energy. Praying the crops and livestock produce a profit; knowing they are responsible for the effort while God provides the wisdom and strength for the decisions and effort along with rain, sunshine, wind, irrigation water, soil, microbes and nutrients.

Growing up, I daily imagined spending my life farming, raising livestock, fishing and hunting on the North Fork of the Solomon River just like my dad and grandpa. I imagined only life on the farm. Once I learned of the necessity of our leaving the farm, I informed God of his mistake numerous times and in a variety of disgruntled tones. Do you find emotional relief in hoping God has a sense of humor? I did and do! Additionally, Christ is full of mercy and grace. Dad began working in Manhattan April 1, 1983, and drove home every weekend. I anxiously awaited him driving down our nearly quarter mile long driveway on Friday evenings about 8:00p.m.

The week following our farm sale, Mom and I visited Manhattan High School. I was 16 and hoping God would miraculously reverse our fate. The enormity of the school frightened me! There were 309 students in our class as compared to 50 in my class at Smith Center High School or 8 at Gaylord Grade School. Leaving the farm and distancing myself from my friends and classmates in Smith County filled my heart and mind with devastating grief.

Mom and I met with Mrs. Nancy Nelson, a guidance counselor when visiting Manhattan High School. She provided a tour of the massive school. Mrs. Nelson asked if I participated in sports. I answered in the affirmative hopeful of my ability to contribute to the 1982 6A State Runner-Up cross country team in the upcoming 1983 season.

Mrs. Nelson suggested we walk through the south gym to the location of Congo's office in the far corner where she planned to introduce us. On the way, she described Manhattan's unique cross country uniforms, powder pink shorts and baby blue tops. Bill 'Congo' Congleton was in the south gym with his sophomore PE class; after introductions he inquired of my previous year's cross country success. I explained that a cold hampered my performance. With an expression in his eyes that later became overly familiar, he replied, "No excuses. Right, Rick Meyer?" He then extended an invitation to his cross country camp in July and stepped into his office for an application. Mrs. Nelson introducing me to Congo permanently and positively impacted my life.

Whose lives will you permanently and positively impact by introducing them to others?

Manhattan

On Saturday May 28, 1983 we relocated to the 'Little Apple,' Manhattan, Kansas. I considered Manhattan a large city, despite a population of under 50,000 when including the students of Kansas State University. Manhattan, nestled in a bowl of the Flint Hills which contains the world's most prolific rangeland. With the presence of next-door neighbors, we adapted to an immediate adjustment. Our closest neighbors on the farm lived over a quarter of a mile in the direction of the rising sun. In the opposite direction, our nearest neighbor was nearly a mile across the river, hidden behind ash, elm, cottonwood and oak trees. We quickly discovered Manhattan's renowned friendly, welcoming attitude and qualities in our neighbors and later among all of the Manhattan residents whom we encountered with neighbors, church members and cross country teammates and their families.

Manhattan: 1983

When we left our farm for Manhattan, God led us away from our homeland. The Bible does not record Abraham complaining to God when led away. My complaining was enough for both Abraham and me. When I read the Bible stories, it seems obvious how the real human characters should respond. We have the benefit of hindsight, and 'God sight.' We hear the story in God's narrative, written through someone else. (If I lived in Biblical times and had been written about; I would have been one whom we read about and shake our heads saying, how many times can he mess up, how long until Rick recognizes that a life lived in obedience with God far exceeds walking a path not approved by God.) Surely, God has a sense of humor. After all, he gave us our sense of humor. I really let Him "have it" when we left the farm. I informed God numerous times of His terrible mistake. Fortunately, God continually extended His patience with me. Do you recognize and appreciate God's patience with you?

God is patient with all who desire to serve Him. Just like a good teacher or coach, he challenges us, drawing more out us than we conceive possible. Today, I cannot imagine life without that chapter. Just like writing this chapter, the work is often tedious while the writing takes place. We question why this is necessary. We all question ourselves at times, questioning is healthy and vital to our growth and well-being. While questioning is good, doubting is bad. Questioning seeks validity and improvement. Doubting presents us a lack of trust.

Joseph, the great-grandson of Abraham, sought obedience to God. He was "rewarded" with being left to die in a well. He was then taken captive and locked in a dungeon because he refused to succumb to the lust of Pharaoh's wife. She falsely accused him of becoming physical with her; in reality he refused to do so. Life is rarely fair! Joseph solved problems while others denied him the credit for his ingenuity of interpreting dreams for 2 years (Genesis 37-40). Have others denied giving you credit for your ingenuity in life, whether at work, home, community or at church?

Manhattan High School was a much larger school than I experienced in Smith Center. My life changed drastically. One morning in September of 1984, my senior year, I walked into Congo's office. We attempted to become the first team to repeat as 6A State Champions. My teammates constantly talked about Wichita East being the last boy's team to repeat the win in the 1960s.

Congo knew how to coach successful teams. His coaching ability lead to many state and national honors for his individual athletes and teams. Congo sat at his desk, reading upcoming workouts or grading papers that morning. Pictures filled his wall with snapshots of the many top performers of his programs, including a javelin thrower who won the 1974 U.S.-Russian dual meet in Dallas, Texas. Other pictures included a 4:56 girl miler from the 1970s, along with a 4:14 boy miler in 1974 and an Olympic marathon champion. This champion stood with Congo at Warner Park, home of the cross country course.

In June, Dad and I worked on the farm each weekend, I stayed with Loren and Mary Jane Zabel. Dad and Loren described each other as good friends who also happened to be cousins. Loren's dad, Otto Zabel, and my grandma, Ida Zabel Meyer, were brother and sister. Their youngest son, Greg, and I grew up hunting and fishing together.
One Saturday evening Dad called Congo to inquire about the camp. I was amazed and encouraged as I sat in the kitchen listening. Dad and Congo primarily discussed farming for over 30 minutes. Eventually they visited a few minutes about the cross country camp. Congo visited our Manhattan home one July evening, sitting and conversing in our lower-level family room with my family for over an hour. Congo grew up on a farm near

Haddam, Kansas. Even though I later referred to my cross country teammates as 'city slickers,' the coach was a farmer. This Manhattan transition might be tolerable after all.

During one of my trips to Manhattan during the summer I had to apply for a job; a new experience. After I completed the application, I was invited to an interview. We visited about a position at a local establishment. I only knew how to work outside. The interviewer inquired about my goals. I shared my farming goals as well as other goals, including one that I set as a freshman to place in the top ten at state cross country by my senior year. I acknowledged that it would be more difficult since leaving Smith Center who competes in 3A; and now running for Manhattan in 6A. The lady conducting the interview began smirking as she viewed this bow-legged farm boy in cowboy boots and a snap western shirt.

She then asked, "Did you qualify for 3A state cross country or track while competing for Smith Center?" I sheepishly responded, "No, I did not. I did watch state cross country in Manhattan last year." She hysterically laughed in my face while summarizing that I failed at Smith Center, yet believed I could achieve an individual top ten finish on a state championship cross country team in Manhattan by the time I was a senior.

I quietly lowered my head, listening to her ignorance and arrogance cackle at my expense. Silently, I knew I would prove her wrong. It is best to perform, while avoiding discussion with someone who believes they know everything: truth is independent of belief and agreement. She never extended a job offer.

MHS – Cross Country

1983 Camp – knee high tube socks & cotton gym shorts.

My introduction to Manhattan High cross country came at the aforementioned Congo's cross country camp in July 1983. Congo immediately improved my running by shortening my stride and eliminating over-striding. Before this correction, I attempted to combined running and aeronautics. With each step, I resembled a mule deer bounding down the road. This over-striding wasted time and effort. While gaining altitude and sailing in the air, my competitors glided along smoothly. Their energy carried them forward with little vertical ascension. Initially, I needed to shorten my stride; this instantly quickened my pace 15 seconds per mile.

Small details determine success in running, as in every endeavor in life! Proper form is attained with a few minor adjustments. Knowing which adjustments are necessary is key. Gaining an extra inch in stride is far from simple. Shortening the stride is sometimes the proper initial diagnosis. Evaluating form requires individual attention. Blanket recommendations of either shortening or lengthening may cause greater harm than good. Would you agree the same is true of most evaluations in all aspects of life?

I rode with Congo in his red Ford pickup to his cross country camp at Rock Springs Ranch, south of Junction City. I arrived knowing only Congo. One guy stood visiting with another about baseball and golf. He followed the Kansas City Royals, as did I. He knew as little about farming as I did about city living; Jon Young and I began running together. During one run, we discussed the 1982 state cross country meet. He was a varsity member of Manhattan's 6A state runner-up team. I related that I attended as a spectator with Smith Center, watching Sara Seamann earn all-state honors: a top ten finish, in the girls' 3A race. I watched all the races in awe, particularly the 6A boy's race. I shared with Jon my amazement at the speed at the start of the 6A race of 1982.

I said, "There was one guy in dead last in the first 440 yards. I might be able to keep up with him." Jon responded, "You are, that was me." As Jon later observed, "Irony can be so ironic."

Do you remember the old Sesame Street jingle, "One of these is not like the others?" As I entered camp, that was me! I was a 5'8" bow-legged farm boy wearing cotton gym shorts and knee high tube socks with the red and green band of the Smith Center Redmen.

Jon Young and I ran 80 miles during the four days of Congo's cross country camp. July 1983 set numerous record high temperatures. The thermometer once read 118 degrees Fahrenheit. I love running in the heat, the sweat cleans out my pores. Congo habitually said these quirky sayings; such as, "Don't be afraid to be great, it all comes down to who wants it the most;" and, "You don't find gold without digging." Inspired and challenged, Jon and I ran 4 to 5 times daily. We discussed a vast array of topics; including the state championship on every run. Congo was a master of internalizing the expectation of greatness, challenging athletes to set their inner thermostat on *greatness* in all they pursue.

Confidence in my ability grew with each run. Whenever we inquired about our chances of winning the 1983 championship, Congo simply replied, "It'll be tough." Jon and I responded as champions, going for another run. Unfortunately, walking proved a difficult challenge for a few days following camp. We were running on faith, focusing all of our effort toward the state championship.

At camp, the boys slept in bunk beds in two rooms on one side of the lodge, while the girls slept in the two rooms on the other side. Wake up call was at 5:00a.m., Congo would say, "Opportunity comes to those who are prepared. Prepare yourselves in such a way as to take advantage of opportunity when it presents itself." Following our morning run, we showered and ate breakfast. Our other runs occurred mid-morning, mid-afternoon, late evening and after 10:00p.m. In between we napped, swam and played the card game War. Several times following Jon's victories over Laura May, Jon burst out in his rendition of ASIA's hit song, *Don't Cry*.

Spring water flowed out of the hillside at the camp, satiating our thirst. One mid-afternoon following a run, several of us sat by the spring enjoying an ice cream cone from the camp's concession stand; a treat of Wamego's coach, Rick Patton. Coach Patton joined us to learn Congo's techniques. Wamego won the 1984 4A championship over heavily favored Colby. Congo mentored numerous coaches, many like Rick Patton, Gary Sigle and Ben Meske won numerous championships with perennial top 5 and state title contending teams.

My improved form resulted in quieter running, this proved interesting on one solo midnight run. As I crossed a small bridge, I met fellow campers and runners, Beth and Lori. Based on their countryside piercing screams, they were surprised by my presence.

Early the following morning, David Pulford, full of encouragement the entire run, pushed me to new limits on my first 8 miler. He logged 100 miles in those 4 days. David's success in regional and national meets, combined with knowing the Nike representative while working at Ballard Sporting Goods store in Aggieville, enabled him to receive gear from Nike while in high school.

During a previous year's camp, Congo once asked a few of the runners to drive the 8 mile route, making a map of the mile markers. The 4 mile marker confused Congo, he asked the girls to explain the map legend. The picture representing the 4 mile marker was of cattle on a hill. These city slickers failed to consider that cattle roam!

On the return drive through the Flint Hills to Manhattan, I asked Congo what he believed my position to be on the team when practice commenced in August. He estimated I would be the team's 10th to 12th runner. His honest response caused my blood to boil. This reply contrasted the Christ inspired goal number 1 set by the windmill tower on the farm in June 1975: Be on a state championship team.

My older cousins and neighbors who were stand-out athletes and edged out of several track and baseball championships at Smith Center added jet fuel to the fire of my desire to be a part of a championship team. Our thoughts are strongly influenced by those with whom we associate. There was only one viable option to Congo's response ... develop the necessary mental and physical improvement to place higher. My goal orientation created a laser focus of me running on the varsity team. I was only in the infant stages of understanding Congo's ability to intensify, maintain and precisely direct our team's focus on the state championship.

I ran very little the first few days following camp due to muscles screaming of soreness. I then ran virtually every day until practice began. The daily temperatures regularly exceeded 100 degrees during this summer, testing my physical and mental fortitude. We develop mental toughness through persevering in daily challenges. I like to call them mental toughness workouts. One distinct workout occurred with the temperature at 118 degrees Fahrenheit. Greg and I worked in an alfalfa field next to the river moving a towline sprinkler along with the accompanying irrigation pipe. The alfalfa's height reached mid-thigh, and the tall trees along the river restrained any movement of the 90% humidity air. These conditions epitomized hot and muggy! Gloves were required to touch the sun scorched pipe.

Another mental toughness workout occurred that summer while baling wheat straw several miles south of Cedar in southwest Smith County while working for Greg Jones. I temporarily replaced Darin Godsey. The temperature reached 114F and 2 hours of work remained after swallowing my last swig of water from my jug. There were no working hydrants or any other opportunity to replenish the water near the field. I continued baling on the open John Deere 4020. Each of these experiences further amplified my mental toughness in running.

Yes, I remain alive and healthy all these years later contrary to what many "experts" try to tell us. After completing the baling, I returned to town feeling like Chevy Chase's character Clark Griswold in the movie *Vacation* after he wanders in the desert. Consequently, I guzzled two 10-ounce Dr. Peppers. Drinking two bottles was a big deal in those days. Today we give little thought to drinking a 20-ounce bottle of soda pop.

Fall 1983

The 1983 cross country season began a week before school in mid-August. This shy, bow-legged boy arrived at the first practice, once again frightened at Manhattan High School. We met outside the southwest corner of the high school in the teacher's parking lot near the tennis courts. I knew the approximate 30 camp attendees. However, another 60 runners (boys and girls) reported to the first workouts.

Dan "Schneid" Schneider sat on the ground stretching with one leg out and the other leg bent to the outside and back, a common stretch for runners. He raised his arm, waving, "Hi! I'm Dan." I recognized Dan from an article in the Manhattan Mercury newspaper in April that discussed their 3200-meter relay that won the 6A state championship, setting a school record.

Much of that initial practice is a blur. In our season's initial run, we covered 8 miles on an 'out and back' course. Even though we began our run in a large pack, we quickly strung out as the run progressed through the town. The pace in the last 2 miles challenged this farm boy. Jon Young and I, along with several others, finished together. Pulford and Schneider heated up the sidewalks with their lively pace while Daniel Wallace and Mark Richter clipped along closely behind.

Several practices consisted of running a warm-up down Poyntz Ave to Manhattan's City Park. Once there we regrouped while stretching and laughing over silly jokes and lighthearted humorous comments of various teammates. I quickly earned the nickname "Pigman" because I raised hogs and was a bowlegged, cowboy-boot wearing farm boy who transferred from a rural Kansas high school. David Pulford, whose nickname was "Buford," along with other boys and girls made fun of the north central Kansas twang in my voice.

Offended

How one handles razzing and teasing separates the champions from the losers. Losers cry in a corner, complaining about being offended. Champions respond saying, "Oh Yeah! You want to make fun of me? I'll show you. I'm proving myself with success!"

Those rooted in Christ cannot be offended because their value originates from God, the Creator who made us in His image. It is impossible to have your value diminished by someone who does not give you value. Plants receive their nutrients which convert into value from the soil holding their roots. A perfect soil will always provide perfect nutrients for the roots. We become depleted and offended from removing our emotional and spiritual roots from Christ and "re-potting" them in the world.

If you allow the world to determine your value then you allow others to offend you. Additionally, those who avoid offense through knowing the source of their value often forget how easily others may become offended. Therefore, another person can only "offend" you when you place your value into the opinions of that person. Does gold lose value when an ignorant person calls it bronze? Of course not! The gold remains gold and retains the value of gold. Conversely, the one who tries to "offend" the gold by calling it bronze has instantly lost credibility with their peers. Jesus offended the Pharisees (Mt 15:12), the Pharisees did not offend Jesus.

Christ's servants focus on serving Him and champions are busy winning! Christian champions exert every ounce of energy they possess in serving and hopefully pleasing our Lord. We have neither time, interest nor energy to join the "I am Offended Foundation."

Fellow champions are more interested in seeing their teammates 'be good instead of feel good.' Being precedes feeling. Additionally, I rhetorically inquired, "Do I like hogs?" *Yes.* "Do I have a twang in my voice?" *Evidently, I do possess this vocal characteristic.* Once I assessed my teammates' observations as accurate, I laughed with them while striving for self-improvement.

After adequately warming-up with strides and stretching, the workout began. We ran six 1.1 mile laps around the perimeter of City Park with five minutes of rest between each mile. Schneider and Pulford circled the park at a near five-minute pace. I ran with several others at near 5:30 pace.

Because we ran 1.1 miles instead of an even mile, I initially thought we ran slowly. Knowledge of the extra distance inspired me. This workout was a 'killer!' The short, uphill cool-down back to the school required briefs walks. I was sick to my stomach for several hours at home that evening. This became a common occurrence following workouts with Manhattan High cross country.

The first day of school arrived. Have you ever desired temporary death? I dreaded this first day. I dreaded walking into this new and enormous school, knowing only a few cross country runners. I drove the 1973 green Ford LTD into the large student parking lot as big as some alfalfa fields on the farm. After finding a spot, I nervously ambled to the school's main entrance in my typical attire. I entered the doors, walked up the stairs and down the proper hall searching for my locker. The hall lockers had built in combination locks that needed correct dialing, each time, for the locker to open. Dorothy and Toto in *The Wizard of Oz* knew they were not in Kansas anymore. Similarly, I knew I was not in Smith Center anymore when seeing the locked lockers.

Virtually everyone I encountered in class and in the halls were strangers. Fortunately, three familiar faces appeared amongst the 30 students in 6th hour history class, teammates Dan and David Schneider and Jacqi

Lambert. Mr. Kolenbrander began calling attendance; he insisted on pronouncing my name as though it were spelled Mayer, with a long 'a.' I was too shy to speak up. Jacqi graciously corrected him several times, saying, "It's Meyer!" I eventually made one or two futile attempts. Mr. Kolenbrander ignored these corrections the entire year, lessening my desire to be in history class. Again, this incident reminded me that I no longer lived in Smith County where names and correct pronunciations are known.

The first school day finally ended. Now, out to my car to get my gym bag, then to cross country practice. Students packed the hallways, walking in every direction. I arrived at what I believed to be the locker room after several minutes of wandering. Scanning the facility, I only saw football players. I asked one of them, "Where is the cross country team?" He politely instructed me that cross country meets in the south gym locker room. I was in the north gym locker room. Seeing my puzzled face, he led me to the proper door and pointed across to the south gym. I arrived at practice anxious to run. During the first day at MHS I was Running on Faith; faith I would somehow survive.

The workouts were tortuous as I struggled to keep up with my fast-paced teammates. Internalized goals continued motivating me to make the top 7, a varsity runner on this state championship team. My state championship goal suffered a blow when one of the top-returning runners chose to participate in other activities. Tom was a member of the school record setting 3,200-relay team and a top cross country runner on the 1982 State runner-up team. Sometimes, internalized goals are not deleted; rather their method of achievement is recalculated.

Congo did not talk about winning the championship. Instead, he prepared our minds and bodies to compete. He continually repeated 'Congo-isms,' such as, "Don't be afraid to be great," and "You don't find gold without digging," along with "It all comes down to who wants it the most." I struggled to understand why anyone was afraid to be great. I firmly believed that everyone desired greatness. Congo inspired us to push ourselves beyond previously known limits, to dig deep down into our souls, finding our Gold Mine of Greatness. He also said, "Don't compare yourselves to other people, their standards may be too low."

My favorite early season workout was the river run; we ran down Poyntz Avenue to the river along the east side of Manhattan. Running a good workout in the river was fun! This reminded me of being on the river at the farm, although this river carried a significantly greater volume of water than the North Fork of the Solomon.

Time Trial

We ran the team time trial at Warner Park on Saturday September 3, 1983. This race would determine the 7 members of each team: Varsity, Jr. Varsity, C team and all others. This was my opportunity to prove myself and attain my goal to be a varsity runner. Dan Schneider asked if I knew the course. I did not. My only previous visit occurred as a spectator of the 1982 State meet. His t-shirt from the 1982 Manhattan Invitational meet included a map of the course. Dan grasped the bottom of his shirt pulling it tight while looking down, grinning and speaking friendly, yet intensely, "Well, here it is. Any questions?" I looked it over despite no plans of leading the race.

The girls ran first, I recall little of their race. Now it was our turn to gather at the starting line. Congo fired his pistol, setting the time trial race underway. I started with Jon Young and Mark Rumsey; believing I could keep up with them for at least for a little while. A group of us ran together for the first half mile. I focused on finishing in the top 7 to earn a spot as a varsity runner. I surged slightly up a dirt slope with rock outcroppings as I approached the bottom of 'mile hill.' I glanced to my right and saw Beth, one of the girl's top runners gathered with a couple of her teammates, giggle as I surged. Maybe the blinding glare reflecting from my bright white legs provoked this giggle. I wore jeans the entire summer on the farm except when running.

Up the hill we ran: this challenging hill tests one's resilience regardless of their level of conditioning. The crest of this hill, while beginning the long downhill, provides a perfect opportunity to assess one's position. I ran among the top 8 or 9 runners. One top runner, Mark Richter, was unable to attend the time trial so Congo held his varsity position. Consequently, the top 6 in this race were varsity for our first meet.

As we came out of the dips with a half-mile remaining: my body hurt, it shrieked!! Jon and a couple of other teammates pulled ahead slightly. I focused on their backs as we circled the starting area, running back on the initial part of the course, before turning the final corner with about 150 yards to the finish. I finished among the top 6, running a personal best time of 10:53 on a tough course, achieving my internalized goal of making varsity. The entire team ran well in becoming the first varsity team in Congo's tenure as head coach to all run under 11:00 in the time trial on Warner Park's grueling course.

Anxiously, I joined my teammates to indulge in the doughnuts and juice brought to satiate our post-race appetites. This moment offered me the first opportunity to meet parents of my teammates. After socializing and eating, my parents and I walked to our home on EJ Frick Dr, less than a block from the dips at Warner Park. Once home, I quickly showered. We returned to Smith County to complete some work on Martha's ground that we still farmed. On Monday, we attended Gaylord's Labor Day Celebration, a tradition that began in 1923. We felt refreshed to visit with friends and neighbors.

We returned to Manhattan on Monday night, I lacked any excitement about returning to class on Tuesday morning; in fact, I was nearly sick from the thought of returning to this large school. However, returning to cross country practice instilled enthusiasm. On the following Saturday we hosted the Manhattan Cross Country Invitational, the media referred to this as pre state where 12 of the top boys and girls teams in 5A and 6A attended. The combined 24 top teams created an amazing atmosphere. The teams arrived to run the state meet course with 7 races in total for the event giving an early season preview of Manhattan's Warner Park's comparison.

We ran intense workouts that week, setting the tone for the remainder of the season, Congo believed in peaking for only one race, the last one: the state championship. During these grueling runs we discussed becoming the first Manhattan boys team to win our own invitational since it became a pre state race in the mid-1970s.

Workouts

On Mondays we ran 2.5 miles to Cico Park. At the track, our workout consisted of 16 quarter-mile runs completing each lap in 75 seconds or faster, followed by 80 to 90 seconds rest in between each quarter. During an early October workout, we completed 11 of the 16 400 meter intervals, each faster than the 75 second goal. Piercing pain saturated our minds and bodies begging us for relief. We cringed at the thought of 5 more 400s. As we recovered between runs, Congo asked, "How many are left?" We replied, "Four," in anguished tones. Congo asked again, "Only four left?" "Yes, coach. Four left." "Okay," Congo acknowledged. As we began running our 12 of 16 quarters, Congo quipped to Assistant Coach Betsy Sloan, "Those who cheat, cheat themselves." This is the *only* time we tried to cheat during a workout during the next 2 seasons.

We understood Congo's message! When Congo inquired during our next recovery, we corrected our "error," acknowledging the correct number of 400s remaining. We nearly cheated our coaches, teammates, family, school, the state of Kansas and ourselves by failing to prepare to the best of our abilities. Every week we ran the sixteenth quarter mile as a 'gut check,' all out. In this quarter, I began breaking 60 seconds for the first time.

Tuesday's workouts often consisted of 6 to 8 miles with fartlek, speed play; or beginning slower than a steadily quickening pace throughout the run. These runs were equally as challenging as Monday and Wednesday.

Often these fartleks were run on the Hudson route. Beginning at the school we ran to Anderson Ave then to Denison heading north past Ahearn Fieldhouse. While running north on Denison, Dan Schneider explained fartlek was a Swedish term meaning speed play. As we neared Kimball Ave the anticipation escalated as our 2 mile warmup ended and as speed play commenced with the westward turn onto Kimball Avenue. The 2.2 miles to Hudson Avenue challenged our mental and physical fitness, intense running followed by short, slow recovery runs. Typically we chose a landmark to run fast to or until someone said to recover. Kimball Avenue consists of mildly rolling hills. Fatigue transforms the severity of hills from mild to moderate. Once we reached Hudson Avenue, we recovered for a short time before running an average pace over the gravel road with moderate hills to Anderson Avenue. The mile from Kimball to Anderson seemed like 3 miles during this workout. The final 2.6 miles returning to the school were often a matter of survival. We then met behind the school to run the 60 yard dash 40 times! Yes, speed can be developed. This, like most of our workouts, excelled in forging championship caliber mental toughness.

On Wednesdays we either drove or ran to Warner Park, engaging in a killer work out of 8 half-mile runs at 2:20 to 2:30 with 5 minutes of walk-jog rest between each half-mile. Sometimes we returned to the cross country course's start line for each repetition, other weeks we ran each successive half mile around the course. I frequently struggled to keep up with my fast paced teammates. Congo often said to me, "Don't feel sorry for yourself, right Rick Meyer," or "Toughen up boy, this is 6A." Following the 7th half-mile run, Congo directed us to gather at the bottom of a long downhill near the dips. We sprinted 200 yards uphill, jogged down to repeat this excruciating exercise 20 times.

Afterwards we met Congo at the beginning of the course's last half-mile, for the final push. Congo looked in our eyes, setting the stage for the tortuous conclusion. "You are down by five points with a half to go, everyone has to catch one person." This prepared us mentally and physically for the championship run. Congo called out, "Line, set, go." Despite our complete exhaustion, we ran our 'pull-in half,' faster than any of the previous 7 intervals. I first ran a half mile under 2:10 on one of these 'pull-ins' at Warner Park. We daily pushed ourselves beyond previously known limits! Once again, my entire body pleaded for mercy from this agony. If given the opportunity, our mind will take the easy way out from life's challenges. Champions' internalized goals override the body's continual attempts at flipping the 'mercy' switch in one's mind. I anxiously awaited supper after returning home following a shower at the school. The time between arriving home and eating supper moved slower than walking across a disc field after a soaking rain.

We continually focused on running *through* the finish line of every run of every practice. Many good runners diminish their efforts just a few feet from the finish line. In life, like cross country, champions finish strong every time, every day.

Pace

Congo frequently taught us by telling stories of past teams. Among these stories, he frequently told of the outstanding 1979 girls team. Shawnee

Mission East girls entered the state meet ranked 4th in the nation. Their top 3 girls ranked among the top 4 high school girls in America. Can you imagine playing a basketball team with 3 of the nation's top 4 players on one team or 6 of America's top 8 football players on one team?

Congo was the starter and state meet director at Manhattan's Warner Park, consequently he saw very little of his teams during the preceding week. As the starter he stood 150 yards into the race, he invented the rule of the 2 command start and if anyone fell down in the first 150 yards there will be a restart. As the 6A girls warmed up by the starting line, public address announcer Don Steffens likely proceeded through his typical pre-race announcements. Most likely alerting the spectators to Shawnee Mission East's national ranking and to watch for their top 3 to lead the race. Steffens certainly announced the starting positions of all the teams.

At precisely the advertised starting time, Congo announced through a bullhorn, "There will be a two command start, runners set, then the gun. If anyone falls down within the first one hundred fifty yards there will be a second shot signaling a restart." The girls toed the line on top of the hill at Warner Park. "Runners Set!" … Congo's Smith and Wesson echoed across western Manhattan. He stood watching as this race's other 11 teams and individuals ran past him. Where is Manhattan? Girls in all pink uniforms should be easy to spot. Here came his girls, 20 yards behind everyone. "What the *heck* are you doing?!?!!" he shouted. Julie Emry replied, "Relax coach, we know what we're doing." The girls remained in last place at 600 yards, while catching up to the pack. They passed the half mile in 3:00 minutes, maintaining that same pace to the mile marker, up the hill, down the long downhill and through Warner Park's painful dips. As the raced neared completion, John, the head coach at Shawnee Mission East, was jumping up and down as his girls finish 1st, 2nd and 3rd. Suddenly, he looked up seeing a solid line of Manhattan's pink ladies placing 10-11-12-15-16; matching Congo's 1977 championship team score of 64 points. Shawnee Mission East's 4th and 5th runners placed about 58th and 64th as Manhattan doubled the team score on them. Consequently, Manhattan earned the season ending national ranking of 4th.

Congo shared this story continually in emphasizing the importance of controlling mind, emotions and pace in winning championships.

Thursdays provided relaxation and recovery as we typically ran 6 miles at an easy to moderate pace around Manhattan. Once again, we ran 40 repetitions of 60 yard pickups. Fridays consisted of either competing at a meet or running a relaxed 4 miles. On Saturdays we either competed or ran on our own. I accumulated 6 to 8 miles either way. Regardless if we had a meet, I mowed our yard and the lawn of our next door neighbor to the north. If we had a cross country meet, Dad and I cut firewood after I returned home. Once, I attempted to complain to Congo about Dad's extra work after a race. He gave one of those looks saying, "Cutting wood is good for you Rick Meyer. You ought to *thank* your dad for taking you with him."

"Yes, coach," I sheepishly replied.

Sundays provided a needed day of rest after challenging our bodies and minds.

Manhattan Invite

I was introduced to a new term the week of this meet that described a concept I had instinctively practiced on the farm: Visualize. In the early 1980s, speaking of preparing through visualization resulted in people looking at you as if abstract objects grew out of your head. Congo began instructing us to engage in this powerful technique to program our minds for success. "Visualize. Your mind can't tell the difference between a real and imagined event."

Interestingly, Congo received very low grades in Psychology courses at Kansas State. Yet, he taught us that as we lay in bed two nights before every race, to visualize the upcoming race. First, to see ourselves arriving at the meet in our sweats and uniforms; unloading from the bus with calmness and confidence. We continued visualizing our warm-up, and lining up at the starting line maintaining our calm, confident attitude. Congo then instructed us to visualize racing the course to the best of our ability, including hearing our desired half mile and mile splits. This was followed by a strong finish, running through the finish line, exerting all of our available effort. He explained how this enabled us to arrive and race with confidence "You have no reason to be nervous because you have already successfully finished the race in your mind."

Visualizing is engraving one's desires on the stone of your heart and mind. Engraving in your heart and mind, like engraving in physical stone, requires commitment and great effort. Because double minded people lack permanent commitment they find it impossible to permanently etch a message or image in either stone or on their mind through visualization. It is impossible for a double minded runner to permanently visualize a race when teeter-tottering between running the first half-mile in 2:25 or 2:32.

As a child riding through the pasture with my parents and sister, the route of the previous drives through the grass became permanently marked by repetition. The first time one drives through, the grass bends differently than the other grass. When a vehicle is relatively frequently driven on the exact same route the grass becomes permanently flattened and eventually worn down to a bare trail. Buffalo wallows, spots where Buffalo laid down, remained visible in our pasture as well as others in the area. Also, wagon tracks from the Oregon and Chisholm Trails remain visible in numerous locations over a century later. Similarly, consistent and frequent visualization embeds permanent tracks in our mind. Prudence mandates wisdom in choosing the beliefs forever branded on your mind.

When Jesus sent the Comforter, the Holy Spirit, God's law became written on the hearts of Christ followers.

> Because you are sons, God has sent forth the Spirit of His Son into our hearts, crying, "Abba! Father!" Therefore you are no longer a slave, but a son; and if a son, then an heir through God. (Galatians 4:6-7)

These writings on the heart influence our every thought and consequential words and actions. Similarly, visualizing our goals permanently imprints them on our hearts and minds which influences our every thought.

What are you visualizing? Are you visualizing success in correlation with scripture? Beliefs and images contradicting God's character will cause internal anxiety. Just as cold dry air mixed with warm humid air produces tornadoes, an attempt to blend holy and evil in your heart will result emotional, spiritual tornadic activity in your life. Are you beginning to understand the damaging effects of visualizing any thought or activity in disagreement with the Bible?

Admittedly, for much of the 1983 season I was challenged in completing this task of visualizing as I was unfamiliar with the courses on our schedule. Additionally, I fell asleep nearly as quickly as my head hit the pillow; usually by the time I reached the first half mile in my imagination I drifted off.

Saturday finally arrived. Congo instructed us to drink additional water all week leading up to Saturday's race. The 6A boy's race started at high noon when the temperature exceeded 100 degrees Fahrenheit. I enjoy running and competing in temperatures exceeding 100 degrees. Some believe running in this heat is too dangerous, perhaps it is for those who pamper themselves and lack adequate preparation. I viewed it as another day of work. Farmers work during afternoons of extreme heat. They would complete little summer time work if they avoided working on these scorching days. The approximate 103 degrees felt cool compared to the 118 degrees weeks earlier. During Congo's 25 years of coaching cross country, he never had a runner suffer from dehydration or heat exhaustion during the season. He taught us how to run properly and instructed us on staying adequately hydrated. Considering he often coached nearly 100 runners in this meet each year, I believe he knew how to coach successful competition in temperatures exceeding 100 degrees.

Fort Riley brought their 'water buffalo' to the meet, a 250-gallon water tank with spigots to fill Hardee's cups available to runners from all of the competing schools. We entered the season and this meet ranked 3rd in Kansas behind Topeka West and defending champion Shawnee Mission Northwest. This ranking occurred before knowledge of us being without a top returning run became public. I recall little of this race, except in the last half mile when the Manhattan High cross country alumni encouraged us, "Come on pink, catch the purple (Topeka West) and orange (Shawnee Mission Northwest) shorts." While recovering, we received the affirmation we sought: we defeated the best in Kansas! We started the season on the right track to achieve our goal of a state championship. Much work and effort lay ahead of us between this September meet and the state meet on November 5, 1983. This meet provided us with a benchmark comparison with the best in Kansas.

During an early season workout I disclosed my belief that most of the people who placed ahead of me possessed greater talent. I thought they were better runners. Dan Schneider replied, "You can run just as fast when you're hurting, as when you're not!" This revelation revolutionized my running. Many of the people finishing ahead of me did so because of greater toughness. This farm boy was insulted that any city slickers were tougher.

The workouts perpetually intensified each week until late October. The intensity leveled off on a high plateau, while the quantity began subsiding. Our legs began recovering for the state meet. My queasy stomach rumbled for the remainder of each evening from these workouts.

On Friday we traveled to Topeka West's meet at Shunga Park, with a hill called Big Shunga. Once again, many of the best in Kansas conglomerated for a cross country meet. We arrived in a big diesel charter bus carrying the varsity and junior varsity teams. These were rare for high schools in 1983. Another regular school bus or two brought the C team and below. Moreover we wore special Adidas meet warm-ups of silk-like material, baby blue in color with three black stripes down the sides of the bell-bottom pants. The tops were zip-up matching jackets. Typical 1970s! We unloaded the bus then Congo spoke to us briefly.

Earlier in the week, Congo had results sheets taped up on his office wall showing our anticipated individual finishes, resulting in a team win. We always prioritized the team win. Individual goals served as necessary ingredients for a team win, just as properly boiling noodles is necessary for great lasagna. Additionally, he gave us handouts allowing us to study our anticipated finishes and who we needed to finish ahead of in the race. Congo wrote at the bottom of that week's sheet that perennial 4A powerhouse Topeka Hayden led by one of Congo's protégés, Coach Ben Meske, was last defeated in 1981.

We knew this meet offered abundant challenges, however our entire season focused on finishing high in November's state meet. We discussed winning the state championship every day. Each meet, win or lose, would not make or break our season. However, each meet was a tool to fine tune our mental and physical racing skills and strategy. The C team ran first at 4:00p.m. Shortly after arrival, we covered the race course with a walk-jog mixture. We typically walked up the hills to preserve the bounce in our legs; we observed and discussed various portions of courses, such as hills, dips and especially corners. We spoke of the significance of surging at the top of the hills. Surging accomplishes several things. It gaps the competition and quickly forces our legs to regain quick turnover for racing, while also sending a message to the competition that we were aggressively moving forward despite the fire in our legs from the hill.

We also planned strategic surges immediately after turning a corner. Corners often offer a brief moment where a runner is out of sight of a competitor lagging a few yards behind. A timely surge allows us to move ahead with the competitor being aware of our move, when he turns the corner the gap of a few yards has significantly increased. This gained distance often breaks the mental connection of a competitor.

This connection is similar to personal space when visiting with someone. Our distance of separation while conversing influences how connected we feel with that person. In races, each person has a certain distance behind a competitor that they believe they are running with that person, even though they are following. Once this distance is exceeded, the trailing runner loses the mental connection, feeling as if they are on their own; increasing the difficulty and likelihood of the trailing runner catching the leading runner.

Do you surge in your professional life to 'gap' your competitors? Do you exert additional effort in customer service, self-improvement or deepening of faith while out of sight of others? Competitors may believe they are within striking distance of your sales numbers, or gaining your customers. They are surprised the next morning or following a break realizing you gapped them with surges of effort late at night or early in the morning.

Just as a runner surges at the top of a hill, do you surge at the end of the day or end of a project? Do you surge by playing with your children or visiting with your spouse when you are exhausted? Do you surge in living the Gospel with extra efforts of love, forgiveness, gentleness, and boldness when your entire existence simply desires to collapse? Do you surge to open and hold the door open for others, greeting them with a gentle smile and welcoming words? Do you surge to serve in your church, community and school when you have climbed the hill or rounded the corner of a major work project? You, like a runner, have burning arms, legs and lungs; your mind is begging for mercy. Yet, you focus and concentrate, saying, "Here I am Lord, choose Me!"

The average runner and person considers these fatiguing moments as justification for relaxing, for letting up. At the end of "the race" we wonder how others who once were near collapsing accomplished so much more. We must be always running on faith.

Eventually, the boys' varsity 2 mile race was underway, we ran straight for a long stretch, then turned corners before conquering Big Shunga Hill. I was hurting, trying to stay with my teammates who surged at the top. Eventually, I could no longer match the tempo of Jon and Daniel. I believe I finished as our 6th runner. Fortunately, when the team results were announced MHS finished in the top spot with the lowest team score. For the second consecutive week, we defeated the best teams in Kansas. This State Championship dream just might come true after all. Goal #1 from June 1975 just might be fulfilled.

Since this was a Friday meet, I spent all day Saturday with Dad. I missed working with him after school and practice each day as I did on the farm. My participation on this team was only possible because of the tough economic circumstances on the farm as previously discussed. Victory often dwells in wake of great defeat. God's greatest blessings are often through the door of hardship. God's wisdom exceeds our own.

Coach Congo was very respectful of our expressions of faith and allowed us to take ownership of our goals. Through that season, we truly became friends and a team that wanted the best for each other. We peaked at the right time and God blessed our dedication to Him and running and we became 6A state champs. Championships, like all gifts in life, require responsible stewardship of any and all benefits and publicity. The stewardship of champions includes remaining grateful, joyful and prayerful, always.

Figure 9: Goal #1 Achieved --Receiving the 1983 State Cross Country Championship trophy. Jon Young (white patch on the letter coat), Daniel Wallace, David Pulford, Daniel Schneider, Rick Meyer. Not pictured: Mark Richter and Mike Gassman. Photo Credit: Manhattan Mercury, Sunday, November 7, 1983

GOAL #2 – Nationally Ranked Team

The 1984 season brought great expectation with our returning of 6 of the 7 varsity runners from our championship team. The last time a cross country team repeated as the best in Kansas, one member of their team, Jim Ryun, ran in the Olympics before state cross country. Another famous person was also once roamed the Wichita East hallways. Dallas Theological Seminary students, faculty, staff and supporters know him as Chaplain Bill. We endured incredible workouts that season, one workout ended with Congo saying, "Congratulations guys, you just completed one-half of a Jim Ryun workout."

Figure 10: The 1984 MHS cross country team. Front Row Left to Right: Rick Meyer, Daniel Wallace, Dan Schneider, Jon Young, Mark Richter, Paul Mitchell. Bill 'Congo' Congleton sits in the upper-right hand corner.

One September morning I entered Congo's office asking if I needed to be running in the morning. He sat in a polo shirt, wrangler blue jeans and cowboy boots; looking up replying, "Depends on how good you want to be, Rick Meyer." Initially this rhetorical comment rattled around in my 17 year old mind. Most coaches respond with bold commands. Congo, who received a D in psychology, demonstrated why the University of Texas Athletic Director Deloss Dodds refers to him as "…better at coaching young people than anyone." Later in the day, this rhetorical question was like a needle poking my excuse balloon, instantly vaporizing every one of them. The following morning I ran before school, I continue running in the morning on a regular basis.

Chapter 4:
Complacency

The complacency of Fools will destroy them ~ Proverbs 1:32

Junction City High School hosted their annual cross country meet in late September on a Thursday. The chartered bus pulled out of the Manhattan High parking lot, down Westwood Road to the stop sign turning right onto Fort Riley Blvd, K18 highway. After nearly 8 miles we drove on the fork going through Ogden, traversing through Fort Riley on Huebner Rd. General Clarence R. Huebner fought with the Big Red One, the Army's 1st Infantry Division in World War I, while also serving as a division commander during a portion of World War II. On this day I thought little about the Big Red One, rather on the race awaiting us at Milford Lake. Eventually we turned down Anzio Road, where the Allies took a beating in WWII. Perhaps this was fortuitous of the upcoming race. This cross country meet location was about 30 miles from Abilene, KS; boyhood home of the Allied Supreme Commander General Dwight D. Eisenhower; he took command after Anzio began.

This great leader's career as described in his biography *EISENHOWER: A SOLDIERS LIFE* appeared stuck and going backwards at the age of 49. Less than 3 years later, Ike received the appointment as the Allied Supreme Commander. Do you feel stuck, perhaps too old to capture your dreams? Keep Running on Faith!

Equally challenging was this course and competition. The course consisted of rolling hills with hay bales stacked two high, scattered around the course. Running up a hill and jumping hay bales required physical strength and mental focus. Varsity boys ran the last of the meet's five races; the bottom bales were loosened, providing little solid footing by the time of our race. Physically, my strength dwindled due to a head and chest cold acquired by leaving a jacket at home when we moved the interval workout to an evening, avoiding the high temperatures immediately following school. During the 90 minute workout, the temperature dropped rapidly and the sprinklers watering the football field came on, also watering the track. I knew better than to leave my jacket at home, however, I left it any way. The Bible says pride precedes destruction; I declined a jacket offered me by assistant coach Betsy Sloan. My pride severely hindered my running for 4 weeks.

Hays was also a team deserving of everyone's attention. Warm-up consisted of covering the course, and investigating the hay bales. The finishing stretch was a muscle burner, driving lactic acid production into overdrive. This course shot down near the shoreline of Milford Lake, then a left hand loop returned us up to the nearly 300 hundred yard challenging slope toward the finish line. My legs, screaming in pain, possessed the strength of wet spaghetti; mental focus and concentration were compulsory for reaching the finishing chute. My teammates blew around me long ago. Finally the heavy chalked line perpendicular to the course traveled beneath my path. Knowing I ran poorly, I desired to dissolve into the earth. My body hurt too badly to move; emotionally I did not want to face my teammates because I let them down. Would you agree facing those who trust and depend on us is difficult when our performance is poor?

After a brief cool down and the disappointing awards ceremony, we began chanting our season's slogan; "Once more in '84!" Congo was far less than amused with our confidence following a royal beating. He invited the 6 returning varsity runners on the 1983 team to join him on the bus. This was the first time I ever saw Congo upset. His disappointment generated from our complacent attitude as opposed to our placing. Congo stared and spoke with ego piercing intensity, "You were state runner-up as sophomores. You were state champions as juniors; you can easily be state runner-ups again this year. Most people would look at that record and be impressed. But, you will know the difference! Whether six months, five years, ten years, or twenty years from now you will look back and know you could be champions this year. You will have to live with the results. Never be satisfied with less than your best! Now get off this bus and run down this road until we pick you up." We ran a little over a mile before the bus stopped for us. We cautiously climbed aboard, giving serious consideration to having to run back to the school.

We returned through Fort Riley, current home of the Big Red One. The Army's 1st Infantry Division never felt satisfied. When they landed on the beaches of North Africa, satisfaction bore no meaning to them. Another amphibious landing on the beaches on Sicily provided no opportunity for complacency. Making a rare 3rd beach landing on Omaha Beach, D-Day 1944, they fought for their lives, for freedom and liberation. All of the United States Armed Forces chose between complacency and freedom. Complacency will always result in defeat and loss of freedom!

Upon reaching MHS, we unloaded from the chartered bus, entering the locker room off of the south gymnasium. Congo invited us into his office for another meeting. The 6 of us entered, Congo shut his office door, asking us to remove our letter coats. Sewn on the back of the letter coats were the 1983 6A State Championship white patches, with a dark blue outline and lettering. We threw our coats on the table as Congo pulled out a big ten-inch buck knife. Instantly our eyes widened. He seized our coats one by one, cutting off the patches with his buck knife and tossing the patches into the corner. Looking us each in the eye he firmly, yet calmly, stated, "If you want these back, you have to earn them." Often we hear of cutting ourselves loose of past defeats. This is good advice. Congo taught us to literally cut loose past successes, allowing for even greater achievements in life. Clinging to past success restricts our ability to move forward as far as possible.

Would we ever see those patches again?

'84 State CC

Thinking: God has plans for you today!

During our warm-up Daniel Wallace, Jon Young and I each prayed for God's guidance, protection and power during the race. We repeated our season long dependence on Him along with our desire to please Him.

We stood at the starting line of the 1984 state cross country meet at Warner Park in Manhattan, KS. Our Manhattan High team planned to become the first high school cross country team to repeat as the 6A State Champions. Oblivious to the 40 MPH wind blowing from the north. The wind hovered near 20 MPH before increasing to 40 between 10:30 and 11:00a.m. Dan Schneider, our top runner, led us in our 5th and final prayer just 3 minutes prior to the start. We had prepared for this final race for the past year.

On the starting line Dan, Jon Young, Daniel Wallace, Mark Richter, Mike Gasman, Mark Lowenstein and I stood in a circle with our heads bowed. Dan Schneider then prayed, "Lord, help us run to the best of our abilities: let us run a race to glorify you, whether we finish first place or last place." When wavelengths representing the words "last place" traversed from his vocal cords to my eardrums, I wanted to deck him: punch him hard. Let's put this in proper perspective: I never hit anyone in the face in anger in my life, before or after this moment. I also refrained then. How dare he suggest that our team finish in last place! We returned 6 of the 7 varsity runners from the previous year's championship team.

I spent the summer telling anyone who asked or listened, that I trained for one date and one moment. That moment arrived! November 3, 1984 - high noon. The entire season focused on this race; we deliberately and diligently prepared for this competition. During those hot August runs, we discussed our desire to win every cross country meet during the season. However, the competition was fierce as we faced one of Kansas' top 3 teams every week. Because the state championship was only awarded in the last meet, our focus was honed only on that meet. Our mission was winning the state championship!

During the season we often arrived at competition with tired legs. A typical week consisted of running 20 quarter miles at 68 to 70 seconds with 80 seconds rest in between each interval on Monday. This surpassed Congo's traditional Monday workout of 16 quarters at 72 to 75 seconds. On Tuesdays we ran 8 miles with 3.5 miles of fartlek. On Wednesdays we often ran 2 miles to Warner Park where the workout would begin. This was frequently tortuous training, running 8 sets of 880 yard runs between 2:15 to 2:20 with a few minutes of walk-jog rest in between each. After the 7th half-mile, we ran 15 to 20 hill sprints. Our bodies and minds reached their perceived limits. Congo called us over to the beginning of the last half mile of the course, setting the scenario, "You are down by six, everyone must catch one person." I often verbally visualized our goal in imitating the announcer of the state meet, "The 1984 Kansas State High School Activities Association 6A State cross country CHAMPIONS …. Manhattan High School!!" Naturally, the 6 returning varsity runners finished the final half mile at full tilt running through the line in a range of 2:01 to 2:08. Excruciating pain only existed in our lower legs, quads, chest, arms, along with a headache. We ran back to the school after this 'fun.' Thursdays were easy with a short 6 mile run. Fridays were either a race or another 6 mile run. On Saturdays we either raced or ran on our own, usually 8 miles. Sundays we welcomed a day of rest.

The price is accumulated. The championship is about to commence, 11 other teams arrived. They too amassed significant accumulations, some more than others. Who would be willing to spend their entire savings on this championship? Financial planners lay out plans for people to maximize their savings. Real Estate experts know how to purchase more land than 'average' people with the same amount of available money. Our legendary coach, Bill "Congo" Congleton laid out the perfect plan for us to attain maximum value from the physical and mental accumulation attained in training. Our goal was simple: spend every penny of our accounts during this race. We frequently conversed, discussing the inability to walk and talk following the race. This was the only way a possible loss could be acceptable. If we spent every particle of energy in the most intelligent mode known to us, leaving us incapacitated an inch beyond the finish line, the results would be acceptable. Just like auctioning a Picasso, the bidding would be exceedingly high.

We desired to be champions. The painful workouts were necessary. Congo frequently reminded us, "It all comes down to who wants it the most." Our hope resided in the hands of our coach; he prescribed workouts we would have preferred to avoid. I would sit in class anticipating with trepidation the enormous pain generated in the afternoon's workouts. Congo's wisdom of preparing us physically and mentally far exceeded our own. We trusted and obeyed him in workouts. We became champions during the preparation. Is the same true of all success in life? God's wisdom is infinitely greater than Congo's or any other human. We should place our trust and obedience in God in even greater abundance than we do any human. God's 'workouts' in life also test our fortitude, preparing us for the great victories given from God.

Pre-Race Prayer

At starting line, Dan Schneider finished his prayer with 2 minutes remaining before Congo fired the gun. The entire season had focused on prayer and winning. That last phrase that had me wanting to slap him made me think. I stood momentary in shock. Dan was right! First or last, the sincere effort was the heart of the matter. Dan later served in President G.W. Bush's Presidency in various roles from Deputy Secretary of Health and Human Services to personally recommending over 400 Presidential appointees receiving Congressional approval. Because of his bold faith and trust in the Lord Jesus Christ, politicians have mocked him and presented ludicrously false accusations about Dan. "If the world hates you, keep in mind it hated me first (Jn. 15:18)."

A few moments after Dan's prayer, Congo approached us. "Are you ready?" Congo was also the state meet director; as a result we rarely saw him that week. I replied in the affirmative, while staring at his pistol. Being an avid hunter, this briefly captured my attention. I jokingly thought, 'Yeah, I know what will happen to us if we do not run well!' In the background, public address announcer Don Steffens was detailing the teams present and their starting positions as well as those teams favored to challenge for the championship. He did capture my attention when his unique tone, widely known at championship meets in Kansas, announced, "...they won the state meet here, (slight pause) a year agooo." Then, we heard our starting position announced.
Congo returned to his starter's position, 150 yards from the starting line. We quickly tore off our traditional uniform of powder pink running shorts and baby blue tops; we now wore a dark blue uniform. Congo referred to these as our Darth Vader, nasty blues. Our competition keyed on us in big meets: the pink shorts provided an easy target. While undressing, Congo announced over his bullhorn, "There will be a two command start, runners set, then the gun. If anyone falls down within the first one hundred fifty

yards there will be a second shot signaling a restart. Runners Set!," *BOOOOOOM!!!!!* The moment had arrived; the race was underway. Most of the runners shot out quickly while we maintained our intended pace, just as we rehearsed physically and visually. The first corner was encountered 300 yards into the race, then the course quickly narrowed with a hard right turn. As we circled back to the crowd we heard the Topeka West fans, our primary competition, yelling, "They are in blue! They are in blue!"

In the second quarter mile we began working our way through the field, pulling apart runners who were side by side to create a path, allowing forward movement through the pack, towards the championship. Repetition provided our proficiency at creating opportunity. Conversely, most runners use this as an excuse for getting stuck in the back of the pack. Would you agree this is good advice for life – create opportunities?

Near the 700 yard mark, the course made its second hard turn, this time to the left with a short downhill. I swung wide right, as many of the eager beavers at the start now slowed. Unfortunately, a slow poke also swung wide directly in front of me. His calf landed directly in the path of my descending 3/8" spikes. Entering the fast lane in slow mode leads to injuries. Continuing on the outside, the half-mile mark quickly approached, 2:26 as I passed by as the number 2 man for our team and in 56th position overall. This split was exactly as I visualized while lying in bed two nights before the race. The race progressed nearly precisely as I visualized; although, spiking a competitor was unintended. Fatigue began to make its entrance, sustainable, yet present. We prepared mentally for the onset of fatigue, knowing our 'cross country accounts' could handle the required 'expense' of the early pace. My mind remained focused on 2 items: the championship and my dependence on Christ for strength.

Extreme focus allows runners to pass other competitors. A runner must focus to avoid any collisions or falling. My freshman year at Smith Center High School, a teammate collided with a tree during a race. The ambulance ride directly across the highway to the Phillipsburg Hospital cost $50 in 1981. This prorates to over $200 a mile. Avoid colliding with trees! Warner Park's side sloped terrain "claimed me" as a victim the year before, during our league championship. The terrain conquered me once, but not again. Shortly before the mile, the burning sensation from the lactic acid intensified. The mile marker rested at the base of a challenging

100 yard hill. I specifically stated, "Lord, I *need you*!! Now more than ever before."

Congo later told me I was in 27th position. The Lord's power overrode the painful sensations. Running on pure faith, I surged up this incline and over the peak. In life and racing, prayer for strength is most powerful when followed by a surge in faith-filled actions. Although screaming spectators packed the hill, I heard nothing except for my name yelled by a high-pitched cheerleader, then I heard my dad cheering: all else was silence. A long downhill was next on the course, in excess of a quarter mile. Surprising to non-runners, this is also painful. I counted my position, just as I mentally preprogrammed with visualization, I was now in 12th place overall. In the previous 1,000 yards, I moved up 44 positions. At the bottom of the long downhill, the brain's pain sensations neared overload, reminding me of chasing the calf on the farm.

Then I saw our neighbors from EJ Frick Dr., Gordon and Karen Hibbard, along with their 3 year old son Jonathan, standing at the corner cheering. Their encouragement and strong faith served as a powerful reminder to 'keep the hammer down.' I believe I spit as I went by, no reflection on their presence! Jonathan would later run around their yard spitting, following the example set by us runners. Our actions impact those with whom we associate, even when unintended; 15 years later, Jonathan was part of the 3A State championship team at Riley County High School in Riley, KS. Jon later served in Iraq as a member of the United States Army. He fought for the world championship of liberation and freedom.

Following this corner was a short mild incline before progressing through 2 tough dips. The dips were roughly 50 yards from apex to apex, about 12 feet deep. The slopes were mostly steep, gradually down, quickly up, quickly down, quickly up. Then came a gradual uphill while turning right into another long, gradual incline. This base represented a half-mile to go in the race. We trained mentally and physically for this moment. When I later described to my dad the extent of the pain experienced coming out of the dips at Warner Park, I said I do not believe I could be in worse pain, even if my mother's life was at stake.

Little did I realize how the assessment of similarities between the pain of that race and the pain of losing a parent were accurate. One's entire body is on the verge of collapse. Only 2 other moments created pain of this magnitude: once at the top of the Boston Marathon's Heartbreak Hill as dehydration began taking effect. The other was immediately following the phone call of my dad's passing away.

As we rounded the corner into the 40MPH headwind, the C team runners stood holding a sheet with our 1983 State Championship patches sewn on by Charlotte Congleton. The C team members screamed, "Do you want these back?" Once again I pleaded, "Lord, I NEED YOU!!"

I blacked out from unimaginable pain, heading up the hill and around the left hand turn at the top, followed by another left hand turn. Suddenly with the crowd's deafening roar, my cognizance returned. "Schneid must be close." I thought of Dan Schneider's race for the individual championship. Congo let Dan choose between two tactics for Dan's state race. Dan could go with Robbie Hays of Topeka West and dual out for the individual title, yet risk the team title should he fall back and lose positions from extreme fatigue of a fast early pace. Or Dan could run patiently, securing second then if possible make a challenge for individual title near the end; the latter strategy drastically enhanced our team title opportunity. He chose the latter. Dan possessed tremendous speed; he once ran the 20th quarter mile of an interval workout in 51 seconds! Prudence required the strategy, as it required all season, of prioritizing the team championship above individual glory. Does this epitomize selflessness?

My regained consciousness alerted me of the remaining quarter-mile. If any pennies remained in the bank, now was the time to make the withdrawal, the bids of all runners escalated. I drove as hard as possible as we retraced our footsteps of the course's beginning. While blacked out, I had passed a runner. I turned left into the final 150 yards and the headwind. Then up the slight incline, I spotted 3 runners ranging from 20 to 30 yards ahead. They crested the slope. Igniting the afterburners, all fuel reserve valves fully opened, now was the moment I had dreamed of since I was 8 standing by the windmill tower on the farm. Once again, the course lined with screaming fans, though I heard not a discouraging word because nothing registered audibly.

This bow legged Kansas farm boy let it all go in that final stretch, catching 2 runners from Overland Park and Wichita schools, driving through the finish line, a couple of steps behind the 3rd person I saw entering the stretch. Nearly collapsing in the chute, stumbling forward, progression was painful, yet mandatory as other runners were finishing behind me. I was unable to speak, yet I heard we probably won. While unaware of the other teammates' places, I remained cautiously optimistic. Was our bid the highest in this auction?

Someone handed me a card indicating my place in team scoring ... 6th ... this place is used to calculate team scores. Soon I learned I placed 9th overall. I fulfilled my goal of a top ten state finish. Dan Schneider finished 2nd place individually; he missed the championship by a step in a "photo finish". The same roar that regained my awareness, alerted Rob as he held off Dan by a step. Teammates Jon and Mike finished in 12th and 16th overall, while Daniel, Mark and Mark ran close behind. The interviewer

regarding the employment opportunity in Manhattan, who uncontrollably laughed in my face 17 months before, was absent. She failed to believe a bow legged, cowboy boot wearing, transfer from Smith Center High School (class 3A) could compete and place among the top ten runners in 6A. This Manhattan business closed in the late 1980s. Do you laugh at the goals of others? Does anyone laugh at your goals?

Figure 11: Rick sprinting to the finish line of State Cross Country at Warner Park in Manhattan, KS; moving into 9th place. Photo Credit: The Manhattan Mercury

I remember little of the next 15 minutes. We probably walked over to the starting area to reclaim our pink and blue uniforms, as well as the silk, light blue, bell bottomed sweats. Soon someone announced the unofficial results to us, we won the championship! We placed the highest bid! We achieved the goal of repeating last year's win! At the awards area, the top ten individuals received their medals, followed by the team results. We visualized this so many times! As Congo frequently declared, "Your mind cannot tell the difference between a real and an imagined event."

The Lord prepared us in numerous ways; blessing us with terrific coaches, Congo as well as the assistant coaches, Larry Anderson and Betsy Sloan. Betsy played on the great Lady Cats basketball teams from 1979 –1983. Desire for greatness and the expectation of winning radiated from Betsy's presence. Her eyes illuminate her instantly contagious passion for excellence. Avoidance of inspiration from Betsy necessitates mental death. Her facial expression magnifies the stupidity of any excuse for complacency.

On April 1, 1985 the quarterly edition of The Harrier arrived in Congo's office. This edition included the alphabetized list of the Best Cross Country Teams in America for the fall of 1984; included in this list was Manhattan High School, Manhattan, Kansas. This national ranking fulfilled Goal #2, "Be on a nationally ranked team," set by the old windmill tower on the farm.

Figure 12: Photo Credit: The Manhattan Mercury

Additionally, virtually every day I continue asking this question, "Should I give the extra effort?" *Depends on how good I want to be.* "Should I read the Bible an extra thirty minutes today?" *Depends on how faithful, obedient and available to Christ I want to be.* "Should I wait an extra minute to hold the door open for an approaching lady?" *Depends on how much I want to share the love and hospitality of Christ to her (even if a stranger).*

We stood on the awards stand listening to Don Steffens the announcer, present the team results. In contrast to 1983, we needed to force ourselves to generate exceptional excitement. Instead of effervescent excitement, our emotions overflowed with a sense of achievement and gratitude. We had visualized this presentation and receiving the championship trophy dozens of times during the season, including following our previously described repeat 880s on Wednesdays at Warner Park. Our minds had previously accepted our winning as chiseled in history, God willing. This aided in our intensity and drive in our daily practices.

Today, Daniel Wallace serves as the Director of Gull Lake Ministries near Battle Creek, Michigan. Daniel gave up his position as a CPA for the largest accounting firm in downtown Dallas in the early 1990s to pursue ministry at Pine Cove Ranch outside of Tyler, Texas. Jon Young owns a Real Estate management company in Olathe, Kansas. Dan Schneider is the Executive Director of the American Conservative Union.

Trash

Congo allowed us to celebrate about 5 minutes. "Congratulations guys! Pick up the trash." He asked us to pick up the trash strewn across Warner Park. The approximately 4,000 spectators and fellow athletes failed to connect with the trash barrels around the park. The various paper cups graciously supplied by Hardees must have been heavy. Why else would they be located on the ground instead of carried an extra 20 feet to the trash barrels? Congo taught us that champions must clean up after themselves and others. Christ declared, "The greatest of all, is the servant of all." Congo taught us to be humble and serving even in victory.

Performing the duties of state meet director, Congo was active with many tasks that day. He did not have to serve as the director. He chose to because he believed in serving his sport in addition to coaching. I do not believe he found time to fully enjoy the championships until all the equipment at Warner Park was returned to the school. In 1984, in addition to the boys winning, the girls fought through an injury-filled season to place a pleasing, completely unexpected, 3rd in the team standings. Years later, Congo shared that due to their injury-plagued season, the girls' finish was nearly equal in achievement to our championship.

The same events take place at football and basketball games. Spectators cheer, expecting maximum effort from their favorite teams while leaving plastic bottles, popcorn bags and candy wrappers in the bleachers. The prevailing attitude believes someone else will clean it up. We believe someone earns money to complete the task. Do we believe we are too good to clean-up our messes?

Lyle Claussen set an example for the University at Nebraska Kearney athletes. Following a long run of 20 miles with his All-Americans, Lyle led them around the coliseum on campus picking up the trash of other students and administrators. *He that is greatest of all is the servant of all.* Too many view this upside down; believing, 'he that is greatest is served by all.' I am unaware of any other coach in the University of Nebraska athletic program, much less a hall of fame coach as is Lyle, who regularly leads All-Americans around facilities picking up trash.

After picking up the trash at Warner Park, we met at Pizza Hut. Upon arrival, waiters served us relatively quickly. However, many of our stomachs remained unsettled nearly 2 hours after the race. We could usually eat more than our fair share of pizza and any other food. The following day, after attending church together, we dined at Valentino's, making up for our lost appetites by raiding the buffet. That afternoon a few of us each grabbed several guns, headed to a farm west of town towards Keats, shooting away at various targets.

Our cross country team only participated in activities involving church, family, school and cross country. Several of us thoroughly enjoyed hunting. We delayed all hunting and shooting until after the season ended. We knew the only way to the championship involved faith, vision, discipline and diligence.

We held a faith in our creator and Savior in our hearts. We had faith in God's power, faith in each other and faith in our coaches. DeLoss Dodds describes Congo in a letter dated October, 30, 2001: "He cares about young people, and he knows how to coach them better than anyone else." A former world-class athlete, coach and athletic director at Kansas State as well as the long time athletic director at the University of Texas, Mr. Dodds knows hundreds of coaches, including the top coaches in both the prep and collegiate ranks.

To increase my faith during the season, I read the entire New Testament (King James Version), except for Revelation, beginning in August and ending a day or two before the state meet. I read slowly at that age. I opted to study scripture instead of some of my homework. Both in the state race and in life, I relied on scripture thousands of times for strength and comfort. I have yet to call upon any readings from British Literature when in need of inspiration or sustenance. To be fair, an understanding of British Literature aids in scripture comprehension. The Holy Spirit internalized the scriptures of 'all things are possible through Christ who strengthens us.'

Because of our faith in Congo as a coach, we did not question his wisdom. Congo's ideologies are summations of proverbs. Wisdom lies in understanding a concept well enough to relate it in a vast array of circumstances in language understood by the target audience. One of Congo's masteries is his ability to plant a seed of thought, and allow the seed to germinate and grow while dwelling on the message. As an example, he would frequently say, "Don't be afraid to be great." Who is afraid to be great? I believed everyone desired to be great. After much pondering, I realized that everyone wants to be good; but few are willing to pay the price over the long term for greatness. Most people would love to own a Mercedes, but few are willing pay for it. Being great involves challenging ourselves, pushing ourselves beyond previously known limits. We did this nearly every day in practice.

While crop consulting, one gentleman did not want to accept the advice for which he paid me. I spent significant time in the alfalfa fields making frequent checks, stopping the blue Yamaha two-wheel-drive four-wheeler, to throw a 3 foot by 3 foot square made of plastic pipe to check the cutworm level of infestation. If levels were above the economic threshold, a recommendation was made for spraying these cutworms. He did not want to spray, failing to believe cutworm were the economic problem as outlined. After some discussion, he would pause and say, "You know, we should spray for cutworms in this field. They can be a real problem – you probably are unaware of the significant problem they can be." I learned to forget about seeking credit, rather agreeing with his terrific idea. Mark Kottmeyer once wisely told me, "The majority of the times, a person's most powerful ideas are their own." Congo was a master at making those seeds of thought germinate and grow to become one's own.

Congo's response of, "Depends on how good you want to be." Had me ruminating about most authoritative figures preferring to tell people what to think instead of how to think. Most people like to be told what to think instead of learning how to think. Are there times we should tell people what to think? Are there moments when we just want to be told what to think? Most of us answer 'yes' to each of these questions, at least under specific circumstances. With that statement, Congo taught me how to think!

Figure 13: May 2002 Wichita, KS. Frank Perbeck, Bill Congleton, Rick Meyer, Jon Young. Frank Perbeck won the Javelin throw in the 1974 U.S.A. vs. USSR track meet in Dallas, TX.

Figure 14: May 2002, Wichita, KS. Gary Musselman and Bill Congleton. Congo's Hall of Fame Induction.

Would America and the world be better off if more people learned how to think? Adolph Hitler once said, "It is the good fortune of rulers that most people do not think for themselves." Why do so few choose to think for themselves? Thinking requires effort!

As a 17 year old C student, this challenge permeated my soul, piercing my excuses like a pin to balloon. This challenge reminded me that I needed to think, I was responsible for my own success.

How good do you want to be? Are you willing to invest the extra time in your relationships? Life is about relationships! What are the two greatest commandments? They include Matthew 22:37-39, Love the Lord with all of your: heart, soul, strength and mind *and* Love your neighbor as yourself. These are both relational commands. God created humans for a relationship with him. We blew it. How did God respond to our sinfulness, our brokenness? He sent Jesus, his son, to live with us, then die and take the blame for all of our sins. Loving God with all of our energy places the desire to please God above all other desires. We fail in these efforts.

We need to care as much about our neighbors as we do ourselves. If we want to know and serve God, we should also yearn for our fellow man to do the same. Loving our neighbor as much as we love ourselves, desiring success for them as we do for ourselves, and our families, is contrary to selfishness. Love involves craving the absolute best for each person. Developing into the absolute best is a painful process. To forge iron, the blacksmiths began applying heat to the iron, applying appropriate pressure until it conforms to the desired shape. Scripture clearly illustrates God as the potter and we the clay. God determines and allocates the proper heat and pressure for each situation. As iron sharpens iron, so one man sharpens another[1].

Loving our neighbor as much as ourselves is caring less about our own feelings and egos, and more about their souls; their success. A coach who allows athletes to avoid pain is a poor coach. The great coaches, teachers, friends and bosses are those who encourage you to keep going long after the pain starts. "Rebuke a fool and he will despise you, rebuke a wise man and he will be wiser still"[2].

Just as physical pain is needed to maximize physical fitness, emotional discomfort is necessary to maximize emotional capacity. The pain in workouts is more tolerable when a goal is kept in constant view. Desiring success, pleasing God, requires continually seeking godly wisdom. Those seeking success and wisdom focus on being better, rather than feeling better. The wise person understands the process, accepts and then implements advice received from wise associates.

How would you like to go through life believing $2 + 2 = 7$, because your associates failed to correct you out of concern for your feelings? Do you want to live or work in a structure designed by someone who had inaccurate mathematical beliefs? If this person became an engineer and his

---

[1] Proverbs 27:17
[2] Proverbs 9:7-9

inaccurate calculations caused a severe accident, would we still be delighted that we made him feel good even when he was wrong?

Ultimately, no one contains the power to hurt another's feelings. The 'victim' relinquishes this power to others. Being thin most of my life, except when a toddler and after I discontinued running high mileage consistently, I endured many jokes. Plenty of jokes were made concerning my low weight, low body fat, big ears and bowlegs. Hearing of the big ears did grow tiresome; however I did not choose my ears, yet I did choose to have them remain the same. The option of surgically reducing my ears never became a viable choice. They are no longer big in comparison to my head.

My active lifestyle and eating a great deal at every sitting, including all of the fat available on meat led me to being thin. The bow legs are just me. All these flaws I learned to accept and felt no desire to change. After I drastically reduced my running mileage at the age of 30, I gained 30 pounds. When teased, I knew it was a result of my decisions. Consequently the teasing did not bother me. If you want to change, and no affordable options seem available, recognize this and move on. Move on to find the solution. Choose to be happy. Whether you like it or not.

If Winning Were Easy, Everybody Would Do It

I first spoke these words to my teammates in 1983 and 1984 as we ventured into competition as I reflected on the faith, commitment, energy, diligence, persistence, vision, discipline and toughness necessary for winning championships. These words however, ring true outside of athletics. They are true for success in *any* endeavor. The higher the stakes, plus the more difficult the task, requires greater staying power.

A common game among young people is Freeze Out. It is a game about staying power. Freeze Out involves turning off your vehicle's heater, rolling down the windows and driving in frigid temperatures until someone gives up and requests turning the heater to high. The winner is the one who endures the discomfort the longest. The winner is the one who proves his staying power.

Achieving success is similar to playing Freeze Out. Only now, the game might be called Challenged Out. The greater challenges we face and endure, the greater success we achieve in the end. Limited success, at best, is the realization of those who find themselves challenged out, as the challenges grow too big, or too insurmountable, for them and their staying power wanes.

While growing up on the farm, we invited friends out to hunt. Jim was one of those friends and hunters, and he knew a thing or two about staying power. Jim was the first scientist in the United States and 3rd in the world, to successfully genetically fuse a tomato and potato plant. Jim tried to teach others the process he used to accomplish this feat, but others' attempts to duplicate his efforts skipped necessary steps in the process. They allowed the challenges to overcome them, thus their staying power simply gave out.

Jim's strong sense of staying power enabled him to create genetic fusion of this new plant. Jim underwent approximately 12,000 laboratory attempts on his journey to success! He was the first to create an albino potato plant. He states it is difficult to know the precise attempts due to numerous concurrent attempts. Throughout this multi-year process, many tried to steal his research notes and some even broke into his laboratory. Jim was able to succeed at world-class achievements because he had staying power. Jim related in recent conversation, the key is achieving and recognizing progress, while maintaining focus. He willingly endured thousands of repetitions in order to achieve the desired result.

How about you? Are you willing to endure thousands of attempts at your goals, enduring several years, in order to achieve world-class success? When confronted with challenges, remember the greater they are, the greater your success will be. Most of all, keep pressing on. Rejoice in your staying power because after all, if winning were easy, everybody would do it!

Farmers' Faith

As previously discussed, Christian faith is knowing that the Lord Jesus Christ is one of the members of the trinity of God. Jesus is the word made flesh who created everything and possesses command over all of creation (John 1:1-3).

Faith is like shooting a basketball in a gym with no baskets while believing a basket will appear when your shot arrives if a basket in this gym and moment agrees with God's plan. Other times, we simply cannot see the existing basket due to an obstacle blocking our view. Numerous times I joke, "I do not mind living on faith, if only I could know what is going to happen." However, failing to act before knowing God's specific plans creates paralysis. Paralysis results in disobedience because we then fail to serve and glorify God. Rather, we have to trust that God will provide regardless of what we see or understand.

On the farm, I learned the hard lesson that it takes less time to show caution than to fix a piece of machinery. My angry father failed to understand why his 12 year old son did not stop the tractor and walk over to inspect the location of a tree stump's position relative to the harrow on the disc when leaving the field through a narrow opening. After spending 3 hours that afternoon fixing the harrow, Dad passionately explained how to avoid an accident and tearing up equipment by engaging less than 5 minutes of caution. I do not need a doctorate in mathematics to determine that 5 minutes is less than the 180 minutes spent repairing the harrow.

Living on a farm requires faith!

Farmers pull drills and planters with their tractors to plant seeds in the fields. Close examination of this process illuminates the verification of faith. Farmers purchase viable seeds at escalating prices, partially due to the technology invested in crop development. The farmer pours these expensive seeds into the planter or drill, which in turn buries them in the ground. For corn, this is roughly equivalent to burying a penny every ten inches. The distance between seeds varies depending on the row width, desired plant population, the climate, soil type, soil fertility, irrigation capacity along with expected rainfall and the specific seed purchased. Imagine burying pennies in this manner. Those passing by on the road viewing this act might question your sanity, particularly as you explain that you expect each penny to transform into five hundred to eight hundred pennies by October. Furthermore, you will pour additional money onto these pennies throughout the year in an effort to control weeds and insects to assure that you receive as many new pennies as possible. Would you agree this epitomizes faith? Life offers no guarantees! Each seed's yield depends upon having the appropriate sunlight, nutrients and moisture. Numerous details exist within each of these three categories.

As previously noted, the Apostle Paul shares an agronomic truth in the Bible that the crop's yield comes from God working through the farmer to illustrate an equivalent truth in evangelism (1 Corinthians 3:6-9). Farmers know God's intervention produces each kernel of grain. The farmer manages the crop as a response to his faith. Without God's intervention, the field grows into weeds and falls to damaging insects. If a person doubts this truth in farming or any business, he could try this litmus test: Ask God to stay out of their business. Is requesting God to remove His presence a good idea?

Reading

One of the keys to growing in our relationship with Jesus Christ is reading the Bible. Reading other books and articles strengthens our professions including our relatability with others. Relatability enhances discipleship and evangelism.

An 1800s version of the Webster Dictionary defined leaders as readers. Reading enables us to figuratively cozy up in a recliner by the crackling fireside with a cup of hot coffee while riding a horse through the flooding river and timber along the Louisiana and Texas border with Ulysses S. Grant or shivering while crossing the Delaware with George Washington.

For example, General George S. Patton studied past wars and battles dating back 2,500 years for 20 years before World War Two commenced. Considering that imagination enhances reading and reading enhances our imagination and that our mind does not differentiate between a real and imagined event, we should not be surprised that he believed he personally fought in those ancient battles. We can only speculate the significance his reading and studying played as his Third Army marched across Europe. Have you considered that God may be preparing you for tasks 20 years from now through placing books and other learning experiences in your path today?

In addition to increasing our knowledge and perspectives, reading also increases the gray matter in our brains which increases our ability to think, which increases our wisdom and discernment. Do you desire to increase your wisdom, knowledge and understanding? If so, read! Reading the Bible along with an intimate relationship with Jesus Christ provides effervescing godly wisdom, knowledge and understanding.

As a child I enjoyed adventurous stories of hunting and the great outdoors gained through reading. Unfortunately, reading for extended periods of time often generated headaches. This painful and discouraging trend continued through college. Once on my own after college, the headaches mostly subsided and my reading escalated. I then realized that reading in dim or soft light caused my headaches, whereas white light or "day light" bulbs yielded delight in reading for me.

Because I strongly desired to raise hogs as a child I eagerly scanned through new issues of Farm Journal and Successful Farming for articles about hog farms. My passion for hogs probably derived from my dad raising them until I was 4. I could barely contain my excitement when I purchased my first bred sow at age 12 from my cousin, Tim Kahrs, for $200. As the herd increased to 4 sows and a boar, I continually dreamed and planned for expansion. Little did I realize how caring for them also provided benefits for my future passion of pursuing Christ through running.

In addition to asking my dad, uncles, grandpa and older cousins countless questions about raising hogs, I read everything that I could get my hands on about hogs. I craved the material printed by the Super Sweet feed and management guides for hogs, reading each booklet at least 100 times. I diligently studied a book written by Harvestore about their role in feeding hogs and the various building designs in the back of the book.

Additionally, I also devoured articles regarding deer and elk hunting in Outdoor Life and Field & Stream. From them, I created exciting adventures in my imagination, hunting alongside author Jim Zumbo on many elk hunts, as well as Jim Carmichael and others.

The above topics, along with books covering outdoor adventure and running, represent more than reading; I experienced many adventures through my imagination as a result of reading these descriptive adventures. Conversely, I despised reading school assignments because I deemed them tedious and laborious, absent any adventure.

Today, I typically read 2 to 10 books a week, covering topics such as ancient and recent history, science, scripture and personal growth. I prefer reading about great servants and leaders instead of books about leadership. What changed in allowing me to capture and appreciate the adventure of virtually all reading material? My expanding perspective! What about your perspective? Does it allow you to enjoy a wide range of topics?

What Size Of Fuse Do You Possess?

Before buying my first sow from Tim, we needed to update the original wiring in the old chicken house built in the late 1940s due to the fire hazard it presented. Dad attempted to teach me about wiring, unfortunately I lacked the necessary interest to fully learn at the time. However, I did capture a few lessons and resulting life applications, such as fuses.

Fuses played an important role in the older buildings around the farm. Few fuse boxes still exist, most are now replaced with breaker boxes. The fuses in automobiles are much smaller than those used in buildings. Fuses limited the amount of electricity, measured in amperage, flowing through them into the wiring. The wiring's length and gauge (thickness) determine its amperage limits. Amperage above the limits creates excessive heat, raising the potential for fire. Fuses prevent any extra amps from flowing through the wiring by "blowing;" or today we may hear of throwing a breaker.

If more electrical demand lands on the circuit than usual, the fuse blows, or the breaker is thrown. For example, the wiring can safely handle 40amps. From this electrical wire a toaster, refrigerator, air conditioner and microwave demand roughly 28amps. Then we decide to add a dishwasher and computer to the same circuit, this surpasses the 40amps. Consequently, we blow a fuse or throw a breaker. We then visit with our neighbor who offers a simple solution. Put in a bigger fuse or breaker; then it will not blow. We realize this is terrific advice!

We grow disappointed with the electrician for attempting to limit the circuit's capacity. Why should we call in our electrician to add circuits when all we need to do is increase the size of our fuses? We continue to add various appliances and lights to the circuit, until we have an 80amp fuse. Suddenly, with an overloaded circuit, we smell smoke. We look around; unable to see anything wrong, yet we know the smell of smoke should not exist. Finally flames burst out of the walls and our home burns down. Either more circuits should exist or heavier wiring should be installed.

Wattage / Voltage = Amperage
Typical Amps for Household Appliances (Home Wiring by Handyman Club of America)

Toaster	8.75
Refrigerator	5
Air Conditioner	8.3
Circular Saw	10
Microwave	6.7
Dishwasher	12.5
Computer	6
Table Saw	18

We do the same thing in our lives when we take on more than we can handle. Either our bodies break down or the projects we oversee fall apart. Instead of increasing our carrying capacity, we take on more tasks and responsibilities while leaving our *carrying capacity* constant. Good news exists in that God designed our minds with plasticity, the ability to grow and adapt to changes. Additionally, God expects Christians to continually grow and mature in His image throughout our earthly life.

Studying and internalizing the Bible, prayer, associating with mature Christians and all other intricacies that develop our spiritual maturity effectively increase the size of our internal fuses. As long as the focus remains on Christ, reading books and listening to recordings of Christian spiritual wisdom increases the capacity of our fuses and our internal wiring. The greater the capacity of our spiritual fuses and wiring, the greater is our ability to serve and glorify God. This includes solving more complex problems for both yourself and others whom God places in your path and life.

Hogs

After my first sow had pigs, my herd began expanding. I kept my hogs in the barn and the old chicken house that Grandpa Meyer built in 1946. During World War II resources such as building materials, fuel, steel and ammunition were available to the general public on a very limited basis. Consequently, new buildings, automobiles and home and farm improvements reignited after the war in 1946.

The 60' x 20' chicken house consisted of two 20' x 20' rooms and a 10' x 20' feed room. Solid internal and external walls stabilized the building and provided a draft-free environment, as did the several feet of straw above the chicken wire ceiling for insulation. This offered temperature benefits during the scorching summer *and* the frigid winter. Occasionally, a big rat scurried from the straw ceiling through the approximate 1.5 inch diameter hole of the chicken wire to the floor. I remained anxiously cautious **about** whether one would attempt to scamper up my pant leg. Fortunately, this never occurred.

Because hogs have a high susceptibility to disease, Dad insisted I thoroughly clean and disinfect the correlating pen in the chicken house or barn before we moved a new group of feeder pigs or gestating sows into the pen. I initially cleaned the pen with a shovel and pitchfork, then swept-up the remaining loose dirt and dust with a broom, followed by a hand whiskbroom along the edges and in the corners. Dad inspected my completed work. The rare times of passing the first inspection generated celebratory elation. Yet even in these moments, he never declared the barn or chicken house perfectly clean. I then sprayed a disinfectant designed to kill critters, bacteria and viruses—on the floor and lower portion of the walls. Once the disinfectant dried, we moved the hogs into these pens. Interestingly, sunlight is also a powerful disinfectant.

Similarly, regardless of our greatest efforts, doing every possible *good* deed and going to church every Sunday, we will never cleanse ourselves of sin. Despite our best efforts, God still declares us as contaminated with sin. Our souls also require disinfection, found only in recognizing our sins and submitting ourselves to the light of Christ, including His death, blood and resurrection. Once we accept and internalize salvation through Christ, He immediately accepts us as His children and later into His kingdom at our physical death (John 1:1-13).

Faith

Fortunately, Jesus shares enlightening insight into faith with the disciples shortly after the transfiguration when Moses and Elijah also appeared. After the transfiguration Peter asked Jesus about building a shelter for Jesus, Moses and Elijah. Before Peter finished speaking, a voice then came out of a cloud affirming Jesus' identity, "This is My beloved Son, with whom I am well-pleased; listen to Him!" (Matthew 17:5) Shortly after this, a discussion occurred on why the disciples were unable to heal a man's demon-possessed son. Jesus then provides perspective on faith.

> And He said to them, "Because of the littleness of your faith; for truly I say to you, if you have faith the size of a mustard seed, you will say to this mountain, 'Move from here to there,' and it will move; and nothing will be impossible to you. (Matthew 17:20)

The inquisitive reader asks why Jesus chose the mustard seed to use as a comparison. What do mustard seeds, seeds in general, reveal about faith? What do you see in a mustard seed?

Earlier in Matthew 13:31-32, Jesus explained in a parable that even though the mustard seed is the smallest of seeds it grows larger than the all other garden plants, becoming a tree large enough to support the birds of the air and their nests.

Mustard seeds are the smallest seeds of garden plants, yet possess all the components of larger seeds. The seed's complete genetic code resides in this tiny capsule. This genetic code determines the plants leaf shape and structure, the internal chemical properties of the plant such as its pH which determines it acidity. For example, years ago plant scientists at Kansas State University developed grain sorghum plants with resistance to devastating chinch bugs by altering the pH of the plant's internal fluid. The chinch bugs hindered crops by sucking the fluid out of their leaves. Their long, flexible siphonatorous mouth bent around the plant's cells like a plumber's snake bends its way through twisted pipes before reaching the plants' xylem and phloem channels. However, once they reach their destinations, the altered pH disagreed with the chinch bugs' taste buds.

The Holy Spirit who dwells in all who know Jesus Christ permanently changes the internal "pH" of believers' internal hearts, minds and souls. This spiritual alteration enables the believer to lose their appetite for the deeds of the flesh. "Now the deeds of the flesh are evident, which are: immorality, impurity, sensuality, idolatry, sorcery, enmities, strife, jealousy, outbursts of anger, disputes, dissensions, factions, envying, drunkenness, carousing, and things like these, of which I forewarn you, just as I have forewarned you, that those who practice such things will not inherit the kingdom of God," (Galatians 5:19–21). Additionally, non-believers reject those who belong to Christ because they become a like an "aroma of death to death" (2 Corinthians 2:15-16) just as the chinch bugs reject the altered, distasteful sorghum plants.

The genetic code of small mustard seeds allows a mustard plant to grow up to 10 feet tall[10] and produce an abundance of new mustard seeds in favorable conditions for mustard plants.

We naturally ponder how the smallest seed grows into the largest of garden plant. Where does the newly germinated plant receive the plant material to reach up to 10 feet tall and be strong enough to support birds

---

[10] Louw, J. P., & Nida, E. A. (1996). *Greek-English lexicon of the New Testament: based on semantic domains* (electronic ed. of the 2nd edition., Vol. 1, p. 30). New York: United Bible Societies.

and their nests? Once germinated, the mustard develops roots which serve as support for the plant as well as the mechanism to transport nutrients and water from the soil into the plant. The naked eye cannot see these soil nutrients. By the way, have you ever seen a clothed eye? Additionally, the plant's leaves absorb sunlight for photosynthesis. Admittedly, we see light as a whole, however we do not see individual particles or wavelengths of light.

The mustard seed relies on those things that one cannot see to become a large plant that supports other life such as birds of the air. This complements Jesus' message (Matthew 6:26), "Look at the birds of the air, that they do not sow, nor reap nor gather into barns, and yet your heavenly Father feeds them. Are you not worth much more than they?"

God may use your mustard seed sized faith to move mountains, feed and provide housing along with anything else He desires for His creation. These birds may later provide nutrition to other portions of creation, including man, along with providing beautiful decorations with their feathers. Yes, submit your tiny mustard seed sized faith to God and you will play a role in impacting the world for generations upon generations. This *does not* promise popularity, glamour, fame or financial wealth in this life. Rather, God mercifully chooses to use your obedience to make a splash with perpetual ripples in the water of life. Let us always remember that God does not *need* us for anything. Because, God is *complete* in every holy and righteous attribute that far exceeds man's greatest imagination.

We may safely assume that the resulting mustard tree also provides shade for small animals and perhaps a few people. Moreover, plant roots descending deep into the soil provide an efficient highway for rainwater or melting snow to seep between rocks, pebbles and stones in the mountains. A wet soil shrinks and swells more than dry soil. This shrinking and swelling is powerful enough to move rocks within mountains over time.

How does this analogy apply to our faith? We must seek and internalize beneficial *nutrients* that we cannot physically see. Additionally, we too need the light of Christ who is the light of the world.

Chapter 5:
Expecting to Win:
Power of Associations

Gaylord Friends

An old adage states that we become like those with whom we associate. This observation includes that most people's income is an average of their 5 closest friends. However, our relationship with God through Jesus Christ by the power of the Holy Spirit far exceeds the significance of our income or economic status.

> No one can serve two masters; for either he will hate the one and love the other, or he will be devoted to one and despise the other. You cannot serve God and wealth. (Matthew 6:24)

> For the love of money is a root of all sorts of evil, and some by longing for it have wandered away from the faith and pierced themselves with many griefs. (1 Timothy 6:10)

These passages amplify the significance of keeping our focus on God instead of money or any other type of material wealth. We manage our physical possessions in response to our relationship with God. The two greatest commandments consist of loving God with all of our heart, mind, and soul; and loving our fellow man as much as we love ourselves. Living out these commandments produce record yielding relationships and associations.

God blessed me with abundant friends and teammates who challenged and encouraged me to achieve higher levels of performance. These interactions with high achievers began as early as I can recall. Associating with high achievers, especially those who expect greatness from themselves as well as those with whom they associate probably attributed to my walking at 7 months of age.

Jim Muck, a long time Gaylord staple, positively influenced many individuals over the years. Mr. Muck, as known by his students, was a stern disciplinarian who expected only two things from students and athletes: Knowing fundamentals and giving your best effort! This applies in junior high math and science, football, basketball, high school track or peewee baseball. Consequently, his teams consistently contended for victories and championships, regardless of talent level. He coached me in many sports where I gave great effort under his tutelage, but they never became spots in which I was able to excel.

Mr. Muck frequently shared stories of excellence in his classroom. Multiple times he told of being an assistant track coach to Alex Francis at Fort Hays State University. Jim's responsibilities included driving an old Jeep lacking a heater along the road from Hays to Ellis virtually every morning as John Mason engaged his morning run. Mason became one of several Kansans, and among the first Americans, to run a sub 4-minute mile in the 1960s.

Basketball

In basketball, Coach Muck led us to consecutive league tournament runner-up finishes. My basketball abilities remained consistently poor. Fortunately, my teammates possessed great talent. One night I dreamt that the basketball flew between my arms during my attempt to catch the pass while I stood just south of the half court line while we practiced breaking a full court press. The following day we practiced breaking the full court press! I was told to stand just south of the half court line on the west side. One of my teammates passed the ball to me, I raised my arms; the basketball flew between my arms and towards the door to the school's kitchen. As Yogi Berra once said, "It was *Déjà vu* all over again." I frequently reflected on whether the dream was portentous or if my mind accepted the mistake as reality and then commanded my body to cooperate in fulfillment of this mistake.

During another basketball practice of running our offense, I played the point guard position, passing the basketball to my teammates. Soon the defense began tipping and stealing my passes. Coach Muck instructed me to alter the type of pass I threw because the defense anticipated consistent patterns such as the straight chest pass, thus tipping or intercepting the ball. This lesson lingered with me! Whether in conversation or presenting before an audience, prudence encourages altering our verbiage and sentence structure. For example, one of my pastors frequently used the word "very" in sermons. Such as: "It was very cold out" or "They were very tired." The word 'very' is a very fine word to use when used in moderation. What other descriptive words convey your message? I once repetitively used 'redundant!' Does this illustrate irony? Additionally, do you inadvertently use predictable tonality patterns, gestures, and facial expressions when talking?

Kent Frieling and I began kindergarten together and remained classmates through college. He was competitive in athletics and academics. He now focuses that competiveness in business. Our friendship began early. Kent's grandma, Anna Zabel Frieling, and my grandma, Ida Zabel Meyer, shared parents. Consequently, our dads are first cousins and were Best Men in each other's weddings. As children, Kent and I attended church and Sunday school together. I mention the family relationship because the Bible emphasizes the significance of family through numerous references to family lineage.

Kent and I both had a degree of orneriness in school. However, Kent's wisdom prevented him from membership into the 'welcoming committee' for the Gaylord Grade School principals. The teachers frequently sent me to the principal's office. My grades allowed much room for improvement. Kent often pointed out that I failed to apply myself academically. Do you give your best in every aspect of your life? He challenged me to challenge myself in the classroom. I failed to understand the significance of a formal education for my life ambitions of farming, hunting and fishing. Acquaintances often tell you what you want to hear, while *friends* tell you what you *need* to hear. Champions focused on serving Christ always crave life-enhancing truth.

Can you imagine a doctor and parent agreeing to avoid giving a child the anti-venom for a rattle snake bite because the shot would hurt? Yes, the shot and the truth often hurt. I hate needles! However, both the anti-venom and the truth provide life over death. How should Christians determine whether to share the truth with others? We biblically and prayerfully seek whether this truth serves and glorifies God. Does sharing this truth with a person(s) in this moment please God? If no, let it go. If yes, profess.

How do we discern what pleases God?					
1.	Does our message agree with God's character as revealed in the Bible?				
2.	Is our message spoken with love (1 Cor 13)?				
3.	Is our message filled with the fruit of the Spirit (Galatians 5:16-18-25)				
➤ Love		➤ Patience		➤ Faithfulnes	
➤ Joy		➤ Kindness		➤ Gentleness	
➤ Peace		➤ Goodness		➤ Self-Control	
4.	Does our message promote deeds of the flesh which oppose God (Gal 5:19-21)?				
➤ Immorality		➤ Enmities		➤ Dissensions	
➤ Impurity		➤ Strife		➤ Factions	
➤ Sensuality		➤ Jealousy		➤ Envying	
➤ Idolatry		➤ Outbursts/Anger		➤ Drunkenness	
➤ Sorcery		➤ Disputes		➤ Carousing	

Kent knows and shares my competitive nature. As a senior in college, he offered me a new perspective. He invited me to view academics as competition with the professor. This new perspective included viewing exams as the professor's attempt to beat me with tough questions and problems. I readily comprehended and applied this revelation. My grade point average quickly escalated with me achieving an A in an agronomy course. I graduated with a relatively low overall GPA, while Kent graduated *Cum Laude* in Finance. He won the competition with the professors. I continue studying intently every day, including reading about a book a day, regardless of the demands of my personal and professional schedule. The salt Kent began throwing on me for academics in grade school, retains its saltiness to this day. Because Kent is filled with the Holy Spirit, he passionately desires success for others. Today, as President of Feather Petroleum, he continues challenging others to perform at their top level using the gifts God gave each of them. As iron sharpens iron, so one achiever sharpens another.

Greg Zabel and I spent much time hunting and fishing together while growing up on the farm. We began hunting together when I was 5 and he was 7. We either hung out on the North Fork of the Solomon River by our farm or Beaver Creek (Crick) that ran through their farm.

We initially used BB and pellet guns on our early prey of sparrows, pigeons, rabbits and squirrels. We later graduated to rifles and shotguns. He used a .22 caliber rifle; I used my Uncle Richard's single shot 410-gauge shotgun. We remained completely safe and healthy in all those hundreds of hours together with guns. However, the same cannot be claimed of golf clubs. One summer afternoon in Zabel's yard, he taught me how to swing his brother's golf club. I accidentally hit him in the head on the back swing. Greg received stitches on that summer day in 1978. His senior year in high school the championship came down to a playoff. Whenever we played sports against one another, regardless if we played basketball, ping pong, Atari video games, baseball, football or sprinting - he clobbered me.

These beatings served as salt on a wound. They burned with pain each of the countless times he out performed me. He was faster, quicker, a better shooter, a better hitter and better strategist. Even though I despised losing, my disappointment was always on myself instead of Greg. Each loss added rocket fuel to my internal fire of desire to improve. He too was driven to win. I would have been furious with Greg if had let me win, we loved competition. Greg never let me win. He knew I preferred another embarrassing defeat instead of an unearned victory. I knew the key to winning was improvement.

Our conversations usually began with the results of the previous night's results of his old brother, Ron's, basketball or baseball games. Ron graduated from Smith Center High School in 1978. The results of their games seldom wavered from: They won. Once they lost in the sub-state basketball tournament. Ron explained the team walked into halftime with a sizeable lead, and became too comfortable. Their baseball teams lost one state championship game and placed 3rd the other 2 years of American Legion Baseball. Ron played catcher, rarely allowing the opponents to steal second base. Greg informed me of Ron often hitting a ball to the 'warning track' along with the number of runners he threw out at second base.

Most people probably thought Ron was naturally talented; he may be, however, he worked diligently to further refine his skills. They tied a bicycle tube to one of the support beams next to the weight bench in their basement. Ron used the tube to strengthen his throwing arm. He was quick, strong and accurate. Surrounded by terrific teammates, they rarely lost.

Other's Influence On Me

Maury and Mark Dannenberg lived directly across the road from us, just 700 yards away. They are 1 and 2 years younger than Ron, graduating in successive years of 1979 and 1980. They epitomize the pursuit of excellence. They excelled in academics, track, baseball and basketball.

Their American Legion baseball teams also earned a state runner-up and two 3rd place finishes. Maury and Mark were team pitchers, Ron was the catcher. Maury commented on the benefits of familiarity that Ron served as their catcher since they began playing baseball on the farm as young children.

Mark was a member of Jim Muck's great track teams, often missing out on the state championship by a few points following the last event, the mile relay. Coach Muck provided Mark with old hurdles to line up along Dannenberg's driveway. Mark used a 200 yard grass strip to practice running hurdles. Mark is the only person I am aware of who lined up hurdles along his farm driveway. Jim Muck told of a high school track meet in Nebraska where the sponsoring coach suggested skipping hurdle prelims because he knew of Mark's reputation of running through hurdles which was to hit them with his front foot, sometimes breaking them.

After completing their day's work on the farm, Maury and Mark played catch with the baseball, played basketball, practiced hurdling or ran several miles on the limestone country road. I often heard others of all ages speak of the natural talent that Maury and Mark possessed. Like Ron, I knew they worked diligently to consistently contend for state championships. I had the benefit of witnessing their vast preparation.

They, along with their younger sister Marsha, earned the title of Valedictorian or Salutatorian of their high school classes. Whenever I walked the nearly half mile to their home for eggs, they were working, studying, practicing their band instrument or practicing athletics. For some reason I avoided picking up their academic and musical habits while particularly admiring their athletic endeavors. Maury, due to an injured back, was among the last players cut from Jack Hartman's 1979 Kansas State basketball tryouts. He missed being a part of teams reaching the Sweet 16 and Elite 8 in the NCAA tournament.

Their dad, Max, erected a basketball goal for them. The height matched regulation of 10 feet. Maury said he practice year round, trying to get the ball up to the basket. Maury confesses learning fundamentals of sports, music and academics provided a significant key to their success. He also agreed a healthy expectation of winning helped. Their Gaylord, KS, pee-wee baseball team qualified for the state tournament. Gaylord's population was barely 210. Maury acquired a B.S. in Crop Protection, followed by a M.S. in Plant Pathology. He later returned for a degree in Electrical Engineering.

Most of the time when I asked how they did in their last competition, whether in the storm cave or at the end of our driveways awaiting the school bus, they responded, "We won." Those few times of confessing a loss, they offered no excuses while fully praising their opponent's worthiness. Moreover, the next day they were once again practicing to become even better. As iron sharpens iron, so one champion sharpens another.

Denton and Lyle Schoen lived up the road from us about a mile and a quarter north, just past the occasionally used railroad tracks on the east side of the road. Some argue Lyle was the best player to ever suit up for Smith Center's football team. While that is arguable; his competitiveness, drive, toughness, quickness and determination were well documented. As a freshman, he ran on a state placing 4 x 100 relay: the team won the state championship. During Lyle's senior year in high school, they ended the season as the undefeated 3A state football champions: including a victory over 4A state champion Norton to claim the league title.

Anyone who observed these two brothers separated in age by 4 years, realizes Lyle's achievements are largely due to Denton. Denton toughened Lyle up with some good whippings as older brothers sometimes do. Denton chased him with a board when Lyle placed another board with nails sticking through the other side behind Denton's car tires. These two became efficient at fixing screen doors because there was no time for Lyle to slow down with his older brother in pursuit. To be clear, this was all fun, the results never included broken bones, permanent deformities or any other serious injuries. They would often laugh about it after the fact.

Lyle and I maneuvered through old farm buildings, pulling ourselves up and over interior walls in an old granary. We jumped off the top. When at rivers, we jumped off the bank and off tree limbs, measuring our horizontal distance, competing against one another. I seldom won. Another talent of Lyle's included catching crawdads at the creek by his home using liver as bait. Crawdads resemble miniature lobsters, complete with pinching claws.

The best mistake Lyle and I ever committed occurred when I was 12, Lyle was 10. We grabbed some cigarettes and matches, taking them behind one of the farm buildings at Lyle's. After a few failed attempts, our cigarettes ignited. Initially we puffed without inhaling, we then decided to further engage with a deep inhale. I watched my dad blow smoke through his nose: I thought this was cool. However, upon attempting to practice what I witnessed, I prayed for death. Perhaps only partial death: temporary relief from the intense lung, throat and nose burn. This was a terrific mistake *because* I felt no further interest in cigarettes afterwards. Nearly 40 years later this experience remains burned on my memory. Learning the hard way is sometimes the best way.

Denton, weighing about 155 in 8th grade, was in the same grade as Darin Godsey. During one week of practice involving tackle football in the fall of 1978, a drill consisted of one person standing in the middle of a circle with the football. Coach would then signal for 1 or 2 people to tackle the guy in the middle. On one occasion, I was the guy in the middle when coach sent both Denton and Darin from opposite directions. They understood trigonometry well enough to collide from opposite directions with me in the middle. Growing up on the farm and working around livestock, one quickly learns the lesson of leveraging with your legs. These two also understood leveraging very well. I related to Wily the Coyote after being tricked by the Road Runner, with circles of stars sailing around his head. These two locked their opponent seeking missiles on me, responding to my every movement. Despite falling down quickly upon impact, I felt as if they launched me for a journey around the moon. During another practice, Denton accidentally stepped on my hand with his cleat shoes while blocking. The hand nearly returned to full functionality after the swelling subsided 10 days later. Toughness was mandatory at

Gaylord Grade School. As iron sharpens iron, so one champion sharpens another.

Another neighbor continually won as well. Don Dannenberg's # 44 race car either won or landed on its side or top. When I asked Kaid and Kris the results of the previous night's race, they too nearly always responded in the affirmative. When they tested the car, I felt the breeze as they cruised within a couple of feet. The cool breeze generated by the car gave me a good, temporary relief from the hot, stagnant summer air. Don enjoyed driving up behind me in his pickup, then laying on the horn. After recovering from the surprise, I turned to see Don laughing heartily. Having fun is an important ingredient of any task. Due to this initiation, running in city traffic fails to bother me.

When Don's son Kaid began driving, similar results continued. Don liked to drive fast, while lacking enjoyment of doing so with other cars by his side. Dad told of him and Don cruising in high school in the early to mid-1950s. My dad was driving, unable to keep up with the car in front of them with the speedometer reading 100mph. Don believed he could catch the other car; naturally they slowed down to 95mph and switched drivers. Dad always followed up those stories with, "Don't you ever try that." They had internalized goals of winning. Dad and Don survived that night and many other wild adventures: including sliding down a barn roof. Dad's sister, Berniel, graciously removed the numerous splinters from their posteriors. I could write of many others in Gaylord who positively impacted me, directly and indirectly. Coach Muck, Kent, Darin, Lyle, Denton, Greg, Ron, Mark, Maury, Don along with many others I fortunately knew in my life, believed in challenging themselves and others.

Did You Do Your Best?

"Less than our Best is Failure!" Our 1981, 8th grade class at Gaylord Grade School chose this as our class motto. I do not know who originally stated this line; however their message strikes the bulls eye of truth. My parents always believed in one standard of success for my sister and me, they simply asked, "Did you do your best?"

This correlates with the parable of the talents in Matthew 25:14-30 where Jesus compares those that fully invest because of their desire to please their master in faith with the one who fails to invest, he fails to do his best because of his fear of failure. Doing your best, fully investing yourself in anything requires effort, faith and a desire to please the master, the Lord Jesus Christ.

My parents asked me this question after badly losing in the 75 yard dash at the Gaylord Grade School Field Days, as well as later when I won a very competitive race. My parents did not attend many of my cross country meets because many of the meets fell on Saturday mornings during busy chore time.

He asked me if I did my best, and I always answered, "No." We then discussed what challenges needed improvement to make it my best race. I usually found no challenges with my first half mile of the races. At times, I moved too quickly in the middle of the race, while other times, I failed to increase the pace with my teammates after the first mile. Dad and I discussed each race all 4 years of high school, seeking any and all opportunities for improvements. The first 33 of the 34 cross country races of my high school career, I confessed that I did not do my best because tactical mistakes were made. Following my final high school race on November 3, 1984 I answered Dad's "Did you do your best?" with a resounding "Yes!" I would run that state championship race the same way if given another thousand opportunities. My discussions with my dad on how to improve after each race over those 4 seasons proved profitable.

Knowing you did your best is the best therapeutic elixir in existent. Your mind fills with hope; your immune, respiratory, circulatory, digestive systems and metabolism run at optimal performance. We acknowledge that life owes us absolutely nothing other than the pursuit of happiness or the opportunity to create opportunity. We owe life every ounce of energy we possess to expend that energy in answering and in responding to the commands of Christ.

At the beginning of each day, ask yourself the following questions.

- How good do I want to be today?
- Do I have the desire to increase my imagination, creativity and resourcefulness?
- Am I willing to program my mind, for success through visualization?
- Am I setting and internalizing goals without limits, requiring me to bend on my knees in prayer, then leaping toward the goals on faith?
- Am I putting myself in a position to win by creating a hope filled environment and avoiding second hand negativism because I know friends do not let friends live complacently.

As the Bible (Proverbs 1:32) says, "The complacency of fools will destroy them." Am I willing to pick up the trash since less than my best is failure?

At the end of each day I invite you to ask yourself this same question my parents inquired of me: "Did You Do Your Best, Today?"

Chapter 6:

Power of Associations

Now Is The Time To Set Goals

When did you begin setting goals? Or have you? I set 5 major goals at the age of 8. I did *not* write the these 5 goals on paper or in any other physical form. I wrote them only on my heart **and mind**, permanently internalizing the goals. The time to set a goal is the instant you realize something is a goal, it is never too early or too late.

1. Compete on a State Championship team
2. Compete on a Nationally ranked team
3. Place high in the Boston Marathon
4. Place high in the New York City Marathon
5. *Remains unlisted until Achieved*

These goals came to me through hunches and ideas. I did not intentionally choose to set these or any other goals until my teen years. Rather, God placed them in my mind, heart and soul.

> Even before there is a word on my tongue, Behold, O LORD, You know it all. (Psalm 139:4)

These goals and my talents were encoded before my birth. Additionally, through His perfect and infinite wisdom, God planned my life's and your life's events and interactions before our birth as well.

> Your eyes have seen my unformed substance; And in Your book were all written The days that were ordained for me, When as yet there was not one of them. (Psalm 139:16)

Despite my deficiency of talents, I possessed a high level of endurance which proved beneficial as others became tired.

We turn to scripture and point out that Christ said, "Simply ask for whatever you desire and you will receive." This invitation can be understood literally, however the *catch* exists in the word *desire*. What do you desire? Do you desire material wealth? Good, as Dexter Yeager states, "God made the materials." The Bible directs us to 'love God with all of our hearts, soul, strengths and minds." We are to submit ourselves to the Lord, giving thanks in everything, seeking his wisdom at all times and in all places. We are to offer ourselves up to the Lord, seeking his will for our lives.

- What are we to think in our hearts, our deepest thoughts?
  - o We must internally saturate ourselves with God's word.
  - o When we are full of God's pure word, we desire to please him, achieving his will for our life.
- Is daily studying scripture wise?
- Is daily seeking God's wisdom worth scheduling in our day?
- Are any expenditures of time more valuable than with God?

Desire

Desire is at the root of all successful endeavors. Do you have the desire to obey and respond to God? Do you have the desire to accumulate the price for success? The price for success consists of physical, intellectual, emotional and spiritual attributes. We must be physically able to perform the necessary tasks; most tasks require some physical skill whether typing, speaking, calculating, measuring, running or hitting. We must intellectually accumulate the required knowledge to achieve our desired success. Emotional maturity and stamina are as necessary as any of the other attributes. Do we have the maturity and stamina to remain at a task through completion? In running, this is called staying power. Seeing the bigger picture requires maturity. One of the techniques of success requires us to breakdown a large project into smaller steps. However, without emotional maturity, we begin to look only at the small steps, forgetting the significance of each step.

The Cove -- 2007

In late May of 2007, I attended the Billy Graham School of Evangelism in Asheville, North Carolina. Asheville lies secluded in the Blue Ridge Mountains. Upon landing at the Asheville airport, I claimed my luggage, then reported to the Avis car rental booth. While walking to the luggage area, an ambitious young man spotted the Kansas State polo I wore. Recruited by the Wildcats to play cornerback on the football team, he inquired if I was the Kansas State football coach; I find this flattering because it is rare a marathon runner is mistaken for a football coach. His ambition was impressive.

The Avis attendant, a lady full of southern hospitality, informed me of an upgrade from a compact to a Jeep Cherokee. I was grateful. The walk from the counter to the vehicle was relatively short. Trees filled the landscape during the 22 miles of interstate driving to the Billy Graham Training Center, seeming as if I vacationed in the middle of a forest instead of a city. Asheville is both. I arrived at the outer entrance of the Billy Graham facility where a friendly gentleman awaited at a booth. He checked my name on the list of expected visitors, handed me a parking pass asking if this was my first time at the facility, then gave directions to my assigned lodge. After following 2 miles of winding, scenic driving, I arrived, parking in a large lot bordering the lodge and convention center.

Elderly, yet young in spirit, greeters in wooden rocking chairs just outside the building's entrance greeted all those entering and ambling along the sidewalk. Once inside the lodge another host who epitomized warm, southern hospitality welcomed us, giving me the key and directions to my room. I opted for an elevator ride to the 2nd floor, lightening the load of my luggage. The lobby of the upper floor contained an array of beverages ranging from a variety of fountain sodas, juices, hot tea or coffee. The room included a table adjacent to a picture window, offering a picturesque view of the Blue Ridge Mountains.

A full schedule of events on the evening of arrival prevented me from running. I chose not to run on the unlit roads in an unfamiliar area. I suffered from too many 'dumb' injuries from such attempts. The following day during the long lunch break, I threw on my running shorts, a tee shirt and laced up New Balance shoes, anxious to hit the trail. The literature describes Overlook Point as being 3.5 miles away. The altitude gain is about 1,600 feet in those 3.5 miles with a constant uphill grade. If the elevation rise were uniform, one would gain nearly a yard in elevation in the distance of first down chains - ten yards: a gain of 26 feet in elevation between the end zones on a football field. Warnings stated only those in excellent health should attempt this climb.

The climb was erratic; the beginning revealed frequent sharp turns limiting visibility, dictating a slow early pace. A sharp eye looking for the signs directing the proper path was mandatory. The meandering trails eventually led to vehicle paths with longer stretches, running became easier, though not easy. Signs were less frequent, yet equally significant. The gravel or rock roads through the Blue Ridge Mountains provided challenges, as my calf muscles contracted. The foot extended and pushed off, thus the toes felt measurable slippage with each step. The climb continued at a near pedestrian pace. Due to a few winter related injuries, such as falling on ice in the dark, my body was not as well conditioned as I preferred. Of course, as Dawn, a wife of a former UNK runner Todd Fuelberth, once inquired of me when I ran over 130 miles a week: "Rick, are you ever in as good of shape as you want to be?"

I later realized at least 2 different routes presented themselves in the first miles. I hope I chose the most difficult. The greatest challenge was challenging myself to become the person God created me to be; opening ourselves to his 'workouts.' The sign signaled a left hand turn to Overlook Point. Nearby was another sign informing those driving vehicles now was the moment to shift to four-low. The message was clear: if four-low was not available, do not climb. The slope was steep, the terrain loose. I shifted into my running version of four-low; one I mastered as a child going up and down river banks, along with a few of the hills in our pasture. This portion of the trail was a few hundred yards in length; which seemed like 2 miles while running up. Success called for short, quick strides, along with intense concentration.

I entered the mental command: Running is the only option. Our minds will always take the easy way out if given the opportunity. Moreover, the commands must be given in the affirmative; as our subconscious deletes negative words such as 'not.' For instance, had the command stated: "Walking is *not* an option," my subconscious would have recorded, "walking is an option." I remembered an old tale, assumed true, of a baseball manager walking out to visit his pitcher when the game was on the line. He instructed the pitcher, "Do not throw to the outside edge of the plate on this guy." The pitcher's subconscious mind started to work, as it does on every pitch. Obeying the manager's command, the pitch flew to the outside edge of the plate. The batter drove in the winning runs.

I finally reached the top of this extraordinarily challenging portion of the trail. An ample challenge remained between this spot and Overlook Point. The incline provided a test of the heart. My heart was pounding; as Jim Ryun says, in his book In Quest of Gold: The Jim Ruyn Story, "not knowing whether to cry from the pain or to laugh because it's so much fun."

In my life of running, this statement frequently proved true. Climbing up this incline provided an experience of simultaneously producing adrenaline and lactic acid. As I scanned through trees on my right, a beautiful lake appeared in the magnificent valley. A few moments later, an epiphany revealed why these mountains were aptly named the Blue Ridge Mountains. The hue of the trees is an ocean blue, while the lake I witnessed was a mirage.

Minutes later, 8 turkeys crossed in front of me on the trail consisting of a mom and her young ones. Growing up in the 1970s, one of my favorite TV shows was *The Waltons*. They lived in the Blue Ridge Mountains of Virginia. One episode involved John Boy and Grandpa Walton going turkey hunting. I always dreamed of being in the Blue Ridge Mountains, here I was at last. *Where is this Overlook Point anyway?* I began to question if I overlooked a sign. Pun intended! The running continued, as did the desire to walk. Desire for greatness drowns out the voice of dissent. Temptation to turn around came sporadically: the closer we near the great achievements God creates for us, the more tempted we feel to quit.

Why?

Because these awe striking scenes are often unseen, and the fatigue becomes daunting. A properly programmed mind is essential. An Overlook Point sign lie directly ahead; finally I neared the destination. When we see signs while running on faith, it is best to read them instead of assuming the content. Fortunately I read the sign before reacting: a half mile to Overlook Point! Numerous times over the years, I would 'drop the hammer' down for the final 880 yards of a run or even a turn around. The continued incline feasted on my afterburners; this last half-mile seemed to go on forever. Overlook Point appeared, I had arrived. I walked on the platform, taking a quick glance in the spirit of Clark Griswold at the Grand Canyon in National Lampoon's movie *Vacation.* Our minds permanently capture the movie of our surroundings better than a camera. The sights, sounds and aroma of the moment are available upon request.

The descent to the lodge began. Even though the road literally declined all the way, I needed to be equally focused running down. The loose gravel required immense concentration. More than once my downhill skiing skills of maintaining balance while sliding paid off. I approached occasional corners; I did not want to overrun these! Most research reveals the mass of a solid tree seldom, if ever, loses when met with the mass of a moving person. The section requiring the *four-low* of an off-road vehicle equaled its challenge traveling in the opposite direction. Leaning back, keeping my weight balanced above the hips, rather than ahead, was mandatory. As a kid on the farm, I occasionally ran through mud too fast; toppling over in forward summersaults. I remember these painful falls on the flat limestone drive. No, tumbling down this slope was not an option. Aesthetically, this run remains in my all-time top 5. I reached the lodge and clicked my stopwatch; 50 some minutes elapsed over this 7 mile run. I received no windburn from speed. Although late to the next session, it was worth the time and effort to enjoy the surroundings, attain a workout and a good challenge. I ran on faith.

Auction

Have you ever experienced an auction? A couple of friends, Bruce and Jon, are auctioneers. Bruce placed among the top 5 at the World's Auctioneer Championships on several occasions. They begin by fluctuating the price, until someone places the first bid. The bids continue to climb when at least one other bidder also expresses a desire to obtain the item. The rate of increase with the bidding is co-dependent upon the item, and those bidding. Once the bidding appears to cease, Jon will say, "One more time around." If no one offers another bid, Jon or Bruce point to the high bidder declaring, "Sold to number 135." Bruce and Jon will tell you that the buyers possess two qualities: the ability and willingness to pay the price. Success in any endeavor goes to the highest bidder. If we attempt to pay for success in life with anything outside of the realm of what is legal, moral and ethical; we pay with counterfeit money. Purchasing an item anywhere with counterfeit money or a bad check results in a visit from the law. Be assured, eventually the consequences do catch up to us for our poor behavior.

At 15, I legally drove home from school in the 1973 Ford LTD. After school, I attended track practice; then rehearsal for freshman prom servers following track. Afterwards I drove home in the rain, with a beverage in hand. Looking down at the drink, my eyes temporarily left Highway 281. My sight returned to the road in time to see the car about to drop the passenger side tire off of the pavement. I overcorrected, causing the vehicle to veer to the left. This led to overcorrecting another time or two before the tires slid on the wet pavement, sending the LTD spinning at 60mph. Everything moved in slow motion. Eventually the car left the roadway, went over a steep incline, sliding backwards in the east ditch before resting between a telephone pole and an iron post. Even though I only travel by this spot once every few years now, I remain impressed by my skill. Okay, I received some divine guidance when placing the car between these two items with little leeway on either side.

I drove up the steep ditch to get back on the road, but due to the rain, I made two runs before making it. I stopped by our pasture at the Junction of Highways 281 and 9 down the road to inspect the car; everything appeared to be fine. Despite knowing better, I said nothing to my parents. The next I did not drive to school. The activities bus dropped me off after track practice. I walked into the large kitchen of our farmhouse. Dad, who was planting corn, left a note on the kitchen table, instructing me to place my set of keys on the table. I lost my privilege to drive or participate in any other non-school activities for 2 weeks. Dad explained he noticed brome grass between the rims and the tires; he then opened the hood of the car. The spinning caused the battery to slide over, hitting and ruining the regulator. This resulted in nearly $200 of damage; a sizable amount in

1982. He was upset at my attempt to hide the accident. He felt disappointment because he knew I failed to tell them about the accident. My hiding the truth resulted in more punishment. When we attempt to hide the truth, the price accumulates with compounding interest.

Only with the proper understanding of value are we willing to pay the necessary price for success. The greater the vision, the quicker the value becomes recognized. Others at auctions may recognize the value of an item (goal), but lack the ability to pay the price. What price are you willing to pay for your desired success?

Chapter 7:
Goal Achieving:
Greatness Occurs After Logic

Why do we set goals? Is it really worth the effort? There are an abundance of statistics showing the benefits. I have rarely been motivated by statistics. How many non-statisticians are bored with statistics? I do not know either. As Mark Kottmeyer of Central States Agronomics stated on numerous occasions, "Figures do not lie, but liars can figure."

The Bible's statistics are much easier to read than those in a research paper. The Bible states specific actions; attitudes and beliefs lead to success, while others will result in disaster. The success or failure, as defined in scripture, is often delayed. Proverbs is full of statistics such as complacency, lying and adultery resulting in disaster and death. Prudence, diligence and submitting our goals to the Lord always lead to long-term success. My parents did not rely upon statistics to persuade me to take action. Action was based on right and wrong, including what they wanted accomplished.

Let us examine goal setting logistically. For years, I have asked audiences how they determine the route to drive to a chosen destination. Many confess to using a map. There are those occasional free spirits who just get in the car and drive to wherever they feel like. They readily admit this fun way of traveling lacks efficiency.

In March 1998, I prepared to set out in my 1990 Ford Thunderbird, leaving Kearney, NE, for a convention in Augusta, GA. Before leaving I had the oil changed at a shop on Kearney's 2nd Avenue. The previous night I had driven 470 miles round trip for an appointment, returning home in the middle of the night. Before leaving for the appointment, I submitted my plans to the Lord. I asked, and then continually thanked, Jesus in advance for keeping and protecting my vehicle from any breakdowns and from all evil. I also asked and thanked Jesus in advance for keeping all animals off the road in my path. Around mid-night while traveling on Highway 24 east of Beloit, Kansas, at 70mph I had a strong hunch to slow down. I was the only car on the road and at least 15 miles from any town. Like most hunches, logic was absent; experience taught me intuition trumps logic. As I was slowing, I crested a terrace in the road before descending into a dip; at the bottom stood a black-angus steer whose weight exceeded 1,000 pounds. I beeped the horn while coming to a near stop, the steer ran off the road; the remainder of the road home was clear.

The owner of the service shop in Kearney entered the office about 4:00p.m. reporting the car was finished. He also informed me of a leak in the transmission line. I asked how long it had been leaking. He said it must have just started because driving more than 100 miles would have ruined the transmission. He then called a transmission repair shop in Kearney who just happened to have the right curved high pressure tube in stock and could fix my car that day if I went immediately. I did, and they did. The bills for an oil change and the installation of a new partial transmission line totaled less than $100.

Imagine the cost and time of repair had the transmission oil emptied while driving; ruining the transmission. Imagine the cost and time of repair if I had hit that steer? Submitting our plans to the Lord involves diligence and prudence. God allows us to face challenges, along with the solution of time, supplies and money necessary for resolving them. If I had arrogantly ignored the voice to slow down, I would have collided with the steer on the highway. If I had been slothful in servicing my car or foolishly ignored the service man's warning, my car would have broken down, requiring expensive repairs. God says when we submit our plans and goals to him; he will direct our thoughts. We must remain humble to hear his voice, while responding in obedience.

The number of times I have seen deer on the side of the road at night is amazing. I occasionally have the urge to honk while driving near rivers at night. Does this prevent a collision with deer? I have yet to smack one. In the past 24 months two deer appeared on a direct colliding course with my car; running all out from a ditch towards the side of the car. They made cuts barely imaginable by great slalom skiers and running backs, missing the car by a fraction of an inch. Some say coincidence or luck, I say, "Thank you Lord!"

What 'near misses' have you had on your journey? On our journey for goal attainment, we will face many close calls. Always give thanks and credit for blessings of life's near misses to Christ.

Would you agree pursuing goals in life are similar to planning a road trip? Do we dare avoid "refueling" our minds and bodies? What is the cost of waiting too long? How do side trips correlate with our primary goal's timetable and route? Sometimes we arrive quicker than planned, while other times our plans are delayed due to circumstances beyond our control. Flexibility is vital lest we become complacent when ahead of schedule or discouraged when delayed.

Goals 1

Bill Congleton taught that one should share unachieved goals only with those who may willingly assist in attaining these goals. As a child, I frequently ran around the farm in cowboy boots; however, my longest race as an eight year old covered only 220 yards. I was among the last to be picked for teams at recess or any other pickup games whether on the playground or at a church function. Each of the five newly defined goals appeared unattainable and unimaginable for this uncoordinated, bow-legged farm boy boasting tortoise acceleration in June 1975. While playing soccer with cowboy boots during recess at Gaylord, I possessed greater proficiency in inadvertently kicking my competitors with my cowboy boots than the soccer ball.

These goals were set in response to several people. Hearing of Doug Phelps becoming the first high school athlete in Nebraska to clear seven feet in the high jump provided my final impetus. I first met Doug in 1999, 24 years after he inspired me. Kansas' legendary miler Jim Ryun strongly influenced my initial consideration to run as well as the perpetual desire to succeed. I first met Jim in November 1984; nine years after setting these initial goals.

Our performances, character and attributes may influence people years or decades before we meet them. We may never meet others to whom we are an influence. Our citizenship in Christ obligates us to perform each of our actions and relationships to glorify God. Consequently, we should consistently seek to attain Christ's love, wisdom, strength, power and mercy. This necessitates recognizing and submitting to the indwelling Holy Spirit.

Submission to the Holy Spirit resembles connecting farm equipment to a tractor both physically with a hitch pin or three-point hitch and with hydraulic hoses. The hitch enables the tractor's power to maneuver the equipment directionally, while the hydraulics allow the fluid power from the tractor to raise and lower the equipment to achieve the desired depth for optimal tillage in the field or all the way up when transporting the equipment. Equipment disconnected from the tractor or another power source simply fails to serve the purpose for which it received design and creation from the manufacturer.

My dad occasionally told stories ending with, "don't you ever try that." When dating my mother in 1962, he drove 23 minutes on way. Is this feat outlandish? Their homes were separated by 43.2 miles. This route consisted of 7 turns and 2 stop signs. The highway at that time contained even more rolling hills than the current road. Both the old and current highways are as narrow as a possible for a two lane road. Considering the vast rolling hills, combined with Dad's racecar speeds; is it safe to wonder if the car's tires were in contact with the pavement at all times? Going an average of 112 MPH; he arrived for their date. Yet, he was reluctant to top 100mph a few years earlier with Don. He always wanted to be early or on time for everything during the time I knew him.

He cleaned the "cobwebs" out of his car that night. Dad's fire of desire sparked by an internalized goal of seeing his future wife triggered his racecar driver instincts. Once parked, he probably meandered to the house wearing cowboy boots, denim jeans and a snap western shirt.

Our ultimate internalized goal is obedience to God's word. What triggers your fire of desire? Do you put the pedal to metal in developing and deepening your relationship with Christ?

Goals that become achieved are first written on our hearts with crystal clarity, internalized into every fabric of our being. The goals occupy our thoughts, directing our choices and consequential actions. God wrote His law on our hearts. In the book *The Hidden Face of God* Dr. Gerald Schroeder illustrates that the world is more a thought than a thing. He further explains all existence is the expression of information. The world was created with God's spoken word (John 1:1-3). Information consists of wavelengths; our thoughts are also composed of wavelengths, as is our voice. An earthquake is wavelengths vibrating out of sync. Are you still surprised Christ said, "Say to this mountain be removed, and it shall be removed." The fig tree died after Christ condemned it, the Bible says nothing of Jesus using the herbicide Roundup, rather spoken words. Did Jesus commit this to a written goal first? No. He spoke from His heart.

Internalized goals set our wavelengths through thoughts and the spoken word into action in the proper direction. The probability of achieving your goals increases exponentially with your determination. In the book *Ship of Ghosts* a story of Pat Rack after being taken captive by the Japanese during World War II, "His resourcefulness and guile existed on a plane far removed from the one where the beatings mattered." In the Jungle of Kwai, American prisoners were pressured to complete work in a year that normally required five years of labor. Japanese officials communicated a clear message: it will be done (P.253). As with many powerful instruments, internalized goals can be used for evil as well as good.

Are your goals internalized with crystal clarity to have an exceedingly high probability of realization? My first 4 goals were achieved between 8 and 21 years after setting them. Time was required for the proper crystallization as well the necessary time for God's plan to unfold. My body required massive physiological adaptations. My physical and mental fitness required development. Moreover, God is always concerned with relationships; this is why He created us. Godly success involves Godly friendships. Jesus spent time with the disciples, Mary, Martha and a number of others. In the Old Testament, Jacob was thrown into a well by his brothers and left for dead. In the end this relationship was restored when he provided food for them during the 7 year famine.

Before my goals were achieved, I formed a friendship with new teammates and coaches at Manhattan High. Before achieving the marathon goals, I formed friendships with the UNK runners and Lyle Claussen. I had to learn to trust Lyle when he suggested I back off of the heavy training. Initially I thought he was trying to hold me back. I have successfully proven my excessive exuberance on numerous occasions, this was no exception. Lyle was a proven runner and coach. After suffering from several over-training injuries, I began to listen and trust him completely.

Trusting God was a prerequisite in all 4 goals. I had to trust God in the mental, physical and spiritual power and strength He gave me. I had to trust God to keep me healthy in all aspects. I had to trust God with the teammates and training partners He surrounded me with. I had to trust God with the coaches and mentors He placed in my path. I had to trust God with His timetable, as it did not correspond with my own timetable. Guess whose timetable is off? Hint, when human desires conflict with God, God is always right and always prevails.

What prevents us from internalizing our goals? Distractions! Distractions oppose achievement. Gossip, television, negative conversation, anything other than a goal achieving thought or action is a distraction. Gossip, Lust, Alcohol, Greed, Envy, Adultery and Lying are the root of distractions. Idolatry originates from us focusing on creation rather than the Creator! These prevent focusing on God and His will for your life.

Jesus teaches focusing on the desired results, then submitting your plans to the Lord in constant prayer. Larry Goering of Platte Center, Nebraska, says on his successful farm he attempts a goal three times while submitting his plans to the Lord in prayer. Either he will attain his desired goal within those attempts, or he will confidently know God is pointing him in another direction.

Figure 15: Larry Goering (November 1948 --June 2017) Photo Credit: The Columbus Telegram

It is okay to have goals written down. If you struggle with maintaining focus, written goals can assist in retaining focus. An organization or business can have written goals assuring everyone's focus and conversation is aimed towards a common target. If speaking or visualizing your goals fails to create excitement, then reevaluate your goals for challenge, belief, desire and faith.

Terrain

In war, terrain is among the important factors considered for a route. The majority of people who travel through the state of Nebraska view the state as primarily flat. Interstate 80 has about 200 miles without hills except for an occasional overpass. Even the remaining 250 miles has few significant hills. Much of the Interstate runs along the Platte River, its flood plains are flat. However, within a few miles of I-80 one enjoys a rollercoaster ride in many places. Nebraska consists of river valleys and hills; some of the hills are big and frequent. Why was the Interstate built along this flat terrain? In part due to lining up with Iowa and Wyoming, that could have been achieved by sending it through some hills. Travel efficiency increases in flat terrain. Driving in a blizzard or ice storm is stressful and hazardous in any terrain. However, if given a choice, anyone would choose relatively flat terrain versus rolling in inclement weather. I have driven on Interstate 70 through the Colorado Rocky Mountains in a blizzard several times. If I am denied future opportunities my feelings will remain undamaged. While attempting to match the tempo of the other traffic you hope your tires hold on the corners as well as the vehicle in the lane beside you. Every few miles vehicles are stranded that apparently played bumper cars.

Just like General George S. Patton knew the best method of moving army divisions based on his intent study of battles and terrain over years of steady reading and visualization, we too can benefit by studying the terrain of our desired goals.

In running we refer to running the tangent where we runners try to scope out the shortest possible steps we can take on each curve and obstacle on our route. Upon arriving at a cross country meet, we warmed up on the course as all teams do. We studied every curve and corner on the course. Just as in football or basketball, one must stay within the boundaries of the course defined. We desired to run as straight a line as possible on every curve and corner when running in a pack. When approaching a corner with a tree, we sought to brush our inside shoulder against the tree; when running on the outside of the pack this forced those on the inside to slow and drop behind us.

In marathons an unbelievable amount of people run down the center of curved roads, following the yellow line. Over the course of 26 miles, 385 five yards and 2.25 inches, it is easy to save at least a hundred yards by running the tangent versus following the yellow line. Race courses are measured by riding a bicycle over the tangents, following the yellow lines of streets or highways is extra distance and wasted energy and time. The key is keeping one's eyes up and looking ahead to the next turn or the next key point. We pick a point and run to it. *Is this step directed to get me to the finish line as quickly as possible?*

We also run tangents in life, by avoiding thoughts and actions incongruent with our goals. We evaluate a racecourse. Should we also evaluate our life course? **Consider:** What does this thought or activity accomplish? Is it directed towards the most efficient route of goal attainment? Which goal am I achieving with this thought or activity? This too requires keeping our eyes up and looking ahead. If a thought or activity is unrelated to any of our goals, why are we engaging in them? Prudence demands choosing goal-achieving activities.

I rarely watch or read the news of the major media, I am careful about which television programs I watch. I have a few that provide some entertainment for relaxation. The networks often quickly cancel programs without sex and swearing. Consequently, I watch very little television. What goal does a program or reading material help you achieve? Does the topic of conversation step directly toward a goal? Farmers frequently discuss weather because it does affect their goals. Will they be able to be in the field? Should the irrigation start today or in a week? What precautions are needed with livestock to lessen the effects of severe weather on all spectrums? Blizzards, ice storms, excessive heat or cold all dictate alteration of care when possible. However, to someone working in a cubical in a non-agricultural industry, the weather has less chance of directly affecting their business goals or even daily routine. Naturally, this depends upon their product or service. Their personal goals may be influenced if they enjoy outdoor activities, including traveling.

In cross country practice we rarely discussed our competition's work ethic. We frequently discussed how to improve ourselves, maximizing daily improvement. We controlled our efforts in stepping directly towards our goal of being champions. Energy and focus wasted on gossiping or idle discussion diminished our improvement. We discussed how to outrun certain individuals, focusing on solutions. Solution orientated thought achieves goals.

Keep your eyes toward the finish line of each goal to avoid unnecessary steps. Run the tangents on your life's course for goal achievement.

Internalizing Goals

My sister and brother in-law had their first child, Wyatt, at the age of 41. Despite this later age for having a child, Brian and Dee fed, clothed, loved, and changed Wyatt. They do not have their goal of loving Wyatt written down. Yet, they continue to achieve this goal every day.

Do you have written goals concerning the feeding, clothing and nurturing of your children? I was once less than 10 years old; yes it is true, weighing about 60 pounds, possessing only the essential body fat. One summer evening, about 9:00p.m., we entered the house after irrigating which required carrying muddy tubes further down the ditch to water more corn, consequently we were often muddy upon finishing. Dad and Mom usually remained much cleaner than my sister and I. My parents' maturity lessened their desire to intentionally seek out mud. Spiritual maturity lessens our desire to seek emotional and immoral mud.

The enclosed porch of our farmhouse provided an area to remove dirty, muddy boots. My mother lacked a pleasant disposition if I stepped on her freshly mopped floors with boots carrying mud or manure. Yes, I tried that *once*. The path from the porch went east through the door into the large kitchen. I immediately turned to the south, past the cupboards and sink, past the stove on my left. The smell of dinner cooking increased my appetite. The chimney from the old cook stove was present but covered; last used when my dad was growing up. Immediately past the stove I went through another door into the original restroom, where only a sink against the wall remained.

On the wall opposite the sink, was the door leading down to our unfinished partial basement. The walls and floor were cement; the basement provided storage for canned goods and livestock vaccines. At the top of the stairs was a door to the outside, rarely used in my lifetime. I stopped short of going to the basement; rather I started to wash my hands in the sink. "Use hot sudsy water," Mom yelled as a reminder. I frequently heard these words. I believe a few germs increase one's immune system. My mother disagreed; consequently I washed with 'hot sudsy water.'

Suddenly, a deafening scream erupted from the kitchen, I then felt as if I had been thrown into orbit. As one who was occasionally ornery, I lacked understanding about what happened this time. An 18 inch garter snake had slithered in from the south door, resting underneath the sink. I remain of the opinion a snakebite would have generated less pain. For the record, the only resulting injury was the initial shock of being launched into orbit by that scream.

Over the years when this story is brought up, my mother promptly defends herself exclaiming, "I was protecting my young." My mom's goals were unwritten on paper or stone, her goal of protecting her young, of keeping clean clothes for us were internalized. Mom's goals were intuitively written in her mind. She loved to make cherry pie and invite my grandparents and Aunt Ruth down for Sunday dinner. My grandfather and I battled for the extra pieces of cherry pie. Mom lacked a written goal for making mouth-watering cherry pie for the enjoyment of her parents, spouse, and children; it was internalized. Isn't this true of most mothers?

I spent vast time helping around the farm, including the Quonset where Dad repaired equipment and built various items needed. I also enjoyed playing at the river or in the barn. Scrapes, cuts, and slivers were an ordinary part of life. Scrapes and cuts keep your skin fresh, because new skin is frequently needed to replace the old missing skin. My entire life I have been accused of appearing younger than my actual age. Could this be the reason? No plans exist of advertising any snake oil cures. Every time I entered the house with a little minor wound, Mom sought to remove the sliver with tweezers or put iodine and a bandage on it. She was insistent on keeping me healthy, yet her goals were only written internally.
Virtually every morning Mom prepared pancakes for breakfast, whether we were off to school, off to work on the farm on a Saturday or during the summer. Dinner was ready at noon and supper was usually around seven o'clock. The house was clean and orderly, the garden produced abundant food. This was common among the farms in the area. I am unaware of any of them writing goals for these achievements on paper. Yes, my mother,

along with all of the other moms, had internalized goals. Are your goals internalized and as intuitive as a mother's?

Farmers

Most farmers have planted crops during an optimal range of dates for decades. Most farmers know precisely when they plan to begin planting, weather permitting. For instance, those in Central Nebraska or Northern Kansas will nearly always say they plan to begin planting corn either April 15 or 20th. Mother nature is in charge. Driving a tractor on overly wet soil can harm the soil structure, negatively affecting seed germination, root growth and the ability of the soil to allow proper drainage of water. University research has shown a loss of yield for corn planted after the 5th of May in this region of Nebraska. The ultimate goal is having the corn planted by this date. However, they all allow for delays due to rain or unexpected breakdowns. I have yet to meet anyone who has a scheduled breakdown.

Farmer's internalized goals are growing profitable crops to provide for their family and feed the world. Farmers know better than anyone, the necessity of caring for the land. The land is the goose laying the golden eggs. Farmers are also fully aware God is in charge of the land and the livestock. Most politicians are aware of neither.

Chapter 8:

Move to Kearney

Kearney, Nebraska, significantly impacted my life for a plethora of reasons, ranging from professional, church, athletics and community. These resulted in abounding friendships. I was employed at Central States Agronomics, Inc. as a crop consultant. Owners Mark and Eileen Kottmeyer are first rate people. I completed two summers of internship while attending KSU. They offered me a full-time position during my senior year. During Christmas and spring break I met with clients and collected soil samples. I graduated from Kansas State on Saturday May 19, 1990; moving to Kearney on Sunday and started work at 6:30a.m. Monday.

Initially upon graduating from Kansas State, I planned to run very little; mostly recreationally. However, most nights after work, around 7:00p.m. to 9:00p.m. I quickly changed from agronomy clothes to running shorts, tee-shirt and running shoes. A crop consultant walks 10 to 15 miles a day in May and June; as one takes population stand counts and scouts for weeds and insects. The hunger and fatigue quickly diminished as I ran through the streets of Kearney. Once home and showered, I ate two hamburgers or three plates of spaghetti with meat sauce; along with a couple cans of Dr. Pepper.

Each morning, a Dr. Pepper and two honey buns served as breakfast as I drove to the first field at 6:00a.m. Saturday and Sunday I ran up to 10 miles; I had no television and knew only co-workers and clients. Mark invited me to First Lutheran Church my first Sunday in Kearney. Pastor Ebb remained as the pastor 31 years after his ordination at this church; growing the membership. I arrived at 9:15a.m. in time for 9:30a.m. church … only to realize church had commenced at 8:30a.m. Fortunately, I arrived in time for doughnuts and coffee. Mark introduced me to various members, each exemplifying friendliness. I thoroughly enjoyed worshiping at First Lutheran as Pastor Ebb passionately preached the pure word of God, and the members provided sincere fellowship. Under his 33 years of ordained ministry, the church grew from under 200 members to nearly 2,000 members in the Kearney community with a population of roughly 25,000. During the pause for greeting during worship and afterwards, people were amazingly friendly. This authentic friendly warmth in a worship setting is a rarity. Despite the congregational size of nearly 2,000, the congregation's warmth resembles that found in smaller churches. I thoroughly enjoyed and eagerly anticipated attending this church; the fellowship was simply remarkable. When I later trained for the marathon, I ran 20-28 miles in the morning, often completing the run at 8:15a.m. Despite fatigue, I quickly showered, dressed and tied my tie while driving to church; entering just as the service began at 8:30a.m. Larry, the head usher, frequently found a place for me to sit; and often asked if I would serve as an usher during offering. I joyfully obliged. The pastors and congregants engaged in sincere interest about my running; which did and does serve as one of my ministry tools.

Dr. Toussaint later encouraged us at DTS that 3 reliable components of measuring a church's spirituality is preaching the truth of the Bible, the congregation's singing and fellowship. First Lutheran Church in Kearney possessed all three qualities.

In mid-June I ran my first road race of the summer in Ravenna, a small town 30 miles northeast of Kearney. I won the 5 mile race. The 2nd place finisher was a high school senior who later qualified for the Olympic Trials in the steeple chase.

Winning races provides several benefits, including the opportunity to meet people after the race; particularly when one is shy. I visited with numerous runners in the Ravenna City Park following the race, including Kearney High cross country and track coaches Pat McFadden and Roger Matheson. Kearney High was a perennial state title contender; yet narrowly missed the title annually. They were due to eventually capture this elusive title.

Roger and Pat invited me to join the Kearney High runners on their summer evening training runs. They also told of a 5K race starting at the Kearney Fairgrounds the following Saturday. Despite leg fatigue from walking in the fields and the desire to sleep a little later than normal on Saturday morning; I arose and drove my 1974 Ford Gran Torino to the race. While warming up, I met Lyle Claussen who was the head men's cross country and track coach at Kearney State College. Their cross country team finished 7th in the previous fall's NAIA championship; his 3rd season as coach. We visited about everything from irrigation methodology to running. His knee was bothering him from driving the team's van during the season. This was the first of many runs now totaling over 10,000 miles and conversations with this coaching and running icon.

After the first half mile of the race, I shared the lead with a college runner. Rarely do I visit during a race; this was an exception. Bryan and I measure about the same height, and he too had the build of a runner. We crossed the mile in just under 5:00, proceeding to the turnaround point. We ran together most of the race, I edged him out at the finish line. We continued visiting after the race, he lived in the apartments across the street where I resided, most of his roommates also ran for Kearney State, the non-runner studied journalism. Bryan invited me to call him anytime to run. I did not write down his phone number, yet (308) 234-6383 remains embedded in my mind. I also met Jim and Jennifer, newlyweds from Tribune and Wichita Kansas, attending Kearney State after transferring from Pratt Community College.

Bryan and I ran numerous times during that summer, we frequently pushed the pace; challenging each other's mental toughness. I regularly encountered Lyle and Mary in church throughout the summer. As the beginning of school neared, Bryan and his roommates invited me to join the cross country team's practice. Fortunately, it coincided with the tapering off of the crop consulting schedule. Additionally, Mark Kottmeyer was supportive and encouraging of community involvement. I met Joe Schumm and Darren Barker on the run to the season's first practice.

With Claussen's arrival, as I mentioned, the division for competition changed and was more challenging. How do you respond to greater challenges and increased competition?

Coach Claussen's plan to improve and compete at the necessary higher level included changing their long-time schedule of the "Horse, dog, and pony show." The previous schedule consisted of running against most of the same teams every week at different meets. He maintained high respect for each of those schools, yet recognized the necessity of a variety of competition for the runners to maximize their improvement. Consequently, Lyle altered the team's schedule, running against tough competition every meet, including NCAA D-I schools such as the University of Colorado. They did not compete every week; the team's goal focused on qualifying for and competing at nationals. He taught that improvement in life demands competing against the best.

UNK Cross Country

Mark Kottmeyer encourages his employees' involvement in community, including pursuing their passions. He and Eileen adopted Zig Ziglar's statement, "If you help enough other people get what they want; you can have anything in the world you want." Consequently, Mark encouraged me to train with UNK cross country; especially since we worked out of our homes, setting our own schedules. I frequently began my work day around 6:00a.m., enabling me to attend practice at 3:00p.m. in the fall once our daily time in the field dwindled.

Kearney State became University of Nebraska at Kearney and switched from the NAIA to NCAA-Division II in sports competitions. Several of the coaches complained about the increased level of competition. Coach Lyle Claussen approached it by telling his team, "Hey, we have the ability to compete at this level if we are willing to pay the price in training." He then explained and led them to the necessary efforts. He, like Congo, never raised his voice or "chewed out" any athletes. They both provided sincere assessment and guidance along with authentic motivation. Vision is the nitroglycerin of motivation!

I trained with Kearney State cross country runners as much as possible, including their 6:30a.m. run. Most runs included a healthy dose and balance of laughter and challenge. Lyle was adamant for the guys to run the appropriate pace on the appropriate day. Often, while running beside and visiting with Lyle, he asked me to catch the leaders to slow the pace to easy or moderate. Top coaches, in sports and business, identify and communicate the motivating factors for their teams. These exceptionally driven young men frequently sought to over exert themselves, requiring continual requests to ease up. Are you as eager in your drive to serve Christ?

The regional meet included perennial national powers such South Dakota State and Augustana. Kearney State qualified for the national meet! I was ecstatic upon receiving the news. Humboldt State, in northern California, hosted the national meet. While running with Lyle after church the following Sunday, he stated that if everything unfolded perfectly, they might finish in the top 10 in their inaugural NCAA D-II cross country championships. Saturday evening following the meet, I spoke with Mrs. Claussen, inquiring of the results. The team finished 8th and Joe Schumm placed 25th earning Kearney State's first NCAA D-II All-American placing in any sport. We were elated! How high do you set your goals? Are you surrounding yourself with people who challenge you to pursue grander achievements?

Training continued, at times my weekly miles varied from 40 to 80 depending on the week. However, consistency increased in January. In February of 1991, my conditioning reached a new plateau, running 70 miles a week became easy. I desperately sought running 100 miles a week for two reasons:

1) Desire for rapid fitness increase
2) Satisfaction of achievement

Because Lyle inoculated his team with vision generated motivation, he frequently requested I slow the runners pace on their "easy" days; and even during some of their interval training. How many college coaches consistently request their athletes to reduce efforts due to the athletes' desire to over-train?

I ran approximately 90 miles per week several times in the late 1980s; the lack of consistency proved to be my downfall. One February day in 1991, I discussed increasing my mileage on a run with Lyle Claussen. He strongly encouraged consistently running 70 miles per week. Sadly, my 24-year-old mind thought he was trying to hold me back from higher levels of achievement. Instead of listening to an ultra-successful coach and runner in his early 40s, I relied on my foolishness. I ran 100 miles, including three speed workouts the 3rd week of February. I felt terrific that week running impressive workouts. I ran 14 miles with Lyle and the Kearney State runners the next Sunday after church; suddenly a ligament in my right foot became painfully inflamed. Lyle graciously listened to my disgruntlement, softly suggesting, "That is what happens sometimes when we overdo it in our training." Did I learn my lesson? Yes, at least for that moment.

God intersects our lives with people who possess the wisdom necessary to achieve Christ's will for our lives. Who are these people in your life? Record their names. Are you listening to them? Write "yes," "no," or "sometimes" by each of their names. Reflect on and record both long and short term benefits received. Now reflect and record why you hesitate listening always or sometimes to others. Who has God placed in your path that you avoid developing a relationship with to garner their wisdom, knowledge and understanding?

"Humble yourselves in the presence of the Lord, and He will exalt you," (James 4:10). This includes remaining humble and learning from those God places in your path and life. One of the roots of foolishness is believing that you understand and see all possibilities. For example, experience and wisdom enable you to look at a piece of developed property and see beyond the visible. Do you recognize the physical, chemical and biological properties of the soil you stand on? Do you recognize and see in your mind's eye the water, gas, electric and sewer lines beneath the soil surface and those hidden throughout the house? Greater understanding enables greater ability to define challenges and identify solutions. This illustration applies to every area of life. A humble heart allows you to learn and accept direction from those who see and understand the non-visible better than you do.

Running on faith includes my learning and willingness to trust the coaches God placed in my life. These coaches see beyond the *visible* and immediate to guide runners to maximum performances.
Bryan Danburg served as my intern during the summer of 1991. The temperatures frequently exceeded 100 degrees. We quickly changed into our running gear each night after work, met in-between our apartments, then engaged in a run in the rolling gravel hills north of Kearney. We believed the faster the better. This, combined with our daily walking in the soft soil and mud of the corn and soybean fields, enhanced our fitness.

The cross country team entered the fall of 1991 with great expectations. The transition of Kearney State becoming the University of Nebraska-Kearney (UNK) created additional excitement in the community. All but one freshman from the 1990 top 10 national team returned. The team gained 4 competitive runners: a transfer from Pratt Community College in Kansas, a former team member, along with a couple of talented freshmen.

The team defeated many NCAA D-I schools while competing at University of Nebraska and Colorado. A different runner emerged as the team's top runner at each meet, at least 10 guys contended for the 7 varsity spots.

Augustana (Auggie) located in Sioux Falls, SD, entered the season as the favorite to win the national title; they handily defeated the UNK Lopers in September. Throughout the season's weekly team meetings, Coach Claussen informed the guys the quantity and quality of their workouts matched those of national powers South Dakota State (SDSU) and Auggie. What are you telling members of your team? Are you lifting up their efforts? Insecure coaches attempt to intimidate their athletes due to the coach's insecurity. Great coaches, like Lyle Claussen, lift up their team's intense efforts. Additionally, Coach Claussen knew and implemented a fundamental principle of motivation, plant the seed of authentic belief and expectation early in the season and nurture that seed's development throughout the season. This practice produces resilient belief and desire when needed for the championship races. This same principle applies with employees and members of any organization.

Lyle was very familiar with these schools; he had once been an assistant at SDSU. Before accepting the coaching position at UNK; Lyle coached seventeen years at Brandon Valley High School, on the edge of Sioux Falls. Lyle's high school teams won 2 state track championships, and were perennial contenders in cross country and track. His athletes won dozens of individual championships. One of his distance runners was one of two athletes to defeat future Olympic Marathoner, Rod Dehaven, in high school.

UNK closed the gap on Auggie at the region meet; they both qualified for the nationals in Edwardsville, IL, located outside of St. Louis. During training runs throughout the season, I joked with the guys that the NCAA was holding a top 4 trophy for them, however they needed to compete at the national meet to receive and bring that trophy home. Frequently, I trained with the team during their regular practice, before running with Brad Sherman (Sherm) that night; he worked for UPS in addition to attending school and running cross country. Due to limited scholarships and the cost of attending college, many of the team members worked steady weekly hours in addition to attending classes, practice and completing homework.

The day before the team left flew to St. Louis; I met Sherm at the track to run the team's prescribed workout. This optimistic comedian who later attended a comic school in Los Angeles lacked his normal jovial disposition. Brad recorded on his work calendar during the summer that he would need these few days off to compete in the NCAA D-II cross country championships. His UPS supervisor surprised Brad this day saying that he needed to remain at work instead of leaving to compete in the championships. I firmly believe Sherm was capable of earning All-American honors; he had been one of the team's many top runners. All his dreams and late night preparations were gone, vanished, all for naught. The next morning the UPS supervisor told Sherm he was only joking and was cleared to leave work.

Perhaps humor does exist in this and similar situations for those who never aspire and pay the price to be among the nation's elite. World champion speakers enforce actions among supervisors, management and general citizens as they pontificate that lying and deception are permissible when used for humor. The supervisor and his peers found great humor in their deception. Yet this humor had detrimental effects.

The team believed they were capable of placing among the top 4 if all went perfectly. Did national runner-up seem too good to be true? I predicted they could place 2nd. The night before the race Lyle gathered the team in one of the hotel rooms to discuss the race. Coach Claussen maintained his usual calm demeanor, yet amazingly motivating voice. "If you start struggling, keep your head and eyes up, look ahead to other runners. Just keep plugging away." Coach Claussen taught and prepared us for Plan A, B and C. Additionally, he reminded the guys of his season long message, "You are as well prepared as Augustana, South Dakota State and all other top teams; this is the meet for which we have trained the entire season. Remember, you represent yourselves, your family, your school and the Kearney community. I receive many inquiries and comments from business leaders and members of the community about your performances."

Lyle's message resembled nitroglycerin; small in quantity, yet powerfully and positively life altering. Shivers danced up and down my spine as I listened in as a spectator; those shivers of excitement return in writing and re-reading his message 25 years later.

The pre-national meet rankings listed Kearney in 8th. As teams gathered at the course light snow fell amidst 30 degree weather. Many of the coastal teams and their fans made a big deal of the dusting of snow. We took it in stride, all teams compete in the same environment; the key is optimizing any given situation.

The time for the race's start arrived. Nearly 200 runners stretched across the parabolic starting line atop a hill on the challenging course. At last, the National Championship race was underway. The UNK team ran behind roughly 75% of the field in the initial, moderately descending, stretch. Somehow Tom Schutz inadvertently tripped or stepped in a hole, nearly causing him to fall. This would have been devastating, resulting in possible injury and certain delay. His teammates reactively grabbed and lifted his shoulders, keeping him vertical and running. Do you surround yourself with those who instinctively prevent you from falling when tripping amidst life's challenges?

The men in white over blue, representing UNK, continually marched forward during the race. Freshman Kurt Holiday ran a solid race as the team's 7th runner, Sherm kept plugging away after following off the pace of the team's top 5: Joe Schumm, Derek Bryer, Tom Magnuson, Bobby Brindamour and Tom Schutz. These 5 remained within sight of one another during their drive through the pack. Near the 4 mile mark of the 10K race; it became apparent they were in position for a national trophy; possibly second; if only they could hang tough on this course of hair pin turns following ascents and descents. One edge of the course offered a steeply slanted side slope followed by a hill nearly requiring a rope to conquer.

University of Massachusetts Lowell was running a phenomenal race up front; barring a tragic occurrence, they had the championship in hand. Near the 5 mile mark, the UNK runners began their final drive. Bobby Brindamour began his patented kick, Tom Magnuson and Tom Schutz pursued closely behind. Derek Bryer continued his gutsy performance, as did returning All-American Joe Schumm who battled a hamstring injury through much of the season.

They sprinted the final uphill stretch! Bobby, Tom M, Tom S. and Derek finished as All-Americans; Joe missed the coveted award by 2 spots.

Friends standing near the finish heard Tom Schutz crossing the finish line mumbling, "Hurt bad, hurt bad…" UNK's top 5 runners were separated by a mere 27 seconds after 6.2 miles; an excellent achievement. UNK cross country runners ran on faith. The calculated scores revealed 96 points for University of Nebraska-Kearney: national runner-up. The team, coaches, family and friends exuded jubilation! Afterwards at the hotel, the team threw Coach Claussen into the swimming pool as an act of celebration.

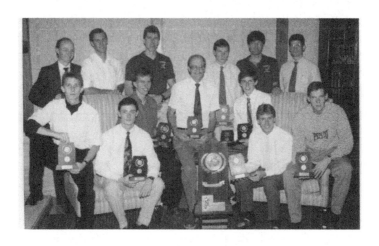

Figure 16: 1991 NCAA D-II Cross Country National Runner-up Front Row: Derek Bryer, Brad Sherman, Tom Schutz, Coach Lyle Claussen, Bob Brindamour, Joe Schumm, Tom Magnuson. Back Row: Alumnus Chuck Stevens, Trainer Jason Coortz, Assist Coach Brian ….., Kurt Holliday, Massage Therapist J. Michael Sobieschec, Rick Meyer.

The 1992 team was arguably one of the best collegiate teams of American born runners in all college divisions. The varsity consisted of six runners from Nebraska and one from Kansas. They entered the national meet ranked only 8th or 9th. Fortunately, rankings carry no credibility. Two weeks earlier UNK placed 3rd at the region meet in Omaha behind Western State and Adams State. Adams State did not run all of their top 7 individuals in the region meet. Slippery Rock, PA hosted the national meet. Six inches of rain fell the morning of the race turning the course into a quagmire. Slippery Rock lived up to its name of slippery. Joe Schumm ran among the top 10 most of the race. Bob Brindamour and Tom Magnuson ran together most of the race. Bob made his strong patented move with about 1 ½ miles remaining. Bob and Joe both finished on the top 15. The team finished 3rd behind a historic Adams State team along with an incredible team from Western State. Adams State achieved an unbelievable perfect score of 15 as their top 5 runners placed 1st thru 5th.

The 1994 season proved a fun season as UNK hosted the national meet. Lyle, as the meet referee, disqualified an Abilene Christian runner who cut on the inside of a 6" tree instead of the outside on the final turn to the finish. This disqualification changed team scoring, moving UNK from 3rd to 4th. The runner's position rounding the tree saved him possibly a yard, with no effect on his position or team scoring. Yet rules are rules and integrity is integrity. Lyle never considered wavering even though his team lost one placing position. These teams are "stars" due to the friendships formed, achievements recorded in the history books and the lessons acquired from association with NCAA All-Americans and their Hall of Fame coach.

Figure 17: The 1994 fourth place UNK cross country team. Front Row: Kurt Holiday, Aaron Ripley, Ivan Ivanov, Tom Magnuson, Bob Brindamour, Erich Whitemore, Todd Fuelberth. Back Row: Head Coach Lyle Claussen, Shelby, Rick Meyer, Brad Sherman, Frank Shorter

Self Talk

The first week of December the flu virus struck, sadly my mind accepted the flu as an automatic annual occurrence. Mark Kottmeyer and I were scheduled to soil sample approximately 3,000 acres west of Ogallala, Nebraska. Mark asked if I was up to the task; I agreed that we needed to complete the sampling. Nebraska weather is unpredictable; major snow storms and a hard freeze that prevents penetrating the soil with soil probes are highly probable in December. We drove separate pickups and stopped several times during the 145 mile excursion to the feedlot office where we met the owner. At each stop Mark inquired of my well-being.

About 11:00a.m. I realized my low energy and lethargic concentration needed to cease. I focused on any and all portions of my body that felt normal, confessing, "I feel good, I am healthy, I am strong. Lord, thank you for restoring my health and energy." An hour later my energy began to increase, by mid-afternoon my health was restored. For supper, my once queasy stomach enjoyed a terrific steak and baked potato with extra butter and sour cream. I avoided sickness for the next 7 years.

Each time a hint of sickness approaches, I confess feeling good, "I am healthy. I feel great. Thank you Lord for restoring my health." Since I feel terrible every single time I become sick, I choose to avoid getting sick. I readily realize and rapidly confess that we lack control over every situation of our health. However, we do contain more control over illnesses such as colds and flu than most of us recognize.

As I write this 26 years later, I have had the flu only 3 times; the last occurring in February 2007. Yes, our attitude and words do carry power over *typical* illnesses. Each of the 3 times that flu struck, I disregarded my instincts of getting necessary rest immediately along with speaking affirmative messages. This may not prevent you from ever getting the flu again, however using our God designed and assigned mind to His glory will reduce your moments of illness.

Overtraining from ignoring Lyle's advice during the winter caused a hip injury. I failed to respond to the injury as I did the sickness. After the pain lapsed for a day, I ventured on an up-tempo 8 mile run 'just to teach it a lesson.' A lesson was taught - I was the foolish student. Proper training ceased for nearly a month. I quickly removed any ponderings of my foolishness being a fluke as I repeated the idiotic behavior several times through the spring of 1994. I continued ignoring Lyle's warnings! He repeatedly instructed, "It is better to err on the side of caution." My running friends continue asking today if I am going to "teach my body a lesson," followed by laughter and stories.

During college and initially following graduation, people frequently asked if and when I was running a marathon. My response remained constant, "Probably in my mid-twenties. I want to be competitive; I don't want to run one just to run one." Competing is fun! I ran my first 20 mile run in August 1993 at a relaxed pace in the rolling gravel hills northwest of Kearney, in 2 hours and 6 minutes. I started at 5:30a.m. and finished at 7:36, leaving abundant time for a cool down walk, to shower, dress in a suit and tie and attend 8:30a.m. church.

Mentally, these runs are amazingly rewarding while incredibly challenging. The mind enters la-la land, a dream state where imagination and creativity soar into frontiers only discoverable beyond one's 5th and 6th wind. Challenging one's mind-body-spirit simultaneously creates exponential benefits. Greatness occurs with Christian faith, recognizing we are created in God's image; fully reliant upon Christ's strength, power, wisdom, knowledge and understanding. Yes, faith is illogical; and greatness occurs when *Running on Faith*.

When the components of greatness combine in any order or combination, the achievements increase exponentially.

Formulas of Faith

Components of Greatness:
    Achievement:
Effort
    10X
Effort + Faith
    100X
Effort + Faith + Desire
    1,000X
Effort + Faith + Desire + Belief
    10,000X
Effort + Faith + Desire + Belief + Vision
    100,000X
Effort + Faith + Desire + Belief + Vision + Coach / Direction
    1,000,000X

$$E=mC >E=mc^2$$
Energy = *mass**Christ (Light of the World) > Energy = *mass**speed of light²

- **Effort** – Magnitude of self-exertion.
- **Faith** – Hebrews 11
- **Mentor** – Congo, Lyle and Charles
- **Desire** – Value determines Price. The higher the Value, the greater enormity and duration of physical and emotional pain you are willing to suffer for achievement.
- **Belief** – Knowing your physical, mental, financial and spiritual resources exceed the price of the achievement; trusting God to provide these resources.
- **Vision** – Submit your boundary fence of possibilities to Jesus Christ and the Holy Spirit.
- **Direction** – The best source of guidance is internalizing the Bible and a communicative relationship with Jesus Christ.

What is your Christ filled vision? Are you fully activating your faith? We achieve Christ's desired greatness in our lives well beyond our 2nd wind. Each wind is the point you desire relief, when your mind and body say *enough*. Sadly, most people make a big deal of attaining just their 2nd wind. Faith, Vision and Desire are essential components of greatness.

Frequently, the mental challenge of running 6 miles or 29 miles resembles a poured, thick cement wall. It appears virtually unbreakable until an exhaustive examination reveals a hairline fracture. Faith, desire, belief and vision are thoroughly mixed with focus and concentration; creating a liquid solution seeping into and through the fracture. Their gradual expansion disseminates the wall. The pristine view of "champion" faintly appears in the distant horizon.

I sometimes acquire 'running closter phobia:' I just want out! This often occurred around 16 miles, my body felt okay with sufficient energy for completing the run. You may experience this at 4 miles, or after completing 4 phone calls to clients or prospects. Ultimately, *running closter phobia* is disproportional to vision. Fatigue, much like temptation, seeps in your mind. If left unchecked, fatigue suffocates vision, displacing faith with doubt; the lack of vision and faith redirects desire for greatness to desire for relief.

I accepted Lyle's invitation to accompany the UNK track team to Fargo, ND, in 1994. North Dakota State University hosted the NCAA Division II Indoor Track Championships. Some accuse me of snoring. Frankly, I have never heard myself snore. I sleep soundly; therefore, these claims rest on a foundation of sand. Just kidding! Some people I travel to running events and business conventions with believe I snore. As much as my dad snored, maybe the trait passed down genetically. One night in Fargo, Lyle claimed my snoring kept him awake; I grabbed a blanket and pillow, and then crawled into the bathtub after closing the door. This prevented my "snoring" from reaching the ears of those sleeping. I woke up shortly before 5:00a.m. and threw on my running gear going for a run. The March morning air in Fargo was a bit frigid at 20 below zero. Patches of ice enhanced my mental focus and concentration during the 20 mile run. Twice I fell down, hitting the pavement in less than the blink of an eye. My knee and pride suffered injuries.

A few weeks later a stress fracture appeared in my left ankle. Lyle said to take daily Tums or Rolaids as a source of extra calcium; along with physical rest. Due to my anxiousness for health and training, I made a rare doctor's visit to an orthopedic specialist recommended by running friends. A brief examination confirmed the stress fracture, along with denying possibilities for expedited healing. This confirmation of prognosis, lack of recommending calcium and failure of remedy for quicker recovery, permanently altered my view of injuries and doctors. Why pay the doctor to be told what you already know?

In the mid-2000s, newspaper articles reported Creighton Medical School's groundbreaking research of taking calcium for prevention and aid of stress fractures. The medical schools' recommendations were at least a decade behind Coach Lyle Claussen's knowledge.

While attending a business convention in June 1993, I purchased a book published in the mid-1900s called *What You Say, is What You Get* by Don Gossett. It was time to re-read to internalize the concepts. He illustrated from actual events the power of scripture in healing our wounds. A few weeks after this doctor's visit, I hobbled along when I decided the following April, I would pursue my goal of running the Boston Marathon. I painfully completed up to 3 miles a day. I began claiming the healing power of scripture. "By your stripes, I am healed," (Isaiah 53:5). The pain remained for nearly 2 weeks after my initial claim.

I allowed only faith to reside in my mind. "Lord, thank you for leaving the pain there to remind me that you are the one who heals me. If your will permits alleviating the pain, you have my approval." We must submit to God's will.

> Instead, you ought to say, 'If the Lord wills, we will live and also do this or that.' But as it is, you boast in your arrogance; all such boasting is evil. (James 4:15–16)

I believe God enjoys honest, tasteful humor. I continually thanked Him for healing me. By June only the calcium deposit remained as indication of this past injury. My training resumed to running 70 miles per week, additionally I walked 70 to 90 weekly miles in corn and soybean fields as a crop consultant.

During the next 31 months innumerable injuries were instantaneously healed. Occasionally, my hip, quad (thigh), calf, Achilles and numerous other muscles, tendons and ligaments began breaking down. Immediately, I confessed my healing by Christ's stripes, praising the Lord for the successful healing. Faith cast off doubt as far as the east is from the west. Jesus Christ provided the necessary faith and healing. Piercing pain and torment always ceased within a half-mile, mere minutes, after the proclamation.

God consistently healed me during this stretch of training. However, He does not promise to heal every single time, if so we would never suffer physical death. Even Lazarus, who Christ raised from the dead, eventually died. Rather, this healing in this moment correlated with God's will within my life during this period of time. Pray for God to show you what to pray for your health. Regardless of what happens, rejoice in Him always.

I discussed my primary goal of running the Boston Marathon with Lyle Claussen. First, I had to qualify for the prestigious marathon. One evening in March 1994 I visited with Lyle in his home when he challenged me to consistently run 70 miles per week. Moreover, he reiterated the significance of taking Tums or Rolaids tablets to prevent stress fractures. This time I listened. My daily workouts correlated with Lyle's wisdom. Consistent intelligent training began paying dividends.

Would you agree diligence combined with wisdom generates success in all of life's endeavors? Within 2 months of struggling to run 3 miles, I ran 20 milers in the hills north of Kearney at an average pace of 6:15 per mile. Running was fun!

Years later, I ran these same 20 milers in less than 2 hours while running over 100 miles per week, week after week. During one 29 mile training run mostly in the gravel hills north of Kearney, I passed the 26 mile marker in 2 hours and 35 minutes (5:57 pace). To be clear, plenty of other runners have run this pace in workouts of long runs. The key illustrated principle resides in contrasting the results between sporadic foolish training, versus seeking and applying wisdom. The Bible says the wise counsel with the wise, and the wise welcome rebuke (Proverbs 13:20; 17:10).

Form

During an afternoon workout, I completed five 1-mile intervals on a country gravel road. Slippage occurred every time my toes pushed off the gravel. The autumn temperatures in the 50s were ideal for a workout. I ran with UNK coach Lyle Claussen back to the school's field house. The fatigue from the workout, amplified with running over 80 miles per week, caused my body's sensory nerves to protest. My head angled downward; the objective, to avoid stepping in a hole or on a large rock. I avoided injury for over 2 years, a trend I preferred to continue. Lyle broke the topic of conversation saying, "Keep your head up." Lyle, a master motivator, was referring to physical efficiency as opposed to inspiration. "Keep your head up" is maintaining maximum efficiency. When the head is up, the shoulders back and hips forward, we maximize our running efficiency. The same amount of energy expended with the head up, shoulders back and hips forward, derives a faster tour of the course than running inefficiently.

What is your proper and most efficient form while *Running on Faith?*
- Love God with all of your heart, soul and mind (Matthew 22:37)
- Love others as much as you love yourself (Matthew 22:39)
- Always be joyful, praying and giving thanks (I Thessalonians 5:16)

Add scripture that is placed on your heart. Keep your head up: Focus on the Lord's path, word and people. Your run on faith will attain maximum efficiency in serving Christ and achieving his will for your life.

Chapter 9:

Marathon

Origination of Running on Faith

"If you want to run fast, you have to run fast." The words were spoken often by hall of fame coach Lyle Claussen. Additionally, Lyle emphasized running slow and running a moderate pace. To become good, one needed to vary mileage and pace.

For example, on Sundays before or after church I often joined the UNK team for their weekly long run of 14 to 16 miles. I later increased my mileage to 28, running with them either the first or last 16 miles helped significantly. These runs were intended as a recovery run, exerting a relaxing effort. Although, too often 'relaxing' dropped off the pace around 15 to 20 miles; leaving us to run with moderate effort the remainder of the journey.

Monday's workout consisted of running an up-tempo 10-miler; usually under 5:30 pace, with some miles under 5:00. On Tuesday's we ran some sort of interval workout such as 10 x 1,000 meters; these were fast and tough, with little rest between each. Afterwards, we ran strides to increase our leg speed, our raw speed. Another day consisted of a moderate run of under 6:00 pace, and another interval workout during the week before the guys raced on Saturday. Each day varied in workout and intensity, the workouts often varied from week to week. Variance created strength, speed and flexibility. Yes, we stretched after each run! Yes, these guys became very good, among the best collegiate teams in America!

How are you becoming good? Are you determined to be among the best in America? Are you varying your mileage and pace? You are probably saying wait a minute, I am neither a runner nor have a desire to run. However, are you varying your topics of study? Do you read a variety of topics written in a variety of depths?

For example, over a couple of hours one Saturday morning I read an Opera Magazine, about 100 pages of a book on Adolph Hitler and various portions of scripture. I am not a fan of Opera, but for a reason unknown to me, I receive the magazine. At first, I discarded it due to lack of interest, Then I read to learn a new topic, expand vocabulary and enjoy new writing styles. How do I become a better writer if new frontiers remain unexplored? Each of these materials expands my thought process, challenges and validates my beliefs.

I began to understand the unimaginable horror in reading of Hitler's antics and mentality. Yes, even though most of us are aware of many of his evil actions and directives; that book provided additional depth into his demonic nature. Why read this horror? Human nature is the same eternally: past, present and future. Many historians illustrate that we either learn from history or repeat history. This history should never be repeated!

Another belief challenge is reading about the grace, love and mercy of our Heavenly Father and His son, Jesus Christ. If ever a "too good to be true" story existed; Christ's death and resurrection for our salvation is it. Fortunately, all is True! Christ did die and conquer death for our sins; you and I can believe, confess and proclaim this Good News. The real message behind, "If it seems too good to be true…" is our inquisition of motive. Christ and salvation are true because of God's desire for us to join him in eternal life. The Bible is clear: All things are possible through Christ who strengthens us. Life's propositions that seem too good to be true are a lie because they originated from an evil heart. Satan is the father of lies and deception. When opportunities are too good to be true, the motives are deception; and a wrongful harvest of gain.

Alter, your cerebral workouts, challenge your mind with new topics and vocabulary. Just as a runner continually seeks greater speed and strength; seek greater depth and breadth of Wisdom, Knowledge and Understanding. Perform 'strides' to increase your mental quickness in resolving issues, your raw mental speed.

Omaha 1993

My first marathon was scheduled; my entry form and fee were mailed. I anxiously awaited Sunday, November 7, 1993. The race commenced by the Civic Center in downtown Omaha, I lodged at the nearby Sheraton Hotel. While traversing east on Douglass Street in my charcoal grey 1990 T-Bird, perplexity struck. Why was on-coming traffic, in all lanes? These Omaha drivers are nuts, yet friendly. Virtually all were honking and waving! Did they know I was competing in the next day's marathon? This ole farm boy returned appreciation of their fine hospitality.

My peripheral vision noticed a sign" One Way. Fortunately I was only going one-way. Can you imagine those who weave or drive around the block several times as their uncertainty prevents driving one-way?

I enjoyed a good night's sleep despite arriving at the hotel about 11:00p.m. due to a business meeting. Coach Lyle Claussen reminded me of the necessity of attaining a thorough night's sleep two nights before the race. Most people's biorhythms cycle every 2 days. Additionally if one sleeps well this night, the inability to sleep well the night before has no significant effect one's performance. The variety of factors influencing lack of sleep the night before a race includes nervousness about the race and nervousness about oversleeping. The latter creates the greatest stress on my sleep.
- Will the alarm sound at the pre-programmed time?
- Will I hear the alarm?
- What if the hotel loses power?
- What if the hotel loses power and its computers?

The race packets must be picked up on Saturday. Consequently, Brad Sherman stopped in Omaha while returning from attending UNK's regional cross country meet in Brookings, SD, to pickup my race packet. He continued home to Kearney, slept for 3 hours. Brad and Lyle departed Kearney at 3:00a.m. to meet me at the hotel at 6:00a.m. The race started at 8:00.

I eagerly awakened at 5:00a.m. encouraged by Lyle in discussions leading up to the race. He completed the marathon in the 2:20's over 20 times in his career. A coach of his magnitude is thorough throughout the season of preparation the message of preparation, along with proper racing, beginning with the alarm clock, was permanently engrained in our wavelengths of thought.

Once dressed in blue Sporthill running pants and a long sleeve t-shirt over a short sleeve t-shirt, I followed his instructions of drinking a glass of luke-warm water. I pulled a stocking cap over my head and ears and put white gloves on my hands, as I exited the hotel onto the streets of Omaha and into the brisk morning air in the mid-20s ^{0}F. I began slowly warming-up while walking a short distance followed by running strides of 100 to 200 yards in length. The alteration of tempo continued for 10 minutes, then I returned to my hotel room. Wow! My body's expedient call for the restroom nearly required sprinter spikes to enter quickly enough. Lyle said drinking a glass of luke-warm water, combined with a short warm-up, would clean a person out. He was right!!

After a soothing hot shower, I began getting dressed. Shorts were the only racing clothes initially worn. The singlet, racing flats and a dry pair of socks were saved until near the beginning of the race. Dressing included copious amounts of Skin Lube on my feet and in-between my toes and arm pits for chafing prevention.

Lyle and Sherm arrived about 6:20a.m. I consumed a banana along with a bottle of Gatorade, since I wanted something light in my stomach. About 7:00a.m. we began walking / jogging the few blocks to the starting line. Brad previously parked his BMW in a strategic location.

Lyle suggested we warm-up, I was in full agreement with his racing advice. We ran 2 miles, then I ran a few strides – short wind sprints. This loosens up the legs, while enhancing the acceleration of the heart rate. Minutes before the race began, I changed shoes and socks; followed by two or three acceleration runs; reaching just beyond potential race pace. I then removed my top and t-shirt, placing on my singlet. The approximate 28 degree temperature when wearing running shorts and a singlet is lower than my preference by 12 to 20 degrees.

The starter called us to the starting line. A number of participants were running a 10K (6.2M) race; yet began with the marathoners. Shivering at the line, I was anxious for the gun to sound; quickly it did. My first marathon race was underway. I consciously, yet silently, quoted a Psalm, "This is a day the Lord has made, let us rejoice and be glad in it." Many runners zipped by me in the first 2 miles, this is typical in the early stages of virtually all races I run. I passed the first mile in just over 6:15 as planned, continuing that pace for another mile. This seemed very slow, as expected. I then began gradually increasing the pace. Sherm and Lyle drove in Sherm's BMW along the course, stopping every 2 miles providing tips and encouragement.

Between 6 and 7 miles I began contemplating the idea of running, of racing 26.2 miles. Quickly experience reminded me to run a mile at a time; just like the old hymn, *One Day at a Time*. My pace dropped to 5:45. As I approached 8 miles, my body resembled an automatic transmission; while maintaining the "RPM" or effort, I naturally shifted to a cadence of about 5:28 per mile. I now moved into 5th position. This was fun!

As we ran north toward I-680, several friends were along the course, including fellow crop consultants assisting with the race. Near 11 miles and running in the high 5:20s, my quads began burning. The pain combined similarities to boiling water in your muscles with acupuncture. There was no logical reason for my legs to burn at this point in the race at this pace. Lactic acid production exceeded metabolism in the muscle. I immediately rebuked the spirit of fatigue and doubt as I pursued the ultimate goal of glorifying Christ.

The burn dissipated, before returning as we turned west up a long hill through a forest of trees and golden leaves to a turnaround near the halfway point of the marathon. Burning lactic acid returned to my muscles on the uphill climb. The Lord led me to mentally picture screw caps on the bottom of my heels. I visualized the removal of the caps and the lactic acid freely flowing through my muscles, out my heels, and spraying the countryside. I quickly regained strength and comfort. I believe I passed the 3rd place runner on this hill.

Running mile splits in the high 5:20s and mostly 5:30s felt good. I went by Lyle and Sherm at 17 miles where they gave me a shirt to warm my back muscles. The brisk air was less than favorable on my muscles. I was laughing sporadically from 14 to 22 miles. At 22 miles, the laughing abruptly halted. My abductor muscle, on the inside of the thigh, became really cold and subsequently tight. This is also part of the fatigue of running a marathon.

Lyle had educated me on the "survivor's shuffle" sometimes necessary in the last 4 miles of a marathon. Frequently many collide with The Wall at 22 miles. I mentally delved into *focus and concentration*: right leg forward, left leg forward. As I ventured around the outer fence of Eppley Airfield, the few miles remaining required running on faith. Going over a viaduct near downtown, I became irate at whoever placed that curb on the sidewalk we had to step up on. This was the most irrational thought process I ever encountered up to this point in life.

- Why am I running in Omaha, anyway?
- Another curb to step on, this is so stupid, don't people think?

With later reflection, these and similar thoughts during the final 4 miles were hilarious, as any healthy person easily and frequently steps up and down on curbs without thought.

We finished inside Omaha's Civic Center. Before entering, we ran up a monstrous hill. Bob Brindamour, a UNK runner, stood cheering. Bob was known for his strong finishes which I also take pride in and enjoyed cheering the UNK runners to strong finishes. As much as I hurt, I surged up the hill, passing 2nd place then driving with all remaining energy through the finish line. My time was 2:30:25; I *really* wanted to break 2:30.

Figure 18: Finishing my first marathon in 2nd place inside the Omaha Civic Auditorium. November 7, 1993.

Months later when I drove up the final hill, abundant disbelief struck of this minor slope being the same as the 'monstrous' hill at the end of the marathon. The difference in perspective illustrates the state of fatigue in a marathon as well as the power of fatigue in altering our thoughts and perspectives.

Omaha 1994

I returned to Omaha for my second marathon in November 1994. Joe Schumm also entered, although he was far from being in top condition. My parents and sister attended as spectators, mostly staying inside the warm Civic Center.

The temperatures were once again in the high 20s at starting time. I do not like cold weather! Governor Ben Nelson was the starter; he was running for reelection on Tuesday. We stepped to the starting line, once again in shorts and a singlet; the starter's gun was raised. Within 15 seconds the gun should fire, and the race begin. Instead, we stood in the freezing cold, on the line in the ready position for minutes. Ben and his campaign staff were assured abundant pictures were captured at the expense of the runners.

Once underway, defending champion Scott Munson along with a past Olympic Trial qualifier, assumed the lead. I once again started slowly. I drank water at every water stop. Near 15 miles a side cramp entered my stomach from excess drinking. I rarely attain these cramps. Despite my legs feeling good, I slowed to **a** walk by 16 miles. My frustration escalated! I regained composure, reminding myself there was plenty of race left. My self-talk reassured me that I felt good; my stomach was relaxing and my legs became fluid and fast.

I failed to pray, at least passionate prayer. In life, like races, discomfort sometimes distracts us from seeking the real source of inner peace and performance through prayer to Jesus Christ. I walked several hundred yards before returning to a slow run, and eventually resumed just under 6:00 per mile. This pace was much slower than I desired, overall my legs felt good. Of course, they should feel good running this slow.

Once again the cold wind tightened the abductor muscle while running by Eppley Airfield. Somewhere around 20 miles I passed the past Olympic Trial qualifier, running in second with someone on a bicycle by his side the last half of the race. I saw the leader, Scott, yet was unable to catch him. We were both in the survivor's shuffle the final 4 miles. I placed 2nd in 2:32:34, failing a second time to break 2:30. I was upset with myself. Yet, concurrently excited as the next stop was Boston!

Figure 19: I also finish my second marathon in 2nd place inside the Omaha Civic Auditorium. November 6, 1994

Chapter 10:

Boston 1995

VISION—Go the Extra FIVE Miles

Without a Vision, the People Perish
~ King Solomon ~

"Are you crazy?" inquired the man digging out his vehicle keys.

"YES!" I answered to this accusation, one of many times over the past 4 decades. This accusation is virtually always a sign of being on the path towards great success.

"No one should be outside in this weather, much less running speed workouts," replied the heavily dressed concerned citizen.

I have trained in inclement weather on numerous occasions this past winter. Most folks asking are those who care, and yet they lack the understanding of what drives a champion to train in deep snow or double-digit below zero temperatures. Occasionally, I find myself reflecting upon a run on New Year's Day 1995. A 20-mile run was scheduled. However, the temperature was 5 below zero with the wind chill at 30 below zero. Additionally, the depth of the un-cleared snow exceeded the top of my knees! My initial reaction was to decrease the run to 15 miles. After all, it was miserable outside and New Year's Day – both good excuses – right?

Some suggested I not run at all. However, since my first hunch was to decrease the run 5 miles, I chose to increase the run 5 miles. Gratification was tremendous when I completed the 25 mile run in miserable and painful conditions.

"How do you do it?" ask those who seek to understand. Several factors led to what many consider insane behavior. One powerful factor is vision. A vision is rich in its minute details involving all 5 senses. In addition to seeing the vision, one must hear, smell, feel and taste everything imaginable with the vision. An effective vision enables laser focus to tenaciously keep at it.

An effective vision generates emotions including laughter, tears, even shivers down the spine. With an effective vision, your performance hinges upon your desire to create the reality of your vision. This means you either go for what you have imagined or you choose to avoid temporary discomfort - neglecting your vision.

· What is your vision? Your dreams will perish without a vision! With an effective vision in any endeavor you will pass the complacent ones who travel only the 'extra mile.' With vision you will traverse the extra 5 miles, a 500% increase in performance generated by your effective vision. Be ready, you may be asked "Are you crazy?" Because, working toward God given dreams appears crazy to those lacking a vision and settling for complacency. Keep your vision on Christ!

You're Getting There...

As Lyle and I run north in Kearney near 27th Street, he utters his frequently recurring encouraging message, "You're getting there!" 'There' was in shape to run the upcoming Boston Marathon, still months away. Each time hearing this, my mind wondered, *Will I ever arrive? Will I ever be ready?* I set the goal of placing high in the Boston Marathon in 1975.

Some claim wind chill, heat index, footing and storm conditions have little effect on those running or working outside. Did you hear about the guy who says his cattle never get out; he doesn't have cattle. Similarly those denying weather's effect on the body are not outside for long periods of time in extreme conditions.

Even though April 17, 1995 was firmly marked on the calendar, there was no guarantee that my condition would 'arrive,' that I would be ready to run optimally in the world's premiere annual marathon; second in overall prestige only to the Olympics. I trained in faith, belief and trust of Christ and his specifically chosen coach for me, Lyle Claussen.

With my internalized vision and Lyle's reminding me that I was "getting there," my training continued through miserable weather, sore muscles, missed social opportunities, tired mind and hungry body. Frequently, I was sick to my stomach at the end of runs; mentally and physically exhausted. Collapsing in the street following a long, hard run was a common occurrence.

These agonies and inconveniences were an expected and necessary part of the journey. The road to being a good marathoner bypasses 'Comfortville'. In fact, meaningful achievements are eternally absent in Comfortville. The greater the achievement(s) sought the further one must reside from Comfortville. Can you imagine the reaction of other runners, if **you** would have only engaged in a light jog each day, yet expected to run a fast marathon? Any experienced runner would have laughed hysterically.

Pursuing the great achievements of Christ's will for our life will require equal, if not greater, training and consequential challenges of training our body and mind for running. Is there a greater achievement than Christ's will for your life? No! Are we willing to endure severe testing of our body and mind? Are we willing for our faith to be tested to the point that we collapse on our knees? Are we willing to be mentally and physically exhausted in our pursuits? Are we willing to be sick to our stomachs as we wonder if it is all worth it? We expect this in athletics. Do we expect the pain in pursuing Christ's desires for our life? At times athletics and Christ's desires for us are the same.

Are you allowing your faith to be challenged to point of utter physical and mental exhaustion? Is your faith training, like marathon training, causing you to miss various social opportunities? Just like marathon training, achieving Christ's will for your life requires avoiding Comfortville. Avoiding Comfortville while training enabled me to visit Victoryville in racing!

Continue focusing on achieving Christ's will for your life, enduring all of the resulting exhaustion and pain; avoid Comfortville. One day, our Savior will lean forward whispering, "You're ready!" Because you avoided Comfortville in faith; you will be welcomed with open arms into Victoryville.

Monday April 17, 1995 was etched into mind as the date that I would run a terrific marathon. My excitement bounced internally, often displaying externally. Goal #3 from 1975 by the old windmill tower on the farm was placing high in the Boston Marathon. I was finally running the Boston Marathon. Just as I read the entire King James version of the Bible before the 1984 state race, I did so again before the 1995 Boston Marathon.

The Wednesday before the Boston Marathon, my workout consisted of a short run, including 2 miles at race pace. The middle 2 miles in 10:30 felt effortless, as if my body were floating through the air while my shoes gently brushed the dirt of Cotton Mill Trail propelling me forward another 62 inches. This sparked reflection of my early high school days when I yearned to run a single 2 mile cross country race in 10:30. I began the workout at 9:00a.m. CT in an attempt to optimize biorhythm synchronization with the Marathon's start time of 10:00a.m. ET. I strongly desired to run under 2:20, qualifying for the Olympic Trials; and placing among the top 10 Americans.

That evening I stopped by Lyle's office as UNK's track practice finished. We drove to Spaghetti Shop where many of us runners enjoyed all you could eat spaghetti nearly every Wednesday. I held the record of eating 4 full plates following a strenuous workout preparing for Boston. This night, I consumed only 2 ½ plates. While eating and reviewing race strategy, Lyle Claussen leaned forward whispering, "You're ready!" Every nerve, neuron and synapse in my spine danced with joy.

The long, agonizing and sometimes lonely runs in thermometer readings ranging from 118°F to minus 35°F, encompassing all hours of the day; along with by-passed social opportunities were about to pay off.

Saturday morning I flew from Omaha to Boston. I arrived in Boston mid-morning, the airport shuttle dropped people off at numerous hotels. I enjoyed the brief tour of this significantly historic city. As I checked into the Sheraton near the marathon's finish line, a lady behind the desk asked, "Do you need to park your kaaaaawwww?" I asked her to repeat the question, I failed to understand. She then spoke much clearer, "Do you need to park your kawr?"

"No ma'am, I do not need to park my car."

An attorney and marathon participant I met on the shuttle was staying at the same hotel. After checking in we met in the lobby then walked somewhere in the buildings connected to the hotel for lunch. He told of his friend, who ran in the 1994 Boston Marathon, she accepted a cup of apparent water from a spectator during the race. It was Vodka! This story generated instant acknowledgement of only taking water from the race's official water stations during the race.

After lunch I walked over to the race headquarters to check-in and receive my packet, this included the bib number, 199, which also indicated one's pre-race ranking. The packet contained a long sleeve, blue tee-shirt. Former Manhattan High teammate David Pulford previously worked several years for the Boston Athletic Association (BAA) Marathon. While visiting with David a few weeks before the race, he suggested visiting a couple of people in management of BAA. I enjoyed a brief discussion with race director Dave McGillivary.

Saturday afternoon, I ran 3 miles around downtown Boston. The statutes are amazing reminders of the town's history. Admittedly, the inscriptions are difficult to read while running. A trip to Boston is needed as a tourist instead of a runner to enjoy the sites. Slivers of doubt attempted to seep in saying, "Rick, do you really think you can compete in the Boston Marathon?" "You are just a farm boy from Smith County, Kansas. What business do you have running in Boston?"

I immediately rebuked these doubts! I thanked Christ for bringing me to Boston, keeping me healthy and blessing my training, including terrific coaching and training partners in Kearney. Following the light run tour, I rested in my hotel room. I reviewed my workouts, visualized the race and pushed play on my Mental Video Recorder to replay various workouts, training runs and motivational moments such as Lyle saying "You're ready!" as well as first setting the goal to "place high in the Boston Marathon."

While resting, I reviewed the literature in the race packet and pinned my race number onto my *Beta Sigs* singlet. The singlet, blue shorts, purple and white Nike Zoom racing shoes and one pair of thin socks were set aside for Monday's race: the Boston Marathon!

Later that evening I walked to an Italian restaurant, cement stairs descended from the sidewalk to the basement entrance. The wait for seating was nearly an hour. I struck up conversations with fellow runners also waiting. One of those I visited with lived in Florida and worked for Bayer, a manufacturer of agricultural chemicals. We discussed the agronomy business and then discovered he was college friends with my former employer, Mark Kottmeyer. We frequently discover that it's a small world…unless we try to walk around it.

Once seated inside the small establishment, the waitress presented me with a menu full of unfamiliar verbiage. "I would like a big plate of spaghetti with meat sauce."

"I am sorry sir, would you like linguini, or fettuccini, or …"

"I would like the one which most closely resembles a big plate of spaghetti with meat sauce, please."

She named something in her Boston accent, the name remains a mystery; essentially it was gaunt spaghetti.

Back at the hotel I reviewed more of the material in the race packet, stretched and then went to bed. My qualifying time ranked about 75th among Americans. Before going to sleep, I visualized arriving at the starting area and the race's start. I continued visualizing Lyle's suggested splits of the 1st mile in 6:00 and 2 miles in 12:00, followed by passing through 10 miles at 55:00. I then pictured the finish along with various other portions of the race. This followed Congo's advice from the early 1980s. I soundly slept through the night. The following morning I ate a light breakfast of a banana and some raisin bagels.

Brad Sherman also arrived to run the marathon, staying with a friend of a UPS co-worker. He said he would stop by the hotel about noon to join me for lunch. Due to a thorough tour on Boston's subway system after getting on the wrong train a few times (easy to do) Brad arrived for lunch sharply at 2:00p.m. Fortunately, this equated to 1:00p.m. Central Time. He planned to simply run the Boston Marathon for fun as opposed to competing, therefore he visited a few historical markers. Additionally, he wanted to visit Boston Garden, home of the Celtics.

Sunday evening I attended the Marathon's official pasta dinner somewhere on Boston Harbor. Once back in the room, I relaxed knowing I had completed my physical and mental preparation.

Monday morning I jumped out of bed at 6:00, simultaneously excited and nervous. A 20 year dream of competing in the Boston Marathon had dwindled to 4 remaining hours. I quickly dressed in running gear different than designated for the race, subsequently drank my glass of luke-warm water. I then headed onto the streets of Boston for 15 minutes. The return to my room narrowly preceded the cleansing effects of that luke-warm tonic.

Sherm and I met by the finish area where a long line of buses shuttled the 10,000 participants to the start in Hopkinton. The bus ride seemed exceptionally long, leading to spurts of thoughts such as, "I have to *run* all the way back."

Brad and I each brought a bottle of Gatorade and a banana. We followed the crowd to the park filled with runners. We found a clear grass area to sit down, stretch, enjoy our banana and sip on our Gatorade. Restrooms, trees and shelter were scarce; men and women abundantly went to the restroom near trees and buildings. Hopkinton on Patriot's Day epitomized the old phrase, "When you have to go, you have to go."

Running a short warm-up was a challenge due to the multitude of participants. Strides were virtually impossible in this crowd. Brad and I received bib numbers low enough, under 500, to line-up in the first corral behind the elites. Shortly after 9:15a.m. we began walking toward our designated starting corral . We were previously unaware that we had to pass 9,500 people on the sidewalks and streets. Suddenly I questioned our ability to reach our start position by 10:00a.m. when the starter's gun would sound.

We arrived ten minutes before the wheelchair racers began propelling towards Boston. This day provided an ideal temperature of 50 degrees. Which direction would the wind blow? Today we faced a mild head wind. One competitor wearing a race number above 500 stood in our starting corral. Officials asked him to move several times, he refused each time. Eventually, they wrote down his number saying, "You will never again race in the Boston Marathon!" I remain perplexed on his unwillingness to comply with the rules and their requests.

Hearing the helicopters overhead served as a reminder of the magnitude of this major sporting event: *I am in the Boston Marathon!* I wore my white "Nebraskans for Kansas State" cap to the line to keep the sun off of my head. A few moments before the race was underway, Sherm and I turned to one another saying, "See you in Bean Town!"

The starter's gun exploded, the Boston Marathon was underway. As with any race, some people believe they have to look good at the start. Just like life, this often originates from insecurity or lacking the ability to perform well through the finish. My pace felt exceptionally slow. I continued holding back despite others speeding around me. I recalled Congo's ideology: Don't compare yourself to other people because their standards may be too low. Additionally, Lyle continually emphasized starting off relatively slow. David Pulford also emphasized the dangerous temptation to rocket out the first 2 miles. "It's easy to go pass the first two miles in near nine flat if you're not careful."

Due to the dense population of runners on this two lane road, I focused on avoiding tripping. The first mile marker quickly approached, I clicked the split button on my watch, 6:00; the second mile came quickly, the watch read 12:00. Both splits matched my visualizations. Near the 3 mile mark, I tossed my cap into the crowd. Shortly after passing 4 miles, the field thinned enough to allow freely running, striding out without fear of tripping.

The miles swiftly passed as my pace gradually quickened. I began mentally praising the Lord for this day and this race. *I am running the Boston Marathon,* my diligent plan was executed as scheduled. By 8 miles, I was passing many of those who were more concerned about looking good than performing well.

By 10 miles I was rolling, passing the marker in 54:57; missing my visualized goal of 55:00 by three seconds. Shortly after 11 miles, water began sloshing in my stomach as it did in Omaha the previous fall. In an effort to avoid a similar side ache; I quit drinking. Lyle Claussen's last advice to me before I left Kearney, "Whatever you do, drink water through 16 miles." For the first time in 3 years, I dismissed my mentor's advice.

From approximately 10 to 16 miles I was running 5:03-5:08 per mile. I was laughing, especially when I reflected back to Gaylord Grade School and my desire to run a half-mile in 2:30. Mentally, I thought, *Here I am in the second half of the Boston Marathon running a faster pace than I could run for a half-mile in junior high.* I felt much better on the two lane highway toward Boston than I did chasing that calf in the alfalfa field on the river bottom on the farm in my blue jeans and cowboy boots.

I focused on running the tangents through the winding roads of Massachusetts. Frequently, I passed within inches of the spectators. The kids put their hands out to receive a high five, I do not intentionally touch anyone during a race. I read a book about Marty Liquori saying that one loses energy in touching others with less energy. These spectators shout heaps of praise, "You are great one-ninety-nine" or "One-ninety-nine, you are awesome!" Normally I do not speak during a race in an effort to preserve energy. On this day, I responded, "It is not me, rather Christ who is in me," "I can't, Christ can, We are." Along with, "I am nothing without Christ," and "All things are possible through Christ who strengthens you." I was *Running on Faith.*

In this race that I dreamt about for 20 years I was strongly led to break a known rule of competition: Don't talk or minimally if necessary. I felt an overwhelming inner voice encouraging me to proclaim Christ and my reliance on Him that day running in the Boston Marathon.

As I approached Newton Hills, my legs began to feel the burning lactic acid. Since I felt this burn much earlier in my first 2 marathons, my confidence soared despite the discomfort. The more I praised Christ the faster I ran, the faster I ran, the more I hurt. Even though my legs were burning from lactic acid through these hills, my strength remained. I was confident about the remaining miles. At 20 miles I heard someone in the crowd yell, "You are near 30th, 199." The crowd was often deafening, particularly going through Wellesley, where they have an all-girls college. Portions of the course resembled the loudness formerly heard at Kansas State University's Ahearn Fieldhouse during many great basketball games.

As I reached 21 miles and the top of Newton Hills, dehydration began affecting my performance. The Boston Marathon offered no additional water stops until the finish. The risk of receiving Vodka from a spectator far outweighed the benefits of receiving water. Have you ever desired to be temporarily dead? I desperately desired temporary death! I began looking for uncovered manholes to drop into and out of sight. Yet, I gave my word to friends saying, "I am finishing." Goal #3 was permanently branded on my mind. The jam packed, cheering crowd prevented stepping off the course anyway. *Will I die, collapse, or somehow, someway finish?*

My word, my goal, the crowd, my faith in Christ's power prevented quitting. Christ arranged and worked through each of these to prevent my quitting. It was the worst pain experienced in my life, surpassing the pain in the final half mile at Warner Park. Then there was 4 miles, then 3, ... 2 miles to go. I rarely hear specifics in the crowd, today was an exception at times. Amidst the roaring crowd, yet resembling hearing while under water, I heard someone say that I was at the Citgo sign, signifying a mile remaining. Every nerve in my body felt as if it were an open wound submersed in a highly concentrated salt bath. The global burn and immense weakness of my body seemed unbearable. Boiled spaghetti possessed greater strength and stability than my legs. *Right leg forward. Left leg forward.*

My pace had slowed to near 7:00 per mile. This race was nose-diving from a dream to a nightmare. Logic mandated quitting. The voices of discouragement spoke:

- You failed to qualify for the Olympic Trials.
- Many people have passed you these last few miles.
- Your body is below empty.
- Give up, you deserve a break.
- You ran good for many miles, but it is no longer your day.
- Why bother to continue running, it is a wasted effort.

Yet, I recalled the one criterion my parents used to evaluate my performances. "Are you doing your best?" My best is *Running on Faith!* Faith mandates trusting Truth who is Christ, the word made flesh.

I had given my word that I would finish. I had visualized finishing several times. Because our minds are unable to differentiate between real and imagined events, my mind accepted finishing as truth. I must continue running until I collapsed or finished. Finishing under my own power was impossible; I called upon the Lord. "Lord, I need you. I am nothing without you. I can't, you can, we are. It is not me, rather Christ who is in me."

The Lord provided amazing, encouraging spectators and strength! Eventually, I turned onto Hereford St, then Boylston St for the final 3 ½ blocks. Running down Boylston towards the finish line, I thought I heard someone scream, "Rick Meyer!" Was this my delusional imagination? Immediately upon finishing, I was thrown into a wheelchair. While being wheeled through the finish chute toward the medical tent, I look up to see a very familiar face. The fatigue blocked my ability to place a name with a friend. David Schneider, a former teammate and classmate from Manhattan High School walked beside me. David is twins with Dan Schneider. David later served on the medical staff of both the Los Angeles Lakers and Dodgers, once attending a Dodgers game with Tommy Lasorda.

David Schneider M.D. responded to my correspondence regarding the finish on the 15th Anniversary of the 1995 Boston Marathon.

"Rick...that is a very happy memory. I was graduating from med school and went on a trip to Boston to see one of the last basketball games in the old Boston Garden. Because one of my buddy's uncles was an executive at John Hancock I had VIP seats right on the finish line, sitting next to the mayor. And here comes Rick Meyer, one of the top American finishers!! I jumped the barrier and followed you into the med tent. We hadn't seen each other in 10 years, so you were a little shocked to see me (besides being in physiologic shock after crushing the hardest Marathon in the world)."

Initially, the medical tent hesitated to allow David's entrance; I told the staff it was okay, he was about to complete medical school. I believe, based on later comments, I even expounded that he was married to Wendy. Evidently I viewed that as making the difference in his admission to the tent. Inside the tent, a nurse placed a thermometer in my ear, my temperature was very low. A reporter from one of the Boston papers interviewed me sometime during my examination. The nurses suggested I drink broth to warm up.

Mumbling in exhaustion I asked, "What is broth?" They patiently explained it is the juice in soups. My temperature remained exceptionally low despite consuming a bowl of steaming hot chicken broth while wrapped in blankets.

David Schneider returned to his friends, it was a pleasure seeing an old friend away from home, following a brutal race.

I complained about the thermometer continually probed in my ear. "Don't you have other options?" One of the 5 nurses, all in their mid-twenties, responded, "Yes, we do have other options. Would you like to roll over?" I mumbled, "You can continue placing the thermometer in my ear." Options provide healthy perspectives.

The nurses announced my severe dehydration mandated an IV. I hate needles! A few of the gals tried to offer comfort as some guy jabbed my arm with a needle as if he were in a dart throwing contest. I screamed due to the pain and dislike of needles; an immense television camera captured the moment from few feet away from my face. The staff informed me that I was the first finisher requiring an IV. The ladies found humor in my screaming disdain of needles. They still stood around my cot, trying help me warm up. I began wondering if I had died and gone to heaven.

The IV bag emptied, yet my temperature remained low. Subsequently they connected a second IV bag. I was oblivious to any other race participants in the medical tent. Hours later, I was released from the medical tent. While departing, the Boston journalist who interviewed me earlier stopped by, "You're still alive!?" I think I ruined his story of a Midwest runner dying after the race.

David Schneider letter continues: "My favorite memory...that night after the Celtics game, I walked back through that huge public square to see the race results posted on dozens of mobile classroom chalkboards, lined up as far as the eye could see. I walked all the way to the first board, and there on the top sheet of paper on the board was your name, along with a bunch of East Africans!! YOU STUD!!! Not bad for the son of a corn farmer from Smith Center, Kansas."

The race was not a complete failure, as I believed the last few miles. I placed 47th overall and 10th American. I achieved one of my goals. When circumstances and discouragement tantalizingly scream for you to give up, perhaps your hope, dreams, energy and bank account are running on vapors, Run on Faith, call upon the Lord. He will provide the vision, encouragement, strength and all necessary resources for you to finish and achieve everything His will desires for your life.

Once I returned to hotel and showered, I called my parents, sharing the results. They responded, "That is nice. Did you do your best?" I did my best in proper physical training, listening to my mentor, reading and internalizing the Bible, praying, setting goals, visualizing, surrounding myself with top achievers, and effort. I failed to do my best in just one area. I failed to respond to my mentor's wisdom of, "Whatever you do, drink water through sixteen miles."

Are you doing your best in training, reading and internalizing the Bible, praying, setting goals, visualizing, surrounding yourself with top achievers and effort? Are you responding to all of your mentor's wisdom? Considering our talents and wisdom improve daily, our best tomorrow will be better than our best today.

Sherm left a message wondering about my whereabouts. He finished about an hour after I did, failing to see me around the finish area as we planned. I took a taxi to Cambridge where he was staying. His friends said the fare should be about $6.00. I mistakenly told the cab driver that I was from Nebraska; the drive took much longer than anticipated, costing $20.00. I was literally 'taken for a ride' by the taxi driver. I hold no grudges, as he will either repent to Christ and be forgiven; or be held accountable if he fails to seek Christ's forgiveness. The same is true for everyone, including you and me.

We were both hungry. Despite this hunger, my stomach remained queasy. A good hamburger, as usual, did the trick. My disappointment in the race was virtually as deep as the nearby Atlantic Ocean. However, Sherm and his friends told the Bostonians whom we encountered of my 47th placing; their reaction suggested I did okay.

The following day I stood waiting for my luggage at the Omaha airport, when someone asked if I had run the marathon, my name and where I was from. "Yes I ran. I am Rick Meyer from Kearney."

"Oh, we read about you in the Boston paper. You are the idiot who quit drinking water after 11 miles."

"Yes, that is me." I refrained from asking where they placed. Evidently referring to me as an *idiot* instead of a *guy, person or runner* empowered their ego. I ran this distance in training runs many times, and in much warmer weather, without needing water. Effort creates thirst. When *Running on Faith*, we thirst for Christ. The more intense we run for Him, the more we need to drink from His word, the Bible, prayer, worship and fellowship with other Christians.

I ran 2 additional marathons in 1995, finishing in the top 30 at the Twin Cities Marathon in Minnesota, and winning the Ponca City Marathon from Arkansas City, KS, to Ponca City, OK. Twenty-eight days separated these marathons of 2:27 and 2:24. The former presented starting time temperatures around 30 degrees. The latter temperatures were in the mid-20s with a 10-12mph head-wind. I stayed overnight with one of my former teammates from Cloud County Community College, Kenny Kaiser, and his family in Augusta, KS. Ken accompanied me to the race. After arriving at the starting line in a small park on the south side of Ark City, I ran a few strides. I then remained in the car with the heat on due to the cold temperatures and lack of shelter in the park. Just before the start, I stepped out the car for a few more strides in my racing flats. I then walked to the white line painted across the road representing the start. Once on the line, I stripped down to my singlet and shorts. The starter fired his gun and I began a slow jog. Surprisingly, I found myself in the lead which is unusual for me at the start.

Additionally, the race director informed me the race included two 5-man relay teams of collegiate runners. Consequently, I mentally prepared myself to run behind them for at minimum the first half of the race. Both teams' lead runners remained behind me, quickly losing contact. I continued running what felt like 7:00 pace up a gradual slope, even though I expected to run 6:00 pace for the first 2 miles. The course contained no mile markers, and the first kilometer (K) marking appeared at the 5K. You can imagine my surprise when I glanced at my watch seeing a 5K split of 16:20 (5:16 pace). "Wow, do I feel good!"

The State Patrol or Sherriff maintained several hundred yards in-between their car and me as we proceeded down the highway. I engaged in my continual focus, concentration and prayer mode as the miles flew by. I recall stepping over a dead armadillo along the shoulder of the highway, the first one I recall seeing other than in pictures. We reached the northern edge of the first town near 12 miles. The patrolman pulled over, his escorting services ended here. I continued through town. I greatly appreciated those who lined the streets to cheer. Upon reaching the south end of town I encountered the course's first questionable intersection. The pavement continued south as well as to the east and west. You do not look at street signs when racing a marathon. A girl generously volunteering to help with the marathon stood at the intersection wearing an orange vest. I looked to the east, west, and straight ahead, "Which way!?"

"I don't know."

"Which way!!?"

She sheepishly shrugs her shoulders, "I don't know."

"Straight!!?"

"I guess…"

I maintained my 5:10 to 5:12 pace while running straight south, the same direction as I had run for the first 13 miles, observing crops on both sides of the road through my peripheral vision. After 300 meters I realized this road dead ends. I quickly turned around, running an approximate extra 600 meters. The race director sat in a car at the intersection profusely apologizing. I rarely become truly angry. I was angry. Do you ever become enraged? If so, what causes your anger? With hindsight, I was wrong for allowing this anger. I failed to remember that when we run to glorify God, we do so regardless of whether we achieve *our* goals. Also, allowing anger in my body opposed my previous positive attitude, relaxed muscles, overall joy and the resulting physical benefits. Shortly after this I began feeling slight fatigue for the first time.

Near 15 miles Ken Kaiser pulled beside me in my Thunderbird and asked if I wanted any Gatorade at the next water station. I drink only water during races. I suggested he mix a cup with half water and half Gatorade. He sped away. It is illegal for anyone on a bicycle, in a vehicle or running without an official race entry to pace a competitor. If Ken had driven by me for very long, the race officials could rightfully disqualify me. When I approached the aid station he handed the concoction to me. I folded the wax cup in half once followed by an additional fold. Former marathon great Benji Durden shared this technique with me two weeks earlier while visiting at UNK's conference cross country meet in Golden, Colorado.

The beverage went down smoothly. Several minutes later, I felt effervescence in my stomach and throat. Without additional warning, Gatorade spewed from my mouth, spraying several feet in front of me. Have you ever attempted to vomit while running 5:10 pace? Not to mention in the second half of a marathon. Not pretty...unless you count the colors in the eruption. Perhaps you now have a new task for your bucket list.

I quickly returned to praying for continued strength. I should have also prayed for inner-peace and a forgiving heart. The bitterness continued, causing my body to slow more than it should at this point in the marathon. Judy Gibbs of North Little Rock, Arkansas, once stated on stage at a business conference in the early 1990s, "You either become bitter or better." My selfishness induced in-grown eyeballs led to my becoming bitter for several miles after the mishap.

Despite my slowing down, I continued a competitive pace through 24 miles where I encountered a long uphill with a respectable slope. My legs began screaming during the climb, running that mile in approximately 6 minutes. My energy levels and leg bounce quickly returned once I conquered the final significant hill. The last mile was inside the city limits of Ponca City, Oklahoma. The final stretch consisted of a long gradual slope. I knew from spectators that I simply needed to finish to win. However, I also knew that my dream of qualifying for the Olympic Marathon trials would once again fall short. Despite the lack of motivation, I felt strong while crossing the finish line of white paint surrounded with a chute inside of cinder blocks with rebar posts inside holding colorful flag ropes.

Meyer Smashes Course Record

By FRED HILTON   "It's a psychological thing when   coln, Neb., was third in 3:01:26

Figure 20: The headline from The Ponca City News, Sunday, November 5, 1995.

Figure 21: Crossing the marathon finish line in Ponca City, OK. November 1995. Photo Credit: Kenneth Kaiser

The first collegiate 5-man relay team finished 20 minutes behind me and the 2nd place individual finished in 3:01. My body shivered from exposure to 25 degree temperatures for the last 2.5 hours. And my leg fatigue resembled a typical Sunday long run. With the exception of the 13th mile through a metropolis and the last 2 in Ponca City, the course followed a rural highway with occasional cheering at the aid stations. Unlike my previous marathons, I was able to walk, talk and stand during the post-race interview. I was tired yet not exhausted. I visited with several cordial locals at the finish who graciously came out to watch and support us runners. I later received a thoughtful note and the local newspaper article with the above headline from a gentleman whom I visited with along with his daughter.

The momentary bitterness reduced my body's efficiency. A powerful reminder that bitterness towards others, even if only momentary and even if justified, damages our efficiency and productivity. Yes, intense disappointment poured over my heart and mind for the next several days. I then began the slow process of regaining perspective. Regardless of our results, God expects us to focus on only serving and glorifying Him. His wisdom far exceeds ours.

New York 1996

My sights were now on goal #4 from June 1975: placing high in the New York City Marathon. I was training injury free since the spring of 1994. The power of God's word is astonishingly real! By his stripes we are healed. My specific goal consisted of running under 2:15, finishing in the top 15 to top 20 overall and first American.

In February, the celebration of my 29th birthday encompassed running 29.99 miles Monday evening after work. The run was miserably cold and at times mundane during the 3 hours and 20 minutes of slow running. I lacked my normal mental focus that night as I first ran 3 circles of the 8 mile loop around Kearney; followed by the 6 mile loop. I rounded my mileage down to assure running 29 on my 29th.
I continued increasing my speed with weekly hill workouts through April. I had difficulty running for a few days before realizing red meat inadvertently escaped my diet creating an iron deficiency. Normally, I consumed 1 to 2 pounds of beef daily.

In mid-April, I was completing about 1,000 daily crunchers of various types. One night while staying at my sister's home before a race in Grand Island, NE, I began getting severe cramps and perhaps Charlie Horses in my abdominal muscles. The previous few days I had challenged myself to 1,250 crunchers. Beginning at supper through the following morning, standing straight and sleeping were difficult. I won the 10K in 32:08, treating the race as a tempo-run workout.

A month later on May 25, 1996, Dee married Brian Isaacson at American Lutheran Church in Smith Center, Kansas. I drove to Gaylord, KS that morning to run a moderate 16-mile training run to complete the first 100-mile week in preparation for the November Marathon. I ran the first 10 miles north, west and south of Gaylord averaging 5:40 to 5:50 pace. With 6M to go, I headed east on Hwy 9, turning south at Hager's. As I passed the end of the sidewalk at our old farm exactly two miles later, I clicked my watch split: *11:02*. Out of nowhere, I instantly recalled setting a goal in 1982 to run that 2M stretch in 11:02--about 30 seconds faster than my fastest 2-mile at the time. We left the farm in 1983. I never did put that goal in writing. I made a U-turn and was so excited about hitting and remembering that goal that I stepped-up the pace a little for the next 2 miles, running miles 14 thru 15 in 9:37.

I then recalled my excitement in junior high when I first ran that 2M stretch without stopping. Whatever your goals, internalize them and keep plugging away! After the run, I showered at Aunt Charlene's in Smith Center before their afternoon wedding.

The weekly miles in mid-May began a rotation ranging from 105 to 135; Lyle Claussen reduced my speed workouts to 2 per 10 days. These included running short intervals such as quarters (12 @ 70 seconds) or 8 x 900 yards uphill intervals; and a longer interval such as a steady state run or repeat miles. Non-speed days consisted of 8 easy miles in the morning before work. After work, I typically ran 10 miles in 51:00 to 54:00 minutes with the last 2 miles under 9:40. Whenever fatigue set in I stepped up the pace while repeating a phrase that I originated in the early 1990s; "Bite off more than you can chew, then chew it." I then ran 10 x 250 yard sprints up and back on B Avenue near Kearney's Good Samaritan Hospital. These hurt and often caused queasy squirming in my stomach each evening, yet I was having a blast! Yes, daily activities form permanent habits which produce lifetime achievements.

Sunday runs ranged from 20 to 28 miles mostly in the gravel hills in the countryside surrounding Kearney, with the average pace usually around 6 minutes per mile. After the first three or four miles, my mind often soared into creative galaxies. Ideas flew in from different dimensions, with each piece fitting perfectly together to form even greater ideas. If only I could permanently etch these thoughts on a hard drive as they developed. I commonly ran the final 2 miles under 10:00. A cool down walk followed each run. The sprint then began, entering the house at 8:15a.m., showering, dressing in a suit, jumping in the car, tying my tie while driving 6 blocks to church, consuming a Dr. Pepper and honey bun. I frequently walked in about 8:28, two minutes to spare. Once seated, standing for hymns, liturgy and walking forward for communion seemed difficult tasks. Larry Neihardt often asked me to help with offering or fill-in for a missing usher.

The first week of June was a 120 mile week completed in 6 days, followed by weekly mileage of 107 and 120. On this third Saturday of June, I ran the race described in the foreword. The last week of June consisted of running 135 miles. The final 15 miles on Saturday morning were painful at times, mostly from dull aches. Overall, I felt good. I strongly desired to run 140 miles the following week. I was feeling good and wanted the proverbial feather in my cap for this achievement. As usual, I asked Lyle what I should do for workouts, expressing my desire for 140 miles. He strongly recommended running 80 miles for the next 3 weeks. Once again, I expressed belief in my ability to run 140 miles the following week.

Lyle reminded me the training of increased speed and endurance is on target. "You have really pushed your body the last six weeks. We should take three weeks off; so let's only run eighty before elevating mileage for two or three cycles."

My mistakes of ignoring Claussen's advice in the early 1990s, remained illuminated with distinct clarity. I listened this time! Do you and I learn from our mistakes of ignoring God's advice spoken through scripture?

The following Saturday I completed my first 80 mile week, running on a sandy beach along the Gulf after a business convention in Mobile, AL. The rest proved mutually beneficial for the mind and body. Roughly, midway through the second week, a few minor tweaks in the tendons and ligaments served as excellent reminders of the importance of strategically placed rest.

I returned to weekly mileage rotations of 85 to 105, with intervals twice per week. The long runs also alternated with 20 miles one Sunday, then 25 to 28 the next week. The 20 mile Sundays provided a nice mental break from the demanding regiment.

Training was going well; the goals remained challenging, yet possible. I was mentally and physically ready for the tapering when October arrived. Grandpa Kenneth Kahrs passed away on October 21st, I visited him in the hospital a week or two before. He asked me to massage his cold, sore hand: I gladly obliged. I briefly reflected on the circle of life. Here lies a man, who along with my grandmother, lovingly raised 6 children, 17 grandchildren. It was now Grandpa's turn to receive care from his descendants.

I arrived in New York City Thursday afternoon, with the race on Sunday. Dan Schneider, a Wall Street attorney, instructed me to take a cab and the fare should be $20 - $25. I stood waiting for a taxi at the airport, a lady who flew in to watch her daughter run invited me to share a Limousine for an upfront fare of $20 each. Naturally, I accepted the offer. We first reached her destination in Queens.

Dan and Giscella Schneider graciously welcomed me into their Manhattan home a few blocks from Central Park. Giscella worked in marketing for Ralph Lauren, while Dan traveled to Wall Street. I read and focused on the race. Watching Seinfeld became even more humorous once in New York. I ran in Central Park on Friday as part of my routine marathon preparation. I then visited the New York Public Library to pick up my race packet. Olympic great Carl Lewis was present for marathon participants to meet. I had no desire to stand in line. I was in New York in pursuit of goal #4, placing high in the New York City Marathon.

Whenever asked about my race expectations, I responded as long as it was not too cold or much of a wind I expected to run under 2:15. After committing my training to the principle "What you say is what you get" by Don Gossett for 2.5 years, I am unsure why I made such a confession.

Sunday morning arrived; thermometers measured the New York air at 26^0 F, with 10 to 15mph winds. Dan awakened as I dressed for the race, suggesting I wear a garbage bag over the top of my gear for wind protection. There was no pre-shower run this morning. I wore only my racing flats on the bus to the starting line, any clothing at the starting line remains on through the finish line, or permanently donated.

I no longer recall whether I took a taxi or subway for the 2.4 miles from Schneider's to the New York City Library. After the 20 minute wait for a bus at the library in the frigid temps, we began the voyage to the Staten Island starting line. At moments, the ride appeared dreamlike. This goal of 21 years was near achievement, the preparation was physically and mentally brutal. Once again, achieving this goal possessed greater priority than the numerous declined social and professional opportunities. What price are you willing to pay to attain your God given goals; His vision and will for your life?

On the long bus ride to Staten Island, discouragement and doubt began speaking,

- Rick Meyer, you are a bow-legged farm boy from Gaylord, Kansas; what are you doing in New York City to compete against the world's best?
- You are in New York City; this is anything but Kearney.
- Do you really believe you can average running 5:07 per mile for 26 miles 385 yards, 2 ¼ inches?

Discouragement and doubt increased. I then reflected on Dan Schneider's simple powerful message in many conversations over our 13 years of friendship: Rick, agriculture is the foundation of our economy. Do not let anyone tell you any differently! Of course, Dan is correct. An economy absent food is soon absent. What is an economy without people? Effectively, New York City's economy would tumble absent agriculture!

I also reflected on a message my dad continually emphasized, "As a human being, you are no better or worse than anyone." Certainly, our abilities, direction, efforts, mentors, faith, persistence and vision separate our achievements, punishments and rewards. God creates everyone, in that we are equal. Do we respond in faith?

Years ago, a speaker spoke in reference to someone less fortunate, "There but by the grace of God, go I."

Initially I struggled to agree before focusing on the discussion in Romans 9 of God raising up people for different purposes. I pondered on another verse where people asked Christ about a sick boy: Which parent sinned to cause this sickness? Christ replied that neither the parents' or the son's sin caused the boy's sickness, rather that the Father may be glorified.

In other words, the Father chose the sick little boy as an evangelist. How is God using your life for evangelism?

My optimistic voice began speaking:
- Rick E. Meyer, you are a child of God.
- Christ is in you; you have continually studied the Bible.

- You received this goal and vision 21 years ago to achieve today.
- This is a day the Lord has made, let us rejoice and be glad in it.
- You are fully capable of averaging 5:07 per mile or faster.
- Focus and concentrate.

I cogitated on running on faith being a step-by-step decision. The human body lacks being a machine where one simply pushes an On button and automation takes over. When the mind and body are fresh, perhaps belief of automation exists. Yet, the greater the fatigue, the greater our awareness of decisions such as 'right leg forward,' 'left leg forward.' Similarly, when our finances and relationships are healthy, most decisions occur 'naturally.' When challenges arise, we consciously ponder each decision: What is best?

After a long bus ride we eventually arrived at Staten Island, we exited the warm bus into the brisk November air. While walking between the buses and the fence to a gate to enter the pre-race area a cup of coffee set on a post spilled onto my right racing shoe. The coffee's temperature lacked being a factor, yet the wetness was a huge factor. My foot quickly transformed from dry and warm to wet and cold. I did bring extra socks for the race, however the shoe remained my only option.

No inside shelter appeared available, we sat on the open grass field. A few 'elite' runners were provided shelter and a normal change of clothes before the race. I attempted to warm-up, however the crowd density proved a challenge. Eventually, I found a building with unlocked doors. I entered, finding several other runners inside stretching and preparing mentally for the task ahead. Warm shelter and out of the wind proved quite comforting. Other than my wet foot, I felt terrific. I chose to avoid dwelling on the foot, rather accept, focus and concentrate.

We began working toward the start area. The final hour before a race is often a Catch 22 because one is excited about the race, yet knows of the mental and physical efforts required to achieve success. Any worthwhile goal requires one being on their knees, at least spiritually, crying, "Lord, I need you! I am nothing without you!"

As we proceeded to the starting line, I slowly progressed forward. Some runners were pushing and elbowing; I slipped by and around them. I stopped once I reached the NYPD runners forming a line in front of my position, directly in front of the New York Police Department runners were the 30 'elite' runners. I stood less than three feet from the starting line of the New York City Marathon consisting of 30,000 runners.

I briefly reflected on being among the last chosen for playground teams, rightfully so; and now stood virtually at the front of the start at the NYC Marathon. A few feet to my right were long-time race director Fred Lebow, nine-time champion Grete Waitz, NYC Mayor Rudolph Giuliani, manager of the New York Yankees Joe Torre, and Olympic Gold medalist Carl Lewis. Each kept their remarks brief, they knew the event was about the runners as opposed to their presence. Carl Lewis said that everyone here today could say we beat Carl Lewis. He could probably lap me in the 100 meter dash, and his long jump exceeds my triple jump.

As with all major races, I visualized every possible aspect of this race. Once again, I recalled Congo emphasizing the first 5 steps of the race. Both he and Claussen taught to run within your ability, until the last one-fourth of a race. Hundreds of competitors instantly passed me; this is a common illogical occurrence. As Congo said many times, "Don't compare yourself to other people, their standards may be too low." I avoided comparing myself to these runners. Who are you comparing yourself too? Do they share or exceed your standards of Godliness, faith, excellence and integrity?

My cadence felt as if I would pass the first mile in 7:30 or slower. I preferred to err on the side of caution, run within myself. If I did cross in 7:30, I knew I could easily gain the 1:45 in the next 25.2 miles. Crossing the mile mark, I heard "5:45," precisely as I visualized in race preparations. Hitting the desired and visualized split creates excitement and confidence knowing the race is starting properly. Additionally, the pace appeared to be a slow cool down jog.

I relaxed since the crowd density thinned to allow striding out. New York's streets were drastically wide city streets compared to the two lane roads in the Boston Marathon. Two million spectators lined the sidewalks. The second mile was 5:15, slightly faster than the 5:30 preferred.

Soon I was running with a Kenyan wearing bib #4, a pre-race rank. Within 2 miles we were running 5:00 to 5:10 pace, feeling very comfortable. Dan and Giscella Schneider stood near 8 miles, as we passed Dan attempted to run ahead for another picture. He was unable to catch us. Dan was the only person I trained with and never beat in a race. He was once less than 100 yards of running a 1:48 indoor half mile when his hamstring snapped. Dan could run!

We kept rolling through the streets of New York. Dan and Giscella jumped on a subway to their next spot to watch, Dan also made an occasional call to Congo providing an update on my position and pace.

A gentleman wearing bib #40 joined us for several miles, I believe he was from Ireland. We neared a water station (located every 1 ½ miles), running on the outside of our three abreast group, I was certain to miss water this time. Since another rehydration opportunity would be available in 2,640 yards, I chose to continue running abreast rather than dropping back for a drink. Most marathons position their aid stations 3 miles apart.

As we passed the station to our right, #40 grabbed a cup of water to pass to #4 who passed it me, #186. Number 40 accepted a second cup to pass to #4, before taking a third cup for his well being. The Ireland and Kenyan understood world class competitors run faster together than separately, thus keeping us hydrated enhanced achievements for all.

Additionally, this illustrates the second greatest commandment of loving others as you love yourself.

- In your quest for world-class achievements, are you willing to lovingly enhance the performance of those who God has placed beside you in your Run on Faith?
- Are you willing to share a drink from Christ's well, the water quenching all of life's thirsts?
- Do you, like the Irishman, assist others before yourself?

The latter is easier professed than lived for this author.

I passed the halfway mark in 67:47. The Kenyan and Irishman fell off the pace either shortly before or after this point. Prerace visualizations and goals were reaching the half marathon in 68:00, running negative splits. I was 13 seconds fast, since the second mile was 15 seconds fast, all else unraveled as planned. Are you visualizing your desired results?

Fatigue arrived as anticipated in the form of a dull ache throughout my body. My body metabolized the lactic acid at the same rate as production. I ran through this type of muscle burn many times. Lyle told of a marathoner he once trained with on occasion, whose legs went numb at the halfway mark on his way to a 2nd place finish in a classic Boston Marathon. The wind chill was near 10^0 F this November morning, colder than I preferred while running in shorts and a tank top.

Running through Harlem, gang members lined the streets cheering for us. I later jokingly told Dan, "Those gang members were friendly, I may go hang out with them tonight." Dan's friend, John, who also participated by walking and running told of an older lady saying to him, "Sonny, ain't nobody walk in Harlem."

I passed several top runners who were now walking, and those who simply slowed their pace. All through the race I continued praying, thanking Christ for this race and the ability to run. Once again, confessing numerous times, "Lord, I need you. It is not me, rather Christ who is in me. I can't. Christ can. We are."

Unbeknownst to me at the time, I passed Dan and Giscella at 16 miles, later learning I was in 36th position and moving up. My training prepared my body and mind for a strong remaining 10 miles. A few miles later, a Charlie Horse developed in the right calf. During the previous 31 months, the origination of any type of soreness or potential injury resulted in an immediate confession of healing. "By your stripes I am healed. Lord, I need you. Thank you for healing this…"

In contrast, this moment I responded, "Lord, I don't want to bother you in asking for your healing power. I can handle this myself with my powerful mind you gave me." Less than 6 miles from completing the best race of my life, I strongly contended for Idiot of the Century. Few actions are more idiotic than professing success is achievable without the Lord. As Kent Frieling later suggested, the Lord probably hardened my heart to use in glorifying the Lord by later sharing the results when choosing *self-confidence* over *God-confidence*. Absent Kent's explanation, I am baffled as to why I allowed this lapse in faith after 31 months of instantly turning to the Lord. This further strengthens my belief in Christ as the one who supplies our faith; perhaps he did desire to remind me how little I am without him in every aspect of my life.

Was my self-reliance a product of arrogance? Do we as a nation, as Americans, believe we can achieve success without Christ? How do we attain world peace; except if the world seek, worship and praise the Prince of Peace, Jesus Christ? Confession, repentance, forgiveness, faith, power, healing, hope and love are staple ingredients of peace.

I continued running, the Charlie Horse persisted the remaining 6 miles. Normally, 2 minutes of a muscle cramp is bountiful pain for me. Finishing was the only option; I was achieving goal #4 as written on my mind by the old windmill tower on the farm. Running down New York's Seventh Avenue, I faintly heard several Frank Sinatra songs and the typical marathon sideline entertainment of *Rocky* theme songs.

We entered Central Park; the knotted calf muscle remained excruciatingly painful. Each mile marker now appeared as if they were 5 miles apart. Aunt Ruth Douglass passed away in September, I could hear her advice spoken with a smile hundreds of times during my life, "You just keep putting one foot in front of the other." Despite the pain I was experiencing, it was mild compared to her pain of being in a covered wagon burying her young sister along the trail near Gardiner, Montana, in the early 1900s. A short time later her mother died. About 13 years later, he only fiancé died. Yes, Aunt Ruth understood the wisdom in continuing to place one foot in front of the other. She ran on faith her entire life. I too must continue running on faith, putting one foot in front of the other until the finish line was crossed.

Why was I running in New York's Central Park with a knotted muscle in the right calf, when I could have stayed in Nebraska? What makes these streets so special? These two thoughts danced across my mind like a rock skipping on the river. My lower right leg despairingly begged to cease forward motion. It would be a good excuse. How many of you have ever had a Charlie Horse in your calf muscle? The knotted-up muscle is excruciatingly painful. I reminded myself of the prestige of running one of the world's most respected marathons. I remind myself of all the miles spent preparing and accumulating the price soon to be paid. I am a finisher! We attain pride in finishing tasks, despite opposition. Internal opposition is often greater than external. The entire body aches, including an intense burning sensation of tired legs and arm muscles. The mind fatigues itself from powerfully focusing on the pace, strategy, competitors and accepting the pain.

I lost a high finish along with a fast time, to falling back to an 86th place finish and 12th American. I later spoke on the phone with my parents. They responded, "That is nice. Did you do your best?"

They never demanded I answer them, rather engage in self reflection. Despite the pain, choosing to stop would have been less than my best. Some question why I continued running with the Charlie Horse in my right calf. In addition to achieving goal #4, and keeping my word in saying I would finish; other factors were at play. What kind of example would I set for others if I dropped out? What kind of example do I set for myself in future undertakings? I continued because I refused to give myself the option of stopping during training runs, the price accumulation phase. I ceased from quitting during training runs when my body cried out in agony. We reveal our character to the world each time we choose to persevere or quit when facing adversity or disappointment.

Sometimes the agony resulted in fatigued legs or a cold body. The coldest temperature was 70 below zero (Fahrenheit) wind chill; the actual temperature read 35 below zero in preparation for this race. Other times the agony was dealing with a fatigued mind from the immense effort of maintaining mental focus.

In life, the ache of our physical body during the daily routine may be different compared to running a race. However, the mental focus in life is every bit as rigorous as in a race.

Figure 22: Rick Meyer and Dan Schneider in the U.S. Capital in the presumed position of Thomas Jefferson's inauguration. April 2011

Post New York

My friends encouraged me to date more frequently, especially during the summer of 1996. Yet, working full time and running up to 135 miles per week, in addition to active involvement in church; left little time for a social life. When I did date, my focus remained on my training. Those of us lacking natural physical talent, invest more in focus and discipline. Those who combine talent, focus and discipline are legends in their sector.

During the summer, I committed to date after achieving goal #4, placing high in The New York City Marathon. I fell short of my specific goal. After gaining perspective, I considered placing 86th overall and 12th American as 'placing high' out of 30,000 competitors.

In June, I met a young lady at church, some of the church women told me about her, moving to Kearney after graduating from seminary in Chicago. I called her twice, once asking her for a date that evening, another time for the following night. Can you believe she turned me down both times? Theresa and I began dating in February. I chose to discontinue running in pursuit of our relationship. We married in December 1997.

1999

By the spring of 1999, after three years of little running, my weight ballooned from 150 to 190. Running was no longer fun, I firmly believed the days of running 20 miles in less than 2 hours were over. I made a decision to improve my fitness to avoid potential health challenges. Slowly, I began running; yes it was slow. Gradually the weight began declining.

During the summer of 2000, some of my 20 mile runs were once again completed in less than 2 hours. I was elated! Less than 12 months prior to this, I was struggling to run 10 miles in 70 minutes. In October of 2000, I finished among the top 30 runners at the Twin Cities Marathon in Minnesota.

Staying Power

Do we have the emotional staying power of remaining on task morally when life's secular success looms if morality is left behind? Do you possess greater desire to please God than attaining worldly success? Matthew 6:33 "Seek ye first the Kingdom of God and all else will be added unto you." Abraham sought to serve and obey God; he acquired great wealth after he left his homeland, his comfort zone. Are you willing to leave your comfort zone, permanently?

This approach is also effective in fundraising, as proven at Gull Lake Ministries. Daniel Wallace accepted the executive director position in 2004; leaving his former director position at a camp near Tyler, Texas. Gull Lake Ministries has had its significant challenges, but with their focused and prayerful efforts, Daniel's committed team has seen a renewal take place in the guests, programs and finances.

Last week, I was privileged to visit my former Manhattan High cross country teammate at his Michigan family camp and conference center. I was traveling from a seminar in Lansing, MI, to one in Fort Wayne, IN; Daniel's time was limited because 600 ladies were descending on the conference center the following morning. The 90 minutes we visited were priceless; as it is anytime one is catching up with longtime friends. We reminisced about our commitment to teamwork, giving our best and winning against odds. Daniel used to tap our sternum with his fingers, passionately saying, "You gotta want it."

Figure 23: During another brief business trip to Michigan. Rick Meyer and Daniel Wallace catching up in Kalamazoo, MI. October 2015

Daniel provided a tour of the magnificently picturesque Gull Lake Ministries campus, including the 52,000 sq. foot ministry center built 2 years ago. Donations allowed the completion to be debt free in Michigan, a state suffering from the horrific economic downturn over many years. Moreover, Gull Lake Ministries now enjoys healthy attendance throughout the year and a vibrant ministry serving churches, families and other non-profit organizations in this pristine lakeside setting.

Is Daniel is a great fundraiser? Contrary to secular logic, Daniel readily admits fundraising is not his passion or a great talent. Daniel's focus is ministry! The Gull Lake Ministries' staff assists people in attaining knowledge of Christ and deepening their relationships with Christ once they know and believe. Focusing on fulfilling their purpose for existing has, by God's grace, met real needs for people for over 90 years, which in turn has sustained their existence.

Daniel's passion is to do his best to live out Matthew 6:25-34. He seeks first God's kingdom and righteousness; knowing in faith, all else will be added to all associated with Gull Lake Ministries. Daniel and the entire Gull Lake Ministries staff readily acknowledge that any success is entirely due to Christ's generous blessings.

Do you, like Daniel, have the passion to minister Christ's love and Biblical truth to people? Focusing on and obeying Christ brings His blessing and peace which surpasses all understanding; providing everything you need to achieve Christ's will for your life and ministry.

Are you in financial, spiritual or emotional debt? Do you feel as if you are stuck in a bad situation? Minister the pure Word of God to those placed in your path. Seek Christ first, all you need will be provided with abundance to irrigate souls with Christ's love, forgiveness, mercy, compassion and Word. What is possible through Christ in your life and ministry?

Speaking Faith

Why do we hesitate to speak, act and run on faith? The reasons vary, we are attempting to appear humble, we want to provide an out, an excuse if we do fail; or we simply lack belief. Regardless of the surface reason, our lack of bold faith is lack of faith. We lack faith in believing others will like our Holy Spirit led boldness, our insufficient faith doubts God's voice spoken to our hearts. We question, "Did I really hear God's voice?" We lack faith. Our deficient faith promotes doubt, prompting unbelief. Deficient faith and belief prompts hesitation; we fail to act quickly and boldly.

Imagination

Albert Einstein once said, "Imagination is greater than knowledge." Why is there such power in our imaginations? Imagination allows us to see the possibilities. Imagination is the beginning of the transformation from a thought to a useable item or idea. Since all possibilities fail to fall into moral and ethical possibilities, an active imagination is best for society when the one imagining is able and willing to filter out any image outside the moral and ethical boundaries.

I specifically and intentionally leave out the boundary of legal. The legality of an issue may change from one year to the next, while morality is nearly always constant. Driving 70mph is legal on one highway but illegal in the next. Morally driving 75mph depends on the location and driver's skill and weather conditions. Driving 75mph through a school playground is morally wrong. Driving 75mph on an interstate with a speed limit of 75mph is both legal and moral. Riding in the back of a pickup used to always be legal, now it is illegal in most places. Cheating is always morally wrong! Great imaginations require increased responsibility of understanding right and wrong. The best way to attain this ability is actively pray, as well as the consistent, continual studying of scripture. Laws are simply guidelines set by politicians. Are politicians always moral and ethical?

How do we attain an imagination? Most of us have an active one as a child, and then it dissipates as reality infiltrates our minds. Imagination is similar to a muscle, built with use. How do we build our imaginations? To be a great imaginer, think, prepare and respond as a great imaginer. Associate with those who have an active imagination. Listen to their thought patterns, their ideas. Ask them how they developed their imaginations. Read books about great inventors and innovators.

As a child we once traveled to Denver with my parents where we visited relatives. Also Dad attended the Four States Irrigation Council annual meeting. At least once on this journey, I remarked while driving through western Kansas and eastern Colorado, "There is nothing out here." Have any of you ever made or heard a similar comment? Dad asked if I saw the barbwire fence and the old dilapidated house that looked as if it could fall over at any moment. I agreed. Dad inquired if I thought those structures and fences had always been present. Of course not. One time this entire area was also open range, cowboys and Indians.

He then invited my sister and me to picture in our minds the people building the barbwire fence.

- How many people helped?
- What was the weather, hot, cold or just a sunny day when they dug the posts in the ground?
- Was the ground dry and hard?
- Did recent saturating rains or snow fall, loosening the soil?
- Did they dig the postholes by hand?

He then challenged us to shift our imaginations to the home. We laughed as we looked at the old small house with no windows and perhaps a hole in the roof. We could hardly conceive of this being someone's home. He and Mom reassured us it once housed a family. We imagined the people, who chose this spot to build a home.

- Was it a bachelor, or a married couple with children?
- If kids – how many?
- Imagine their attitudes!
- Did excitement fill their hearts when they began building?
- How excited were they when finished?
- Did they host family dinners for Easter, Thanksgiving, Christmas?
- Picture the relatives walking in carrying food, perhaps a cherry pie – my favorite.
- Imagine the kids running around the yard with their cousins.

The questions would continue because our imaginations fell into overdrive; the miles passed by quickly.

Today I listen to movies and I picture the orchestra. I see trucks and speculate about the drivers, their families, their communities and the cargo.

Imagination – Possibilities

What is possible? With God nothing is impossible! Are we willing to hang onto God's hand? Write down your wildest dreams. Are they congruent with scripture? Do they help others? Any image we create consisting of sin should be immediately deleted from our minds. If this or any evil image returns, ask God for a mental fire wall, preventing images of any sinful activity.

Consistently inquire: who, what, when, where and why. This visit to Colorado in 1978 was the week of the "Orange Crush" of the Denver Broncos playing the Dallas Cowboys in the Super Bowl. Paul and Karen's son, David, was 4; he was as inquisitive as I had seen. On one of the days which my dad did not have meetings, we drove to Winter Park to go sledding. We did not leave until mid-morning, after a big breakfast. My parents enjoyed this leisurely start to the day. I was more like John Wayne, "We're burning daylight!" Eventually we loaded the sleds, and the 7 of us left for a day of adventure. We stopped several times for pictures, once by a huge boulder. Rather ironic, huge boulders just outside of Boulder, CO! David continually questioned the camera's physiology. As soon as an adult satisfactorily answered and explained, he would think for a while, then proceed with a follow up question: How does the camera work? How does the film work? How do they get the picture off of the film? Why do they use film? David went on to graduate from Colorado School of Mines in engineering. He worked for some time in Tokyo; he continues to be a successful engineer today. Most of us will not pursue a degree in electrical engineering like David. However, if we want to engineer the best life possible for ourselves, such as the life God desires for us, we too must ask questions, followed with *more* questions. Do you possess a raging, internal fire of desire for knowledge?

Imagine perpetual possibilities. If an event occurs, what are some possible scenarios, followed by possible scenarios of the possible scenarios? Why do many of us fail to do this? Maybe it is because engaging our brain requires great effort. I readily admit engaging the brain hurts. We can have fun with this whether by ourselves, in an office, traveling, exercising or any other activity. If we are with others, we can make a game out of it, allowing the possibilities to spiral skyward as we brainstorm. The only limits are morality. If you are unaware of existing technology necessary for your possibilities, brainstorm on various advancements for this to become reality. Keep a journal whether written, drawings, voice recording or a combination. If driving, drawing and writing are probably not the best options for record keeping. Just in case you did not already know that. Excuse my dry sense of humor.

Ask what occurs behind the walls in buildings, under the floors, above the ceilings. Here we find wiring, plumbing, heat and air ducts. What goes on underneath the soil surface? What are the microbes doing and why? What types of soil 'critters' do we find in this environment? Where and how do they attain their life-giving energy? Is tillage good or bad for them? Do these microbes thrive in wet or dry conditions? Will a new agriculture advancement help or hurt the soil life in the long term? What does the soil structure look like? How does it compare to other soils? Even if soil lacks an ignition of excitement in your mind, stretch your imagination, creating possible answers and solutions. Remember – we all rely on healthy soil in order to eat every day.

Traveling

While traveling ask yourself or discuss with fellow occupants why this highway was built here as opposed to a few miles in either direction. Why were the towns located at their specific location? If it is because of the location of the railroad, inquire why the tracks were laid there. If it is due to a river, examine the landscape, pondering why the stream flows as it does. Every river has a flood plain; can you see its boundaries? Concrete and steel now cover the plains of the Hudson River, we can still estimate where it first existed. Observe the surrounding vegetation in an attempt to decipher the time of any past floods. How far in the flood plain did it progress? Imagine being a settler on a horse or with a wagon. Imagine settlers seeing the storm clouds brewing in the distance, rolling in their direction. How would your perspective change?

I recently drove north in eastern Nebraska, 5 miles north of the Platte River. The highway left the flat plains, ascending into rolling hills. Several farmsteads rested on top of the first hill. Initially, one may wonder why they chose the higher altitude, thereby subjecting their homes to brutal north winter winds. However, the realization of the flood plain below answers the question of location. Did the river run along that hill at one time? Is it possible? What caused the rolling hills to the north? Possibilities include glacier deposits or windblown soil.

If the river did run adjacent to this hill at one time, when did the flood occur that changed its course? How many times has the river relocated due to flooding? Let your imagination soar. Grandpa Kahrs invited me to ride along with him one day in the late 1980s. I climbed into his 1987 Pontiac 6000 four-door car. As typical of my grandfather, his seed corn cap tilted slightly up and a few degrees to the right. We drove down to a 60 acre field on the south side of the Republican River. He drove his car in the field; fortunately all the gates were open. If a pasture gate was too tight, he used his car bumper to loosen the wires and if necessary, he bumped the gate post. Driving through the corn stubble, the noise of the stalks rubbing the underside of the car sounded as if water ran underneath the car. Once in the middle of the field, he stopped. We exited the car, examining the soil. *Yes, he carried a shovel in his car!* After he bought this piece of land, he said he believed he just bought land that he already owned. Is that a unique paradox? His childhood home lay directly a half mile to the west. He and my uncles owned the land along the north side of the river. The 1935 flood generated an 8 foot wall of water roaring down the Republican River Valley for hundreds of miles. This caused a re-routing of the river channel. The channel shifted to the north several hundred yards. Legal descriptions for land along the river read everything on the north, south, east or west side of the river within these parameters. This shift in the channel shifted ownership of the land. When observing nature's landscapes, imagine the perpetual possibilities.

Radio

When listening to the radio, allow your mind to picture the broadcasted events. Difficult tasks promote growth. Picture the message. If this causes embarrassment or you hope your child does not picture these events, then change the channel or turn off the broadcast. If describing your mental picture to your parents or grandparents embarrasses you, discontinue listening. Use your imagination to picture the singer as if seeing them in concert, along with the musicians, guitar player, drummer and the soundboard operator. How many times did the singer record this song before releasing for production? Why did the songwriter write this song? What sensory inputs amplified inspiration in this song? What inspired the song? What location inspired the song? Why did the vocalist agree to sing this song? Did someone else reject this song, and why? What are the possibilities?

While listening to the announcers, visualize the events they discuss, if you do not know the specifics, imagine various possibilities. As always, use moral discrimination. While listening to a ballgame, picture the players, their colorful uniforms. See the lineman making the blocks, the backs making the cuts. Imagine the linebacker blitzing, the safety breaking up the pass, the defensive tackle creating a pile to plug the hole in the line. Imagine the outfielder running for the magnificent catch.

As a kid on the farm, I listened to Dev Nelson announce Kansas State basketball games while I worked in the hog barn. Kansas State won 10 regular season Big Eight basketball championships in the first 17 years of the conference. I pictured in my mind's eye, Tim Jankovich, Rolando Blackman, Tyrone Adams, Randy Reed and Ed Nealy running Jack Hartman's offense. I could picture them rotating, passing the ball, and Jankovich putting on a dribbling clinic. This was exciting basketball in the pre-shot clock days. Then Dev Nelson would describe the spread offense, suddenly Rolando Blackman would burst toward the bucket with Jankovich, Adams, Reed or Nealy hitting him in stride with a perfectly thrown pass. I visualized their white uniforms or light purple when on the road. My imagination saw the black or yellow of the Missouri Tigers as they battled for the regular season conference championships.

We continually have opportunities to cultivate and increase our imagination. We simply use our surroundings. Our mind, our imagination, is the same as our muscles: employment increases strength and efficiency.

Imagination - Music

Do you notice the background music while watching TV shows or movies? Sometimes I hear the music distinctly, other times I fail to recognize the music as my emotions fluctuate; anxious one moment, gleeful the next. I ask myself, "Self, why do I feel this way?"

Ironically, as I write, Rush Limbaugh plays Manheim Steamroller's *Silent Night*, a tradition on his show before Christmas. This song played by Chip Davis, instigates a flood of Christmas memories. The imagination shifts into overdrive. I see a reflection of all of my relatives who sang *Silent*

Night in Christmas Eve worship services throughout their lives. I see my grandparents, aunt, uncles and dad; who are no longer living. But because of that "silent, holy night, when all was calm and bright as our Savior was born," they are in heaven with that very Savior. I pray for those with hardened hearts, unable to satiate their hurts and fears, because of their blindness to Christmas. I pray this will be the year their hearts; their eyes open to see Christ our Lord. Sadly when people squabble over the recognition of Christmas, demanding to bury it amongst the holidays; they announce their hardened hearts. As Christians we should not feel anger towards them, rather we should compassionately pray for them. I pray the naysayer's heart may be illuminated by the brightness of Christ, receiving a calm heart. Christ does silence our fears with his holy presence, brightening our hope, allowing us to remain calm in the midst of life's storms.

Listening to these songs allows our imaginations to soar. We can reflect on family dinners of past and anticipate family dinners to come. Do we take for granted the presence of each person at the table? Regardless of their age we are given no guarantees of their future presence, or of their future presents. (A little humor is necessary.)

Humor

Family dinners with cousins usually results in painful laughter, especially if told by master storyteller Bruce. His humor results in virtually everyone engaging in uncontrollable laughter. Additionally, Bruce's hysterically humorous messages are pure truth. He once told of his brother Don wanting to throw feed into a pen of boars. For those unfamiliar with hogs, boars and hospitality are polar opposites. Bruce the older, assumed to be tougher, brother; grabs a 5 gallon bucket of feed from Don. He adamantly tells Don, "This is how you feed these boars. They are not going to bother you!" Bruce steps over the 3 feet tall hog panel onto a cement slab. Bruce marched over to the feed trough, and poured the feed. Bruce was correct! The boars did not bother Don: however they did perform a hog's version of liposuction on Bruce. After pouring the feed, a boar clamped down on Bruce's posterior. Even though he never ran the hurdles in track, he cleared the fence with ease and respectable form. Factoring the cost of stitches and a tetanus shot, the hog's liposuction remained less expensive than visiting a cosmetic surgeon.

Wavelengths

The wavelengths of music connecting with the wavelengths of the molecules constituting our eardrums, powers us to alter our emotions. All chemistry boils down to wavelengths; matter comprised of energy, comprises wisdom. Chemical reactions depend upon the specific properties of the chemicals involved in the reaction. Our thoughts are chemistry, the wavelengths of sound are chemistry; consequently we often experience various emotions hearing the same sounds at different times. Equally, two people next to each other may experience different emotions when hearing a song. When speaking at a Memorial Day ceremony and seeing the Veterans standing while *The Star Spangled Banner* plays, my eyes begin to leak.

Conversely, when I stand by Veterans at ballgames, unaware of their past while our National Anthem played; the emotions are less than at a Memorial Day service even though I experience deep respect for America. At times I imagine the battles as described in various books, realizing the full impact of battle from those who participated. When hearing the National Anthem, once again the emotions begin to boil over with deep gratitude for those who served our great country. On the other hand, someone lacking appreciation for the freedom we enjoy in the United States may react completely differently when hearing *The Star Spangled Banner*. Their connection between this song and freedom is absent; therefore their chemical reaction is different than other Americans. Visual connections create emotions based upon their meaning, and the interaction of the meaning with our thoughts.

Christians see a cross as a symbol of Christ dying for our sins. Mathematicians may see it as simply a plus sign. Every person to ever walk this earth may be forgiven if only he accepts Christ's invitation. The meaning of a cross creates powerful emotions for Christians. The cross itself did not die, nor rise. The cross does not supply the forgiveness of sins. The cross simply reminds us of how and why Christ died. Consequently, the cross should only contain symbolic religious meaning to Christians. Mathematicians view + as a component of an equation. Many criminals died on the cross throughout history. Anyone who truly believes that Jesus lived as a normal person will live unaffected by the cross. This leads us to two possible reasons the presence of the cross is bothersome to non-Christians.

1. Their conscience battles God's invitation. God has revealed to them the significance of the cross and Christ, but they reject the message.
2. They detest Christianity and Christians.

In athletics, the offense drives down the field toward the goal, or tries to drive in runs. The defense attempts to stop the offense. The defense only reacts when it competes against a more powerful offense. When overpowered by the offense, the defense becomes the victim.

Dad was in Saudi Arabia for 7 months in the mid 1980s. During his tenure, Ramadan, the Muslim holiday of prayer, occurred. Dad described watching an old man with a cane beat people who failed to pray properly. Is this a peaceful religion? The Saudi's lacked concern about offending my dad or other Christians. Dad felt no offense because their religion possessed no power over him. His power came from the Lord Jesus Christ residing in his heart. I, like Dad, feel no offense at other religions or religious practices. The Holy Spirit resides in me. There are no forces in existence, eternity past, present or future, equal to or more powerful than Jesus Christ and the Holy Spirit.

Consequently, when I allow Christ to control my life, nothing offends me. Nothing overpowers Christ who lives in me. Those offended by Christ, whether by seeing a cross, a nativity scene or hearing a prayer or Bible story simply confess the power of Christ over our sinful nature. Being offended by Christ admits our desire to fight Christ, rather than submit our souls to him. Yes, I find myself disappointed and saddened by various statements and symbols but not overpowered. I am deeply saddened by those who fail to recognize Christ as their Savior. I am deeply saddened by their actions, my sympathy pours out to them; however, sympathy alone is powerless. My prayers go out for them and I pray their hearts will soften and their eyes open. I pray the blind may see Christ and their soul's dependence on our Savior. I pray, they too, will run on faith in Christ.

Imagination - Objects

While driving down the road, I see a truck full of electrical line poles. An ice storm on New Year's Eve of 2007 in Nebraska left many without power, some for days and others for nearly a month. Thousands of poles needed replacing, including some enormous steel poles. The ice accumulated up to 2 inches in diameter. Electric company officials say this added 28,000 pounds to the load of the poles!

A few months before this storm, we visited the state of Washington. We saw numerous loggers and logging equipment. In fact, we spent a few days at the home of a retired logger. Upon seeing these trucks carrying these poles, my imagination began to soar. Where, specifically, did these poles come from? What is the landscape of the area? Did a bear, moose, deer or elk rub against this tree? Who are the people associated with the logging company? Do they have families? What are their interests beyond logging? What are the interests and challenges of the truck driver?

We may ask these questions of any piece of lumber or object. The miles pass by rapidly as we exercise our minds. Our friends in Washington also have a rock quarry. When viewing a building in the downtown of a city, inquire about the rocks. What is their origin? Who are the people responsible for mining those rocks from a quarry, then down the road to the place where they end their journey? Use perpetual imagination.

Think Inside the Bible

My grandparents rode in the front of their 1948 Ford pickup, while my dad and his 5 siblings rode in the back, underneath a tarp. Once or twice a year they journeyed to visit Dad's grandparents in Johnson, Nebraska. This was a 193 mile journey; one way. Dad told this story about 7 months before passing away. If I had known Dad would be gone in 7 months I would have been more inquisitive. The Bible says we do not know what tomorrow will bring. I did respond to my belief that travel was slower in those days. Dad just laughed, "You should know better of your grandfather." Grandpa did not waste time traveling down the road: reports reveal he drove around 80mph on this voyage. All 8 in the vehicle remained healthy and safe during those trips.

Unfortunately, some suffered injuries caused by someone acting stupid: sometimes just a plain and simple accident. We now live in an "it is not my fault" society. This society originated in Eden with Adam and Eve.

The 'it is not my fault society' is full of immigrants from the village: "I am too lazy and complacent to think for myself."

My grandparents thought inside the circle of Christ, inside the Bible, by finding a way for all 8 of them to travel together to family reunions. Others of their generation were also proficient in this practice. The only boundaries are those in scripture. Those boundaries are absolutes! I saw an advertisement on the web with the line "nothing is black and white." Wisdom, knowledge and understanding enable us to see in black and white. When black and white becomes clouded over with gray, we need to put on our lenses of wisdom. Since we possess limited wisdom, there will be a new, further distant point of blurry gray. God possesses all wisdom. God says if we need it just ask. Since God knows everything, he sees all is black and white. For those unaware, God is pure white. To say there is no black and white, proclaims that God is not white, and evil is not black. White is pure unless stained with black. Is God stained with the black of evil? NO! Jesus did become completely black when he accepted responsibility of the sins of all who ever walked this world. However, he defeated evil, death and our sins. The world became pitch black for several hours. Which proves evil is black. If Jesus is not pure white, then he failed to conquer sin. What does scripture say? Does scripture say Jesus defeated death and sin? Was God pure white? Yes! Consequently black and white exists.

White is light: Jesus says he is the 'light of the world.' This is why the world was without light, and dark, for a few hours upon Jesus' death on the cross. As an artist pointed out, light illuminates all of the other colors we experience. Unfortunately, there are those who are colorblind, unable to observe or appreciate the rainbow, the setting sun, the green spring foliage and the colorful autumn leaves. Aside from those who are visually colorblind, there are also those who have colorblind souls. Why? Read the 9th chapter of Romans for starters. Those with colorblind souls fail to see God's presence and blessings intertwined with every aspect of their daily life. Before the rest of us become too proud, we must remember that even those who see color visually also vary in their range of recognition. For instance, I see red, yellow, blue, purple, green and maybe a few other colors. On the other hand, those with more cones in their eyes sees magenta, marigold, cornflower blue, aquamarine, periwinkle and plum, pistachio pudding green, cedar tree green and the 'dog threw-up green.'

Our souls are similar to our eyes; we each vary in our range of recognition. When we lie, exaggerate, cheat, steal, gossip, lust and engage in sexual activities outside of a man and woman's marriage we live outside the circle of Christ. We live outside the boundaries of God's existence. Upon exiting the circle, we also exit out of our relationship with Christ. When we accidentally dangle our legs over the edge, or fall out of bounds, we must quickly apologize to God and return to the field of play within the circle. Christ suffered death and won the battle with his resurrection because he knew we would fall out of bounds too often. The Bible says God chooses us to play on his team. Why does he choose us? Romans explains this is beyond our understanding. If we intentionally walk off of the field, we are on our own at the mercy of evil. Does God welcome us back into his circle? Yes! Several parables illustrate this idea. There are other parables and illustrations which show if we exit the circle by leaving the field of play to return to the 'locker room' because the game is over, our souls are out of luck. We must be on the field when the final horn for our game of life sounds. Unlike an athletic contest, we do not know the stage of the game we play. Each of us receives different lengths of games. This is why is it vital to remain on the field, inside the circle of Christ, where our thoughts reside. So do our actions.

Just like the repenting criminal next to the cross of Jesus, some will live their entire lives outside the circle, only to join the field of play in the last minutes or even seconds of their lives. The Bible is also clear that an "intentional choice" of this strategy will fail. In other words, at the moment of this awareness we should sprint to join Christ's salvation. Would it be wise or foolish to purposely postpone resolving a customer's complaint until they sat in the parking lot? The customer who knows you were capable of offering a quicker resolution, will avoid you while taking their business to someone else.

Conversely, if you are unaware of an existing customer's complaint until he ventures on his way to your competitor; they will probably listen to your apology once you gain awareness.

How does 'Thinking Inside the Circle of Christ,' or 'Thinking inside the Bible' increase possibilities? Remove all interior walls, barriers. The only boundaries are those we discussed previously, and crossing those boundaries will be devastating. The devastation may be immediate. Devastation may be delayed for decades, but it will occur. Knowing all things, moral and ethical, is possible, but what holds us back? Mental, physical and spiritual ambition enables each of us to explore. We must be willing to submit to God: pride prevents submission. Humbling ourselves before the Lord allows God to pick us up in his arms. Imagine a child on a crowded street or in a crowded store. Everyone is at least twice his height. His, or her, view is limited because he cannot see over the people. When the parent picks up his daughter, she sees as the parent sees. Instead of having a limited view, she now becomes aware of the vast space around her. When God picks us up, we too become aware of the enormous possibilities. We arc also able to better understand directions and are able to recognize the boundaries as we approach them. God lifts us up saying, "Go in this direction. Stay inside this area. Those boundaries are there for a reason." God then sets us down, still holding our hands. We set off in the direction God shows us. Obstacles appear in our paths. This is okay, because we know more lies beyond this area even though we cannot see it on the ground. We maneuver around the challenges, and then we come upon a border. We stop; we remain on this side of the boundary. God still holds our hand in his, clasping firmly. We become so over-whelmed by the view outside of the circle.

Humility

We must ask with a humble heart. Examine the leper and the centurion (Matthew 8:1-3 & Luke 7). The leper and the centurion ask in faith. The example in scripture shows our requests based on faith leave out any foolish statements such as "look what I have done…" or "I promise to do…" if you grant me this one request. Christ does not give because we deserve gifts rather he gives out of his abundant love. This love includes telling us 'no' or 'later' sometimes.

One October day, I met one of my fraternity brothers and his family at the Henry Doorly Zoo in Omaha. Danielle, an intelligent, observant and vibrant 9 year old girl, ran from exhibit to exhibit. She placed her face against the glass containers with deadly snakes; Danielle then told the snake she believed it was beautiful. Danielle also ran up to the see the Siberian Tiger saying, "Daddy, Daddy, you have to get me one of these." Everyone in the area burst into laughter, admiring her enthusiasm and boldness; then placing their eyes upon her dad, Wes, waiting for his reply.

Wes simply responded they would not purchase a Siberian Tiger or any of the poisonous snakes she also requested.

Danielle's request came with a humble heart. She did not claim she deserved any of these creatures as gifts, nor did she make any promises if she received any of her requests. She asked in faith, knowing her dad was the provider for her needs. Wes and Heather, being good parents, did not make any plans for granting her requests for these dangerous animals as pets. They denied her requests because of their love for their daughter. They know snakes and tigers may be appealing as pets to a youngster, yet she did understand their potential danger nor the logistics of keeping these animals in a safe place. It is possible Danielle will own, or care for, all of these critters when she is older, if doing so is legal. Perhaps she will attain a degree in zoology, or attain the knowledge to properly care for tigers and snakes.

Fortunately, God also denies our requests for Siberian Tigers and poisonous snakes. In our ignorance we do not recognize the danger of what we ask. God also delays our requests until we have the maturity and the education to properly handle our requests. Just as receiving a tiger or poisonous snake could easily be deadly to a child.

Friends Do Not Let Friends Live Complacently

Just as it is dangerous for friends to let friends drive drunk, allowing a life of complacency is equally disastrous. The devastation of drunk driving is often immediate, while complacency is a slow death.

My Uncle Doug Kahrs, along with his brothers, Bill and Jim, and my grandfather bought another farm along the Republican River. A creek enters this farm on the south, draining into the river on the north end of the property. A dike, made decades before, prevents creek floodwaters from entering the fields. Uncle Doug decided the dike needed lowering. Upon seeing Uncle Doug on the dike with a tractor pulling a scraper (dirt-moving equipment) Grandpa Kenneth raced to shut down the excavating project.

This was the early 1970s; after a great deal of soil conservation work remodeled the countryside. New terraces and ponds, along with better tillage practices were developed across the area. Uncle Doug, like most people at the time, believed the end of drastic flooding from creeks had arrived. Grandpa Kenneth was an eye witness and rescue participant in the 1935 flood along this same river. This river extended hundreds of miles from western Kansas through southern Nebraska back into northern Kansas, all the way to Kansas City. He knew the question of floods was "When," as opposed to "If," the next one would occur. Grandpa also knew floods arrived with little warning. Grandpa Kenneth instructed Uncle Doug to leave the dike alone, it would be needed the next time a foot of rain fell in the drainage basin of the creek.

Twice in less than a month, two 11 inch rains fell: both times the flood waters rose to the top of the dike. Boundaries lie in place from our forefathers for a reason: they remain as the accumulation of past experience, revealing our forefather's wisdom. Some damage occurred from the floods with the dikes in place. Imagine the devastation if the boundaries were nonexistent!

Uncle Doug also shared a story of removing an old fence between their property and a property they rented from another landowner for many decades. With the fence removed, farming on the ends and along the edges of the fields proved much easier. The fence provided obstacles to machinery when working the fields. Grandpa Kenneth once again gave Doug "an ear full," as described by Uncle Doug, for removing the fence. The fence provided the boundary of property lines. Grandpa Kenneth told Uncle Doug they would not always rent from Jess Sr., and the original agreement did die with him! Decades after removing the fence, the property sold to Hank who then sold it to Ben. (Hank and Ben are both fictitious names to protect the guilty). Hank lied to Ben about the property boundaries, because no fence remained. Ben attempted to claim Doug's property since no boundary line existed. Uncle Doug quickly remembers the "ear full," he received from his dad who was also deceased. A great expense for surveying finally settled the dispute.

In life, little good results from removing boundaries. Proverbs warns against removing the property boundaries set in place by our forefathers. More dangerous than removing physical boundaries established by dikes and fences is the removal of the boundaries of right and wrong as established by scripture. Disaster awaits all of us when removing physical or spiritual boundaries.

As my dad told me innumerable times while growing up on the farm and even later, "There's a reason for that!" Have you ever heard this line from your parents or grandparents? I, like Uncle Doug, become completely aware of my dad's wisdom and my lack of wisdom. If time allowed, I would sit and listen to Uncle Doug and others like him for hours. They share the wisdom of their 70+ years of life. Will I learn from the Uncle Doug's of the world, or will I view their wisdom as outdated? Choosing the latter will certainly result in defeat. The same is true for all of us. Time proved Dad right, despite my complete blindness when initially instructed. The Bible is clear when stating the foolishness of God, far exceeds the greatest wisdom of man. God's boundaries in scripture may completely exceed any of our comprehension. However, to remove or ignore God's boundaries is exponentially more damaging than removing a fence or a dike. The consequences of God's boundaries reveal eternal effects.

During my second year of serving as a summer intern with Central States Agronomics, I worked one Friday afternoon in late May checking a corn field belonging to Warren Batie; the famous actor is unable to claim a relation to our Warren. Warren and his son, Don, owned and operated a farm and ranch outside of Lexington, NE. My boss and I were scouting for weeds and general crop health. I began walking across the 40 acre field as instructed. Wanting to assure extra effort, I walked all the way over to the farm house on the field's east border. The farmer in the yard waved while looking at me reluctantly. I then circled around to complete my loop across the field. This field seemed larger than 40 acres, probably because I was beginning to get tired.

When Mark and I eventually met to write the field reports, he inquired how far I walked across this particular field. I proudly told him I went all the way to the farmhouse on the east boundary. He complimented my wonderful notes, before showing me the field boundary. In my eagerness, I missed the field boundary. This field and the neighbor's field border one another, lacking a distinct marker in the middle. If my head would have remained up and in the proper direction, the post on the field's end would have been easily seen.

Our boundaries become blurred and intertwined when we let our head and eyes settle downward. Boundaries are easily detectable when our eyes are up, fixing on Jesus.

Mark, like Grandpa Kenneth with Uncle Doug, quickly forgave me once I apologized and sought to correct my errors, learning to keep my eyes up. Fortunately, once we apologize for removing boundaries and for being unable to see boundaries; Jesus quickly forgives our errors. His mercy and grace are exponential compared to wonderful people like Grandpa and Mark. Study scripture, learn the wisdom of your elders, seek wisdom from the Holy Spirit, and keep your eyes up on Jesus. You will recognize boundaries, and receive God's love even when you make mistakes.

Chapter 11:
Activities For Permanent Habits/Lifetime Achievements!

Activities are words or actions directed by our thoughts. Everything any of us does or says begins first as a thought between our temples. Success occurs one thought at a time. Henry Ford once said, "Thinking is the hardest work there is. That is why so few people do it." At the beginning of my presentations, I often have the members of the audience turn to their neighbors stating, "You are only six inches from the greatest achievements of your life," followed by, "I am only six inches from the greatest and safest achievements of my life." Look in the mirror; tell yourself you are only six inches from the greatest achievements of your life: the six inches between your temples.

Family Changes

June 2005

In the latter part of June 2005, Dad and Mom drove 165 miles to visit us at our home in Leigh, NE. They arrived Saturday morning. Since this was their visit during warmer weather, they wanted see some of the greater area around Leigh. Eventually, we ate lunch in Fremont, afterwards drove by the new large Catholic Church. The doors were unlocked, we entered. Several people were setting up for a wedding later that afternoon.

In an effort to avoid being a burden we quickly took our tour of the church. A hospitable lady approached offering us a guided tour. Dad commented that his right knee was sore from an apparent slight twist while mowing a couple of days earlier. The lady either had experienced a similar injury herself or knew someone who recently underwent successful treatment. She and Dad traded knee comparisons, she continued offering helpful advice. We made a few other stops throughout the hot afternoon with the temperature exceeding 100 degrees. Dad limited his walking compared to normal because his knee continued being sore. At 67 years old, concern was virtually non-existent. He would go to the doctor, who would perform the necessary tasks for repair and complete recovery.

Thursday September 1, 2005 I awakened at 4:02; my body and mind refused to return to sleep. Eventually I went to my office to read, and go on dial-up internet. Dad left a message at 5:28 saying that my Grandma Emily Kahrs died about 4:00. Her passing was a blessing. My cousin Tamra played piano music at the funeral including *Blessed Assurance*, that song adequately describes Emily Kahrs. She quietly lived caring for her husband, children, grandchildren and the community.

In September Dad's knee was operated on. Following surgery, the swelling in his knee and ankle prevented him from wearing cowboy boots. Dad wore boots all his life with the exception of participating in athletics. He also stopped working. For the first time in his life, he was unable to work outside. The previous 6 years we went pheasant hunting together the first Saturday of December. There would be no hunting with Dad in December 2005. I remained optimistic for December 2006. He was challenged to maneuver in church for his sister, Berniel's, funeral, where I was honored with the privilege of reading the eulogy.

He began seeing Dr. Brad Rogers in Kearney. Brad attended First Lutheran Church in Kearney where I had been a member while living there. No medial explanation for his lack of recovery was given. During one of these visits in May or June 2006, Dr. Rogers handed Dad a piece of paper with I Thessalonians 5:18 written on it, "Be joyful always; pray continually; give thanks in all circumstances, for this is God's will for you in Christ Jesus."

On a positive note, Brian and Dee announced they were expecting twins, due December 1, 2006. Towards the end of July, we made travel plans to attend a wedding on a ranch in the Couleville National Forest in Washington State. We were excited, we had planned to vacation in Washington for years. Due to the distance and our schedules, finding time seemed difficult. This time we made a commitment to visiting and attending.

I knew he would be healed, and we would hunt together again. On August 20, 2006 Dad turned 69; the age at which his oldest brothers, Irvin and

Wally died; Uncle Irvin from a stroke and Uncle Wally from dementia. On Wednesday August 23rd Theresa was driving home from meeting parishioners in Columbus when she lost control of her Mazda, spun around to hit a guardrail before flying down a near vertical embankment. The car was totaled! A few things went wrong, while innumerable things went right. The most significant right was her escaping injury.

Days later, we drove to Franklin to stay with my parents prior to attending Uncle LaVerne's funeral. Dad and I, like so many times, sat in the vehicle and visited while Mom and Theresa ran into Mom's work place. We continued our conversation once home, before Dad finally saying it was time for bed.

Once at the church the following morning, we placed Dad in a wheelchair for the funeral. Following the funeral, we drove from Osborne, KS, to York, NE, to serve as greeters at Darren and Jennifer Barker's wedding. We were excited about our trip to Washington in mid-September, she wanted to visit her friends and show me the countryside and natural attractions. She kept a countdown of days until departure. I too was excited to visit an area I never previously been. We said things such as, "I/We can't wait to go to Washington." Have you ever made similar statements? The day for departure finally arrived! We drove to the Omaha airport and flew to Salt Lake City. I saw a tee-shirt promoting polygamy in one of the airport stores; I thought it was a joke; evidently, polygamy is a sincere message for some.

The flight from Salt Lake to Spokane was mostly after sunset. However, raging forest fires appeared as large camp fires from approximately 36,000 feet. On our drive from to Wilbur after landing, I prayed that our time in Washington would be filled with joy, while moving very slowly. Amazingly, both components were answered. I looked forward to sharing our trip highlights with Dad.

The night before returning to Nebraska, my mom calls saying Dee was in the hospital and may lose both twins. I prayed with more passion and energy than ever before. I begged both twins be saved, "at the very least let one live, Lord!" I praised and thanked the Lord in advance for the blessing that at least one and preferably both would be safe.

September 22, 2006 Cooper and Wyatt were both saved. Cooper completed his chores; he provided the nutrients and comfort for Wyatt to arrive and survive before entering eternal Salvation at birth weighing less than 3 lbs. Wyatt weighed just over 3 lbs; he and Dee were in NICU at the University Of Nebraska Medical Center in Omaha for 6 long weeks. Brian and Dee were running on faith. Faith that Wyatt survived; faith of gratitude as friends and neighbors completed sheep chores at their farm nearly 200 miles from Omaha. The generous outpouring of support from friends and family was amazing. Once Wyatt's chores were complete, he left to spend eternity with his twin brother.

Carla Meyer, the daughter in-law of cousin Bob and Karen Meyer, arranged through her work with Coke and the resulting connections with the Kansas City Chiefs for Wyatt to receive an autographed Shadow Doll from NFL great, Tony Gonzales. Tony Gonzales' foundation supports twins who lost their twin. Have you or a close friend or loved one lost a baby?

We returned to Omaha the night of September 22nd, flying through a thunderstorm. This thunderstorm was a portent of the unfolding storms of life. The following morning Aunt Sara called saying that my dad was confused at home while my mom was in Omaha with Brian, Dee and Wyatt. I was confused on why Dad remained at home instead of being at the hospital. The following week Uncle Doug called during breakfast saying that I needed to drive to Franklin to take care of Dad. Within an hour, my suitcase was packed and I was on the road toward Franklin. Yes, Dad was confused, unable to carryon a conversation. He asked why the house was divided in two, along with questions regarding a door on the end of the house where none existed. It was as if he were in a dream.

After supper we drove his pickup through the countryside, there was no meaningful conversation as we had on similar drives. Uncle Jim Kahrs visited us at the house; awaiting Mom and Aunt Susan's return from Omaha. Dad and I had no visit before going to bed that night due to his confusion. I was unable to tell of our adventures in Washington.

The following morning, I thought, "I just want my dad back." Have you seen your parents or loved ones health decline?

Soon we learned he suffered from hydrocephalus, water on the brain; causing the confusion.

Sometime in October, Uncle Doug and Aunt Betty drove Mom and Dad to the hospital in Omaha. Dad held his grandson, Wyatt. His beaming smile resembled the smile of his own dad. Surgery was scheduled in Kearney for November 1, 2006. The pre-operation blood results displayed the surgery could proceed. I stood in the pre-operation room with Dad, in a few minutes the surgeons would resolve the hydrocephalus and Dad would regain his ability to think normally.

The nurse stepped into our area, presumably to take Dad to the operating room; instead she informed us the last minute blood tests revealed pneumonia. Surgery was delayed until he recovers. *Good grief!* While listening, an unexpected and undesired hunch appeared: Dad was about to die. I rebuked the hunch as negative thinking. Isn't Dad going to recover? After returning home that afternoon, Dad was admitted into Good Samaritan Hospital in Kearney the following day. On November 7 he was diagnosed with lung cancer. My body and mind were numb.

The following evening I was scheduled to speak at a church function in Hastings, with nearly 1,000 attending. The engagement was booked in January; my speech was planned, rehearsed and fine tuned. I was looking forward to speaking and seeing friends from our 5 years of living in Hastings. Upon receiving the report of Dad's lung cancer, my desire to speak swiftly dissipated. I scrapped all the planned speech. I mentally responded by reminding myself of several points:

- I thoroughly enjoy speaking to audiences
- Eager anticipation of this engagement
- Gave my word to First St. Paul's Church I would be there
- I speak to serve Christ
- God will provide my strength and his desired message
- Seeing and visiting with friends

We arrived early, enjoying wonderful conversations and catching up with friends. The barbequed meat's aroma and flavor was salivating delicious. The Rally Dinner fall event began in the 1950s, continuing every year with detailed scheduling. The keynote speaker is scheduled for 18-20 minutes of the program. Considering time is life; respecting others' time is respecting their life.

My friend Dean Hawthorne introduced me, after a few jokes I entered a zone, recalling little of what I said. Fortunately I recorded the message. Upon completion, I returned control of the podium to Dean, and then exhaustively collapsed in my chair. The exhaustion originated from the speaking, pouring my heart out when speaking; and the emotional drain from Dad's diagnosis. Everyone stood to applaud.

I rhetorically contemplated, "Are they tired of sitting from my speaking too long?"

We had planned to stay with friends in Hastings that evening, Tom and Carol whom I have known since moving to Kearney, generously invited us to stay at their home instead of the hotel the church graciously offered for lodging. After the program, Dee called from Omaha saying that the hospital needed someone to stay with Dad overnight or they would have to secure him to the bed. We drive the 50 miles from Hastings to Kearney arriving about midnight, allowing Brian to go home and sleep for a few hours before catching up on work around the farm.

We arrived exhausted and the night was just beginning. Dad wanted to get out of bed, "go home and do chores." He believed the cattle needed fed. I told him he is in the hospital; he does not need to do chores. After several times of this I said, "Dad, I finished the chores."

"Did you do them?" he inquired while looking directly and intently into my eyes. A frequent look and question he commonly asked me as a child on the farm.

"Yes, I did." I responded this way in belief that I did feed some of God's people the previous evening with the keynote address. Have you completed your daily chores? Are you feeding the people God places in your life with his word?

Dad slept for a couple of hours. We alternated taking short naps in the hospital chair. The exceptionally friendly and helpful nurses exemplified hospitality. One nurse provided a brief tour of their break room, "If you need anything, just let me know!"

I humorously reply, "I could use a large prime rib, cooked medium rare." Smiling, she quickly corrects the word 'anything.'

After what seemed a rather long night, sunlight bean glistening in the crisp November air. Often when very tired, sunlight provides invigorating physical and emotional energy. Isn't this a reminder of the invigorating power residing in Jesus Christ the Light of the World?

The nurses brought breakfast. Dad said, "We need to pray for Christ's blessings for everyone we know."

We did: Dad finished breakfast. When life's circumstances are grim, and death of life, dreams, job and/or finances appears near; do you focus on Christ's best for others? The Bible tells us in Job 42:10 "After Job finished praying for his friends, the Lord made him prosperous again and gave him twice as much as he had before."

Shortly after breakfast Dad looked intently into my eyes with laser focus. "Always trust God! Remember that son. Trust God, always!"

"I will Dad, I will." Only later, did I recognize this as Dad's final advice to me.

Do you always trust God the Father, the Lord Jesus Christ, and the Holy Spirit? Have you received transformational advice from your parents, loved ones or mentor? Immediately record this advice. What wisdom do you share with those you mentor, regardless of age?

About 10:00a.m. Uncle Wayne and Aunt Loretta stopped by. I participated and observed as the two brothers and one of Dad's classmates took communion together. I continued expecting recovery.

Many of Dad's friends, relatives, former neighbors and classmates from Gaylord visited him signing the guest book. The nurses became concerned because Dad got out of bed looking and asking for one of his guns. Fortunately, Tim Kahrs remained on the floor after visiting Dad, and confirmed they just finished visiting about hunting. Tim's visit stirred Dad's memory and desire to hunt.

The week of Thanksgiving the doctors dashed our hope of Dad's physical recovery, reporting that his plummeting health prevented operating on the hydrocephalus and the lung cancer. I now realized that Dad would most likely live only another six months. They begin radiation the following Tuesday, November 28th. A hunch on Monday suggested I visit Dad on Tuesday instead of waiting until Friday. The following morning, I drove

2.5 hours from Leigh to Kearney. Dad received radiation in the morning; slept the rest of the day.

Dee took Wyatt to his afternoon doctor's appointment at a nearby office; afterwards she visited the hospital. I sat in the car with Wyatt, rubbing his back while praying that Wyatt walks with the Lord Jesus Christ all the days of his long, prosperous life; and the Lord bless his health, along with granting him an exceptional amount of Godly wisdom, knowledge and understanding.

After Dee and other visitors leave, I drove to UNK where I changed into my running clothes in the coaches' locker room downstairs and then ran the old 10 mile route. After showering, I returned to room #339 in Kearney's Good Samaritan Hospital. Dad continued sleeping. I stood by his bed praying softly, yet powerfully, for his complete healing.

Dad woke up, extended his hand to shake mine, looked in my eyes, then spoke for the first time that day, "Good bye."

I thought my prayers upset him and he wanted me to leave. "Good bye, Dad."

My conclusion and his words contrasted his nature that I knew for 39 years. I never recalled him saying, "Good bye." Instead, he quipped phrases such as, "See you later" or "Don't do anything I wouldn't do." I leave perplexed.

In the hallway, I encountered and briefly visited with Eileen Kottmeyer, R.N., wife of Mark Kottmeyer. She said if I ever need a place to stay while visiting Dad, they have an extra bedroom. I last worked for them as a Crop Consultant twelve years ago.

Dad: Death and Funeral

Friday December 1, 2006 I enter the house after retrieving the mail, Theresa shared that my mom called saying the doctor encouraged the family to come to the hospital. We quickly packed, including our Chocolate Labrador, Guinness; boarding him at the Veterinarian Clinic in Columbus. Traveling on Highway 30, I want to pass a couple of semitrucks traveling below the speed limit. Occasional oncoming traffic prevents passing safely.

Dad's firm voice resonates in my mind's ear, "Son, do not risk the lives of others, or yourself. I'm okay, trust Christ!"

As we approach the east side of Gibbon, NE, the phone rang. "Rick, this is Uncle Doug. I'm sorry to have to be the one to make this call, your dad just died." Dad completed his chores.

Do you remember receiving the news of your loved one's passing? One person describes receiving such news as similar to someone ripping out your spine and beating you with it. That is a fair description. Would you agree? I am immensely happy for Dad entering heaven, joining God the Father, Jesus Christ and the Holy Spirit, face to face. I am sad for the rest of us.

Theresa left a phone message for Kent Frieling; then dialed Jon Young followed by Bryan Danburg. Bryan professed empathy and encouragement on the phone as I drove north to the hospital, saying, "Keep going!"

As we parked at Good Samaritan Hospital, I was once again speechless. The perpetually intensifying, excruciating pain resembled lightning bolts piercing my mind and body's every nerve. We go up to Room #339. Numerous family members stand in the room and the nearby lobby. I approach the bed where my dad's body lay.

Uncle Wayne looked directly at me. "It never stops hurting." His statement captures my attention like a hissing bull snake because nearly 31 years has eclipsed since his dad died. I failed to comprehend the residual grief of my dad and uncles throughout the years. Grief is proportionate to value. We must remain joyful and thankful in Christ for the amazing value of loved ones in our lives.

While the preacher lead us in prayers, two calls appeared on my cell phone, which I turned to vibrate. After the prayers, I listened to the messages. The first was from Congo. Twenty-two years after our last state championship, my mentor and friend calls me only 34 minutes after my dad passed away. He received the news from my former teammate Jon Young. Congo left a simple, yet powerful message, "If there is *anything* I can do for you, let me know!"

I recall another Congo-ism, "Don't be afraid to be great!" I will challenge myself, digging deep down into my soul to rely on the gold mine of faith God gives each of us.

Kent Frieling, a lifelong friend and cousin, left the second message. Both request updates of the finalized funeral logistics.

Eventually we leave the hospital, driving to Franklin. I drive Mom's Ford Explorer; Dee rides with Theresa in our Buick Rainier. While driving east on Fort Kearney Road, south of Kearney, a revelation sparked in my mind. I reflect back on my childhood when Dad sent me to church activities despite my begging to stay with him. He did so to encourage and strengthen my eternal relationship with Jesus Christ. He knew that we would spend life together eternally with God in heaven through Christ. He knew this life was temporary, while eternal life exists in accepting the forgiveness of sins from the death and resurrection of our Lord and Savior Jesus Christ. Dad, like many area farmers, gave a much stronger sermon through living, instead of words.

As we walked to the church for the funeral, Kent and his parents are among the first people I encounter outside. We grew up together attending Sunday school, church, confirmation and kindergarten through college – minus my Manhattan years. The faith and scriptures that teachers challenged us to internalize through memorization in our early years, I needed now as much as any time in my life.

Dennis, Barb and Abby Lehmann sit in the back of the church. Memories overwhelm me as I look at each person. Dad's siblings, their spouses and many of his nieces, nephews and cousins also attend. Former neighbors and friends from Gaylord attend, including Coach Jim Muck. Once seated in the front row of the sanctuary, almost as if placed in the display window of a store, I glanced around seeing fellow agronomists Mark Kottmeyer, Bruce Karnatz, Bryan Danburg from Kearney and Darren Barker from York, NE. The latter two also formerly ran for UNK, along with Kurt Holliday from Seward, NE.

About a dozen members of the two congregations I attended in Leigh and Grand Prairie, NE, were present; along with a multitude of others. The sanctuary filled with those Dad impacted, directly or indirectly, the ushers then led those arriving later to the basement. The congregation sang, *Shall we gather at the River,* the song Dad frequently whistled and sang while farming along the banks of the North Fork of the Solomon River.

A pure white funeral alb covered the casket. This symbolizes our pureness from Christ's death and resurrection; receiving the signed receipt of acknowledging our dependence on Christ for forgiveness of sins necessary for salvation. At the end of the service, our family stands to depart from the sanctuary; we walk through the line for inspection. I restrain the sobbing lingering in my throat while wiping away tears in my eyes. I want my dad back. I am Running on Faith.

While exiting I look up and see Congo. Upon making eye contact I instantly think, "Do not feel sorry for yourself, right Rick Meyer."

Congo drove 191 miles from Manhattan to Franklin on this Tuesday December 5, 2006 for Dad's funeral. He stopped by Haddam, KS, on the way to visit his dad. Memories of sitting in the kitchen in our farmhouse, listening to Dad and Congo visit over the phone about farming in excess of 30 minutes in 1983, flood my mind. I initially ponder, later confirming, that as Congo woke that December morning he considered, "Do I really want to drive 3 hours across rural America to attend a funeral of an athlete's parent from nearly a quarter of a century ago? It depends on how good you want to be Bill Congleton." Probably an abundance of others had similar ponderings that Tuesday morning.

Do you ask yourself similar questions before attending funerals or supporting friends in other aspects?

The vast attendees illustrate God's presence, his reminder to "Fear Not." God weaves the attendees and all those offering support, around and through our lives, forming a spiritual and emotional safety net. Christ remains with us always amidst dark, cold, terrifying moments. He exists and expresses his presence in those we encounter. Some serve us, others we serve; yet others - we synergistically serve one another and those surrounding us.

The warm outside temperatures for December in Nebraska provided an ideal environment for visiting those who attending. One conversation occurred with Kaid and Kris Dannenberg, our former neighbors on the farm. Their dad, Don, died earlier in 2006. I view it as somewhat ironic that Dad and Don, who endured much fun as classmates, friends and neighbors; died a few months apart from causes unrelated to driving fast or sliding down a barn roof.

Temptation: Responding

Several times in the next few weeks my mind and body begged to quit; wanting to tell the world, "Go ahead." Just like the races, I felt as if I was about to collapse at any moment. Pain, once again, zapped my every sensory nerve. A mirage of comfort, peace and joy appeared through the path of drunkenness from alcoholic beverages.

These temptations provide logical justifications for drunkenness:
- Is one time of drunkenness really going to hurt anything?
- The alcohol will provide much needed relaxation, which enhances health.
- I will sleep much better.
- I am not hurting anyone.
- I deserve a break after all I have been through.
- My dad would want me to have a little fun.

Have you faced these or similar temptations?

The Holy Spirit combats each of these temptations through various avenues including illuminating his pure word—Holy Scripture—in my heart, mind, and soul. His message reminds me that true comfort, peace and joy exist in a relationship with Christ (Galatians 5:16-18).

I stood facing a fork in the road. Which path do I choose: Alcohol or Scripture? Alcohol presents a broad path, while scripture offers a narrow path.

I choose the narrow path rooted in scripture. "Train a child in the way he should go, and when he is old he will not depart from it" (Proverbs 22:6). Sadly, some "Bible scholars" declare portions of the Bible as fiction; these false teachers encourage others to doubt scripture. This leads many to seek comfort in alcohol, drugs and sexual immorality. The serpent first deceptively convinced Adam and Eve to doubt God's word, the narrow way; this opened the broad path of disobedience and sin.

I continued studying the Bible, reading it cover to cover approximately 15 times in the following year. When the life's challenges cause you to question your ability to move forward, how do you respond?

Toastmasters - 2008

In March 1999, I was introduced to Toastmasters, truly a life changing event. Toastmasters International is an organization designed to enhance speaking for anyone seeking improvement. Eventually, I competed in contests, qualifying for my first District 24 International Speech contest in 2003. District 24 represents most of Nebraska and a portion of southwest Iowa. The International Speech contest accompanies the full gamut of topics or styles one desires to present. Typically, contestants present motivational speeches. In my first trip to the district contest, I failed to place in the top two. I continued sporadically competing.

In 2008, I committed to deliver my best speech at the District 24 contest. Beginning with the club contest in March, preparation included practicing the 7 minute speech at least 1,000 times with over 300 edits.

I elicited help from many, including Doug Hobel a former speech and drama teacher that lived in Leigh, NE. Someone suggested I tell the story about my knee high tube socks; Toastmaster member Jeanne advised my sitting down during one portion of the presentation. Dan Pabian and a host of other Toastmasters offered suggestions to enhance the message. I later diagramed the stage positioning for each portion of the speech, practicing the positioning at least 100 times. When the contest arrived, I was prepared and exhausted!

Every morning at 5:30a.m., I walked next door to the church basement, practicing at least 10 times. I then read aloud from the Bible for 60 minutes. Tonality and enunciation must be fine tuned. I practiced the presentation an additional 30 times throughout the day while working, driving or walking the dog. I desired to taste victory! I visualized every step from introduction, completion and receiving the trophy, just like Congo trained us to prepare for cross country meets and championships.

I won the club, area and division contests. The District 24 contest and conference waited next on the schedule.

Friday afternoon I drove 3 hours to Beatrice, the contest occured Saturday evening. Doug strongly suggested avoiding any rehearsal of the speech on Friday. Friday evening I asked a member of the conference committee which room would be use for the contest. I entered the room, and then rehearsed, walking up and visualizing a room full of people.

The person who directed me to the room stood in the hall enjoying a chuckle. Surely they ponder: Who in their right mind does this sort of thing?"

Champions!

Since I had to check out of my hotel before noon, I took an afternoon nap in my car before the contest. Eventually the time arrived for us competitors to meet with the Toastmaster who reviewed the rules and we drew numbers to determine speaking order; 6 of us provided fierce competition, including professional seminar facilitators, a Past International Director and other talented speakers. As we gathered in the hall, a group of ladies from the Advanced Club I attended in Sioux City walked in after driving 200 miles to watch and support my efforts.

The first 3 contests delivered outstanding speeches. The moment I visualized many times arrived, the Toastmaster announced, "Rick Meyer, Congo's Ideologies; Congo's Ideologies, Rick Meyer."

The audience clapped, I calmly walked front and center. "Bill Congleton, better known as Congo, mastered transforming ordinary people into champions. He internalized the expectation of Greatness." The speech began as planned; each completed sentence increased my confidence. Near the end of the speech, I told of Congo attending my dad's funeral. Tears crept from every eye in the room. I then concluded, "When facing life's challenges, whether dealing with a loss, or struggling to keep up in this fast paced world; are you going to feel sorry for yourself, or EXPECT GREATNESS? It depends, on how good *you* want to be."

As the contest concluded, I knew that I had a chance at winning along with other top competitors. Several attendees told me that I won. The social hour, a banquet and a program delay the announcing of the results for nearly 3 hours. I disliked this facet of Toastmaster competitions; additionally the contest scores remained a secret to everyone except the judges.

Imagine attending a football game, then waiting 3 hours after the game for the officials to add up the penalties and decide which touchdowns counted and which touchdowns failed to count; then announce the winning team without any score or explanation.

Finally, they announced the results beginning with second place, then the champion. Gene Deyoe received second place for his outstanding presentation. A mix of elation and worry fill my rhetorical pondering, *Did I win, or did I fail to place?*

A dramatic pause preceded the announcing of the winner: Rick Meyer. Even though I visualized this victory hundreds of times, hearing my name announced as the winner saturated my heart and mind with elation and gratification. Elation from the victory, and gratification from performing to the best of my ability.

As I left the parking lot for the long drive home, I called Congo, "We won another state championship." He enthusiastically congratulated this bow-legged farm boy who first appeared wearing cotton gym shorts and knee high tubes sock with the red and green band of the Smith Center Redmen. I later sent the recording to Congo, former teammates and friends, each verifing the pure truth of everything stated in the presentation. Since it is impossible for the Holy Spirit to lie, a Spirit-filled Christian seeking to please God speaks truth. To be fair, Dan Schneider said that I should better describe my blinding white legs.

On June 28, 2008 I competed in the Region IV Toastmasters contest in Rapid City, SD. Toastmasters required a different speech. Before the competition, I repeated the message of Dan Schneider's prayer on the starting line of state cross country, "Lord, help me speak to the best of my ability; glorifying you whether I place first place or last." I was the 4th out of 6 contestants. As I stepped on stage to present, I remembered fellow Toastmaster David Deford's advice earlier in the day: Love the people.

All 6 contestants gave outstanding presentations! After results were announced, my dream of qualifying for the World Championships of Public Speaking was torpedoed. The top 3 placers each profusely acknowledged the assistance of contest judges on their speech that afternoon.

I went to my room, changed clothes and ran 5 miles. The Holy Spirit reminded me of my prayer to glorify him, whether first place or last. "Lord, it is much easier and more fun when I win." I am thankful that the Lord of creation included humor with creation. Many outsiders suggested that I give up on my dream of speaking professionally. The Holy Spirit continued speaking encouragement to my heart; this message originated both from the still quiet inner voice as well as from friends and peers who heard me speak.

What are your dreams? Listen for direction and encouragement from the Holy Spirit by studying scripture, internal promptings and through others.

Divorce

One of the reasons I had lacked urgency in getting married in my 20s, is that I despised divorce and wanted the best assurance possible of a lasting marriage. I did not believe in divorce, with the exceptions of adultery and physical harm. Unfortunately, I was blindsided with divorce in August 2008. However, a mature relationship with Jesus Christ demands that we extend mercy and forgiveness to others as God extends His mercy and forgives us of our sins against Him. Chuck Kahl provided great wisdom immediately following this shock. "Rick, whatever you do, do not speak badly about her. What you say about her or anyone who hurts you simply reveals *your* character and relationship with God." Since I am an imperfect person, I pray others will extend mercy and forgiveness to me for my sins against them.

Uncle Wayne

In October 2008, I visited my Uncle Wayne Meyer, a retired farmer, at Good Samaritan Hospital in Kearney, NE. It was the first time inside this hospital since my dad passed away. I inquired about faith's impact on his life, especially as a farmer. He quickly and humbly acknowledged it was God who provided the necessary sunlight, moisture and nutrients for germination, crop emergence, pollination and ultimately yield and profit. A pastor once inquired of Uncle Wayne why he did not spend more time in prayer before getting on the tractor each morning, whether tending to crops or livestock. Uncle Wayne replied, "What do you think I do all day while on the tractor and working around the farm?" Uncle Wayne, like most farmers in the area, prayed without ceasing.

As we have discussed in various events; hail, wind, floods, pests or disease can destroy crops, profit and livelihood in less than 30 minutes. Entire crops are sometimes lost in the blink of an eye. Conversely, amazing profitable crops sometimes emerge from dismal appearances and circumstances. What amazing profitable crop is about to emerge from your dismal surroundings and circumstances?

Chapter 12:
Ministry

A few years after I graduated from Kansas State, pastors and peers began suggesting that I consider attending seminary and engaging in full time ministry. These suggestions of entering the ministry intrigued me because I held the profession of ministry in high esteem. Additionally, sharing the gospel and helping people apply the Bible to their everyday lives ignited my passions even more than engagement in agriculture. New allergies developed during these same early years, eventually forcing me out of agronomy.

Agriculture provides the needed physical food and ministry supplies spiritual food. God implanted my heart with the desire to partner with Him in feeding the world. Food, water and Jesus Christ encompass the necessities of physical, spiritual and eternal life. I tried other professions such as insurance. I greatly preferred visiting with people about Christian faith than insurance or any other business.

Pastors and peers regularly sprinkled encouragement for seminary and ministry. However, I never considered myself worthy to serve God in the capacity of full time ministry. Consequently, I sought excuses and delays on seminary and other options for ministry. I threw down the common excuses of the need for relocation and finances. After my divorce, I decided to try agronomy sales. Perhaps my allergies had expired. I was an optimist. The allergies remained. Additionally, two representatives of major agricultural companies blatantly warned me along these lines:

"Rick, if you want to succeed in this position you must ignore biblical principles such as honesty and stop treating the small clients with the same respect as the big clients. Continuing this will cause you to fail in this position. Success in this position requires mixing truth with exaggerations - stretching the truth." Fortunately, these statements represent only some in this profession and *not* everyone in agronomy sales. Their heart, their inner man, produced thoughts incongruent with God's character.

Shortly after this conversation, I accepted an invitation from my pastor to meet for breakfast. Pastor Larry encouraged me to reconsider seminary. I delayed another year until one fall afternoon in 2010 I decided to apply to Dallas Theological Seminary (DTS). I became aware of DTS from listening to Chuck Swindoll on the radio for the previous 20 years while driving my pickup down the dusty, muddy and snow packed country roads as an agronomist and insurance agent.

I hit submit on the application with hesitancy because of my poor grades at Kansas State and knowing the reputation of DTS as among the best seminaries in the world. I began confession, "All I know for certain is that I am too apply." Much to my amazement, I received acceptance around January 1st. My new motto became, "All I know for certain is that I am accepted." When I finally moved to Dallas and started classes I confessed, "All I know for certain is that I am to attend this class in this moment." I invested virtually all of my time in class, visiting with fellow students, studying, sleeping or eating. I rarely spared an hour for personal enjoyment. I approached seminary as if training for a competitive marathon. Eventually, I graduated while receiving the highest grades of my life. About half way through my studies at DTS, I felt compelled to engage in ministry outside the walls of a physical church. So many in ministry focus on either those who attend church or those who are physically and financially on the down and out. Most mission organizations appear to compete about whose target audience is in the worst physical condition. However, many who look good, smell good and drive nice automobiles also need the gospel and application of the Bible in their own life. Too many presume that if their neighbor lives in a big house and drives a luxury automobile that they're prospering spiritually. They believe in the prosperity gospel!

Consequently, I founded Running on Faith Ministry, Inc. that focuses on discipleship, building disciples and evangelism.

In July 2015, Dee went to the hospital after feeling sick and weak for a few days. The test results revealed a diagnosis of bone cancer.

Figure 24: Memorial Day 2015. Dee and our cousin, Dennis Kahrs in the yard where our mom and his dad grew-up. Only six weeks before her bone cancer diagnosis. Dee, Wyatt and I drove around that afternoon having my fun. Little did I I realize this would be our last outing.

Dee's battle with Cancer and Death

My sister, Dee, lost her battle with bone cancer at her home on Wednesday April 27, 2016 at 2:30p.m. CDT. Her life consisted of abundant cheesecake-type relationships, rich and filling. Dee focused on loving God, His people (Matthew 22:37-39) and her need for forgiveness of sins for eternal life with God only through the death and resurrection of the Lord Jesus Christ (John 3:14-21).

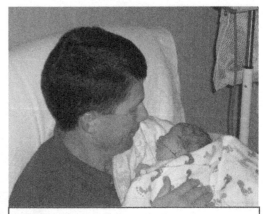

I am holding Wyatt Isaacson, born Sept. 2006 weighing 3 lbs 2 ounces.

Dee maintained her optimism, sense of humor and strong faith in Jesus Christ through the end. She epitomized *Running on Faith*, fully trusting God with all aspects of her earthly and eternal life. She recognized each step and breath, whether healthy or sick, as God's gift of an opportunity to love and to serve.

God enabled us to grow-up in a family and community that hinged on faith in the Lord Jesus Christ. I fondly recall Mom sitting on the dining room floor with Dee and me teaching us to sing, *Jesus Loves Me*. Mom also taught us to read from a Children's Bible as well as numerous books of Bible stories we received from relatives, neighbors and teachers. I last visited Dee Monday night, April 25th, saying goodbye with a strong firm hug then gently rubbing her back. Yes, we love you Dee!

Revised from the original version written December 28, 2015

I learned a great deal about *Running on Faith* from watching my sister Dee battle breast cancer, followed by bone cancer.

Dad and Dee: Christmas 2005
Cherish the moments with your family.

One of the thrills in athletics is pushing yourself beyond previously known limits and watching others do the same. This includes beyond the point of what we previously believed as the point of absolute physical and emotional exhaustion, the point of physical collapse.

Now faith is the assurance of things hoped for, the conviction of things not seen. For by it the men of old gained approval. By faith we understand that the worlds were prepared by the word of God, so that what is seen was not made out of things which are visible (Hebrews 11:1–3, NASB95).

The Greek word for hope, elpizō, is "to be confident and reasonably expectant of a future event."

Dee could not compete in sports due to challenges with her knees, yet she strongly encouraged myself, other athletes and championship teams. Additionally, she truly inspired me in her courageous and faithful battle with cancer. She initially defeated breast cancer from February 2014 thru September 2014. Last July bone cancer chose to challenge her.

The week of Christmas she entered ICU for the second time in two weeks, this time for two or three days before transferring to PCU (Preferential Care). Dee continued her upbeat attitude as her faith remained founded on the solid rock of Christ's words (Matthew 7:24-27).

The hospital released her on Thursday afternoon. She and her smile joined us at my mom's. We enjoyed a wonderful Christmas Day. She continued running an amazing race on amazing faith. By March 2016, she was able to once again able to offer a little help with sheep chores.

As an example of her faith, I never heard Dee complain or ask, "Why me?"

Yes, she faced previous hardships including losing a son and our dad 10 weeks apart in 2006. She kept her faith and hope rooted in Christ.

Dee's iron will for victory over bone cancer illuminated her faith in Christ along with her love of her husband, Brian, and son Wyatt. These types of athletic performances often result in the athlete receiving headlines, their picture in the paper, their name in every major paper around the world, and perhaps appearing on ESPN's Sports Center. Not so with most cancer patients.

Dee your battle with cancer epitomized *Running on Faith* pushing yourself far beyond previously known limits. You inspired me, your friends, family and many whom you have never met.

Chapter 13:
Writing on Faith

This book project began 10 years ago, with completion nearby but just out of reach for a long time. Many re-writes and additions occurred as I survived losing a nephew, my dad and an unexpected divorce. While reading the Bible this morning, the Lord *spoke* to my heart, "Rick, writing your book is like writing your life. You do not rewrite your past, and while we must keep adding new chapters; we must commit our completed work for societal benefit. Rick, it is me, the Lord who gives value to your writing, work and life. Your efforts and every ones' efforts are useless and meaningless absent my presence. Tie-up the loose ends, submitting for my use. You will be amazed!"

Yes, I strongly desire that all who read of this book or hear me speak to passionately engage in *Running on Faith*. Fully exert and submit every ounce of energy you possess to the Lord who further reminded me through His word that He transforms every ones' heart, soul and mind when we turn to Him. It is not you, rather Christ who is in you or awaiting an invitation to each of you (John 15:4-5). You can't, Christ can. Yes, you will also be amazed what God will do in each of your lives. Submit to God and achieve an abundant life with God's riches beyond earthly comprehension (Ephesians 3:14-19; Philippians 4:19)). Most people fail to recognize and enjoy God's spiritual riches because they look only for tangible, worldly riches.

Running on faith requires mental toughness. Mental toughness is faith: Faith God will provide strength. Faith that the effort and agony is worth it, Faith God will always supply your needs – mental and physical. **Faith is staying power!** Do you have the staying power to allow God to work in your life? Are you willing to let God give you the staying power necessary? It will not be easy and it may be painful, however always worth it.

Faith is the substance of things hoped for, the evidence unseen. Faith comes by hearing and hearing by the Word of God. Where your treasure is, there your heart is also. Great men and woman of faith are in the Word of God, internalizing God's Word. Are you saturating your mind and body with God's Word, and the Holy Spirit? When you invest in God's Word, your heart is with God. Everything we do should be glorifying our Heavenly Father. Crops and livestock provide for people's physical strength, profits from any of our endeavors are to nourish our family and selves physically, mentally, and spiritually.

When you are saturated with God's Word, the thief is unable to deceive you. The thief attempts to draw you away from your home; you must cling to God's Word. In ancient Greece, the enemy would try to get the opposing army to open the gate to the city just a little bit. This is true in the story of the Trojan Horse, once the gate is opened by the slimmest margin, the enemy would take advantage of the opening, quickly infiltrating the entire city, allowing them to defeat the city. You must stand firm on God's Word, avoiding those who question the validity of scripture; you must keep the gate shut tightly. Just as the ancient armies would use clever deception to gain entrance into the fortified cities, so does the enemy of God use clever deception to attempt entrance into your life; both with the same motive: the destruction of the occupants.

It takes faith to stand firm on God's Word, it takes faith to invest your life and treasures into God's Kingdom. God performed the impossible when he gave Abraham and Sarah a son, God performed the impossible when he saved my Uncle LaVerne and his shipmates in WWII, and saved Richard from the Japanese. In all instances God delivered life, when all the evidence indicated death.

Go out this day, this week, this year, this life, on complete faith in our Savior, Fearing Not the World; enhance and empower the lives of all those you encounter; as you share the life of faith, absent any fear, made possible by a life in Christ! Knowing God creates legacies, when only death is seen.

God gives you life in your marriage, finances, work, friendships or any other endeavor; despite you seeing no option but 'death' or failure.

What is the price of Freedom? Freedom is religious freedom. Those who confiscate your money confiscate your life. Your money is earned from your sweat and thoughts.

As Ben Franklin once stated, "Only a virtuous people are deserving of freedom." Are we willing to 'Run on Faith' daily! Are we willing to fully exert ourselves to achieve God's will in our lives? Exerting ourselves physically, mentally and spiritually. Let us challenge ourselves in deepening our thought process in our work, with our families, in our communities. As Bill "Congo" Congleton often said, "Don't be afraid to be great." There is no greater challenge to ourselves. Challenging our mind, our body and our soul. We must be willing to push ourselves beyond previously known limits.

In the 39 years of running I have run in nearly every imaginable range of weather. Hurricanes and tornados are the two exceptions that come to mind. In 1995 and 1996 I was consistently running over 100 miles per week. Living in Nebraska and running an average of up to 20 miles every day, means a wide variety of weather is encountered.

Conclusion

Yes, I originally believed that God made a mistake when removing us from the farm in 1983. However, it was His plan before any of us were born (Psalm 139). God specifically designs each phase of our lives for a specific purpose. He expects us to respond by turning to Him, recognizing His holiness, along with our sin and dependence on Christ for the forgiveness of sins and a restored relationship with God.

Everything is *good* when we focus on God. However, just as good running workouts are necessarily difficult and challenging, so are God's *workouts* for those He loves.

Yes, I strongly desired to live my life farming and hunting along the North Fork of the Solomon River, a mile east and two miles south of Gaylord, KS. However, God had different plans. These plans aren't *better*, rather different. Because, God also specifically places others to live and farm that land and area. Since they too are the Lord's, only the arrogant would suggest that one is better for leaving than those that remain. Rather, everyone who pursues and obeys God is living out His plans, thus a good life.

God brought another faithful servant, widower Elliott Nielsen, into Mom's life in 2011. They married that December. Through the hardships and celebrations, she consistently praises and trusts God as she did during my childhood on the farm. Mom serves as a wonderful example that we run on faith every day, fully exerting ourselves in pursuit of our God given goals: God's will for our life. Unlike a foot race, we do not know when we will enter the homestretch with our life's finish line in view. For some, the home stretch is long, too long; for others the homestretch is nearly non-existent; a sharp turn and suddenly the finish line appears; we cross it before we realize what happens. Regardless of how many years we run before entering the homestretch or how long our homestretch is, each of us will cross life's finish line. The best feeling at the end of a race is knowing you did your best, expending every ounce of energy you possess as intelligently as you know how. The same is true of finishing the race of life, it matters little how others view your race; rather, whether you know you expended every ounce of energy you possessed in responding, in answering the commands of Christ.

Appendix
Do you Finish God's sentences?

Do you finish other people's sentences?

Several years ago, following a Toastmasters meeting I visited with a local businessman and philanthropist, Joe, who visited our club to promote a fundraiser. Joe told of attending Kansas State University's world-renowned College of Veterinary Medicine. As Joe began, I was finishing his sentences whenever he paused as I knew exactly what he was going to say. Wrong!!! I did not know how Joe was finishing his sentences.

I normally do not engage in finishing someone's sentences, however the excitement of discussing Manhattan and Kansas State got the better of me in that conversation. Moreover, his favorite professor of Vet Med was the father of two of my friends and high school cross country teammates. The first few times of my interruption, Jim patiently stated, "No, I was going say…" Following my 6th repetition of rudely and inaccurately finishing sentences, Joe politely dismissed himself.

Are you irritated when others finish your sentences, especially when completed inaccurately? Have you ever finished someone's sentences? Others tend to inaccurately finish my sentences when I pause, just as I did when Joe paused. Instead of listening we jump to conclusions. Frequently, emotional irritation is the only damage. However, when continued, we lose credibility as a listener. Even greater damage is possible.

Once in the summer of 1986, Jim and I were instructed to drive a farm truck to Fettger's (the name of a farm) to meet my cousins where we would load straw bales. As soon as Jim and I heard "Fettger's" we stopped listening; because we knew exactly where the Fettger place was since we irrigated there every morning. We jumped in the truck, driving the 12 miles on gravel roads to the Fettger place. We were puzzled because we had not seen wheat on that piece of land; however we were only familiar with the irrigated portion of the property. As we drove we discussed that the wheat and resulting straw bales must be in the dry land portion of the property. Upon arrival we saw no one; 20 minutes later, we still saw no one. We reassured ourselves that we were told to meet at the Fettger place. After half an hour passed, and no two-way radio and long before cell phones; we drove back to the yard; the farmstead where my mom and her siblings were raised.

Once in the yard, we sheepishly began calling for directions on the two-way. My uncles were less than thrilled. We were told to go to a different Fettger place, one nearby; additionally we were to have waited and followed my cousins to the specific field. We wasted significant time, fuel and energy; while generating enormous frustration at us. We finished the sentence of our directions; we failed to listen to the full instructions.

Do you finish God's sentences? I have! At times, I know God is giving me a specific message. I later realize I finished God's sentence instead of listening to the entire message. I inaccurately finish God's messages when he pauses, or when I "know" exactly what He is going to say. But I do not know, as His wisdom far exceeds my wisdom and your wisdom.

Perhaps you say, "But Lord, you told me to accept this promotion, this new job. Why am I miserable?" The Lord says, "No, I told you to *interview* for the position." We say, "Lord, why am I unable to pay for my new car that **you** told me to buy?" He replies, "I instructed you to *visit* the dealership and *test drive* the new car."

The next time our Lord speaks to your heart: Listen! Listen through the pauses; listen to the entire sentence, paragraph, chapter and book. Listening to the entire message enables you and I to be fully in tune with our Savior and the Holy Spirit.

See Christ, Believe Christ, Achieve with Christ!

Altitude & Wisdom

I boarded a plane for a flight to Albany, finding my seat next to the window. The view while sitting at the gate offered a limited perspective of the surroundings. Based solely on this view, Chicago's O'Hare Airport possessed about a dozen boarding gates, with limited airplane traffic.

As we taxied to the runway, I was able to a better view, seeing dozens of additional gates and airplanes; although the airport's size still appeared modest. I would have been a less than adequate ambassador for O'Hare Airport due to my limited perspective. If someone sought my advice for O'Hare's capacity; I would have been very confident, and very wrong. A limited perspective provided the foundation of my assessment.

Approximately 20 minutes after boarding, the pilot announced, "Flight attendants please prepare for takeoff." The jet engines roared as we zoomed down the long runway; with nature's law of lift collaborating with the law of gravity our ascension commenced. My perspective increased exponentially with altitude. Quickly, O'Hare's vastness became apparent.

As our ascension continued the logistics of the entire Chicago landscape became significantly more apparent from the air. After reaching 36,000 feet other cities appeared as a speck on the map, including Detroit and Windsor, Canada. Lake Huron seem not so great; Niagara Falls appeared simply as a nice stream. I now had a greater understanding of how everything fit together geographically. With a view from great altitude, I could have answered any geographical question with much greater accuracy than when on the ground.

When asking questions about O'Hare Airport, the city of Chicago or Niagara Falls; would my answers reveal my altitude? A higher altitude, among many things, allows one's awareness of possibilities to drastically increase.

Would our decision-making ability increase in quickness and accuracy if we had 'altitude' in life? What is life's equivalent of altitude? Wisdom provides 'altitude,' greater perspective, in life. Do a person's answers reveal their 'altitude,' their wisdom? Does greater wisdom allow an exponential increase in awareness of possibilities?

Scripture states that if we desire wisdom, we simply must ask and believe. Attain wisdom for greater understanding.

See Christ, Believe Christ, Achieve Wisdom with Wisdom

Friendships and Corner Posts

Friendships are like corner posts: when dug deeply and solidified, they will withstand a great deal of tension.

Corner posts are pulled tightly by wire tightened with wire stretchers, often in two different directions. If dug quickly and shallowly, and the soil is not solidified from the base of the post up; their usefulness is drastically limited.

Walk with Christ, Talk with Christ, Achieve with Christ!

Bibliography

Andreasen, Nancy C. M.D., Ph.D. 2005. *The Creating Brain: The Neuroscience of Genius.* New York, NY and Washington D.C.: Dana Press.

Blakeslee, Sandra and Blakeslee, Matthew. 2007. *The Body Has a Mind of Its Own.* New York, NY: Random House.

Burns, J. Lanier ThD, PhD. Spring 2013. *Dr.* Dallas, TX: Self.

Clark, E.A. Paul and F.E. 1989. *Soil Microbiology and Biochemistry.* San Diego, California: Academic Press, Inc.

Mathias, Art Ph.D. 2003. *In His Own Image: We are Wonderfully Made.* Anchorage, Alaska: Wellspring Publishing.

Meyer, Rick E. 2013. *The Holy Spirit's Guidance in Max International.* Dallas, TX: Self.

Pert, Candice Ph.D. 1999. *Molecules of Emotion.*

Schroeder, Gerald L. Ph.D. 2001. *The Hidden Face of God: How Science Reveals the Ultimate Truth.* New York, NY: The Free Press.

Spirit, Holy. 1962-1995. *NASB Bible.* Grand Rapids, Michigan: Zondervan.

Swindoll, Charles R. 2000. *Perfect Trust.* Nashville, TN: Thomas Nelson.

Toussaint, Dr. Stanley. 2012. "Acts and the Pauline Epistles, Class Notes."

Toussaint, Dr. Stanley D. n.d. *TAI Series: People Come in Four Sizes.* Millet the Printer, Inc. Dallas, Texas.

Made in the USA
Monee, IL
13 January 2023

25187460R00148